T0140360

Process Assessment and ISO/IEC 15504

A Reference Book
Second Edition

Process Assessment and ISO/IEC 15504

A Reference Book
Second Edition

by

Han van Loon

Leistungs Consult GmbH
Visiting Professor – Nottingham Trent University, UK
Visiting Professor – University of Business and
International Studies in Geneva

 Springer

Han van Loon
Sagenstrasse 35
CH-6318 Walchwil
Switzerland
Telephone & Fax: +41 41 7580826
email: welcome@lc-stars.com

Process Assessment and ISO/IEC 15504
A Reference Book, Second Edition by Han van Loon

ISBN 978-1-4899-9114-0   ISBN 978-0-387-70696-2 (eBook)

Printed on acid-free paper.

9 8 7 6 5 4 3 2 1

springer.com

springer.com

Dedication and Acknowledgements

This book is dedicated to the many professionals committed to improving their organizations through process assessment and quality improvement.

I would also like to thank contributors from around the world who have provided information about the use of process assessment and improvement methods. Naturally my thanks extend to the contributors to the first edition, much of which remains relevant in the second edition. The second edition brings new sections and contributions for this book and the companion practical guide book.

Input was used from the European Space Agency Research and Technology Centre, European Aerospace and Defence Systems Astrium, the Software Engineering Institute, the Software Quality Institute, the OOSPICE consortium, Rational, Audi and the Automotive SPICE group, the United States Federal Aviation Administration, the Swiss Federal Strategic Committee for Information Technology, Philips NV, Credit Suisse, NEC-CAS, and Process Improvement Task Force, Ministry of Economics, Trade and Industry, and Software Engineering Center, Information-Technology Promotion Agency, Japan.

Han van Loon   2007

Leistungs Consult GmbH
Web site: www.lc-stars.com
Email: welcome@lc-stars.com

Table of Contents

List of Figures

List of Tables

List of Tables

Introduction

Introduction to Reference Book

The Reference Book introduces the reader to the concepts of process assessment in general and the various process assessment standards. In particular, it describes ISO/IEC 15504, SPICE variants and CMMI®.

It has a companion guidebook: **Process Assessment and Improvement. A practical guide**

In the first chapter, I look very briefly at the creation of an international quality standard specifically addressing process assessment. I describe the foundations for organizational success in terms of a People-Process-Product model, the concepts of processes and process assessment in general, and how these are achieved in ISO/IEC 15504. It is written in a very general way and assessors, process and quality professional may wish to go to the more detailed sections suggested in the reading guide instead.

In chapter 2, an overview of the ISO/IEC 15504 standard and the structure of the document set are described, together with the reader's guidance to the standard. This provides the reader with a quick, high-level overview of the standard and its parts.

In chapter 3: Meeting the requirements of ISO/IEC 15504, I describe the overall requirements that the standard places upon assessment models and methods, and its role to harmonize across various standards, models and methods. This chapter covers the need for several levels of detail in process models by specifying the requirements for a conformant Process Reference Model that provides process purpose and outcomes, a conformant Process Assessment Model that can be used to assess the processes, plus how to map between the two models. The chapter also specifies the requirements for a conformant assessment in detail. Finally, the chapter discusses certification of assessors and assessment results.

In chapter 4, I explain the major dimension of process assessment: the capability dimension. The measurement framework describes the Capability Levels of ISO/IEC 15504, compares the new standard to the older Capability

Levels in ISO/IEC TR 15504-2:1998, and describes the author's experience of the state of practice for each Capability Level. The way to rate process attributes using the NPLF rating scale is described. This is followed by the way process attributes are collated into process Capability Levels. Finally, I compare ISO/IEC 15504 to similar aspects of ISO 9000:2000.

In chapter 5, I explain the second dimension – the process dimension, as described in a Process Reference Model. The chapter describes several international standard models, particularly ISO/IEC 12207 and ISO/IEC 15288. The chapter then describes some industry and domain specific Process reference Models, including the Information Technology Infrastructure Library (ITIL ®) model, OOSPICE ® and SPICE for ISO 9000.

In chapter 6, I describe Process Assessment Models. The chapter starts by looking at the ISO/IEC 15504-2 requirements for Process Assessment Models, then the nature and use of process assessment indicators. To illustrate what a conformant Process Assessment Model contains, I describe the ISO/IEC 15504 part 5 and part 6 exemplars. I then summarize other conformant Process Assessment Models, including SPiCE for SPACE and its enhancements, OOSPICE for component-based development, and Automotive SPICE. The SEI CMMI® and FAA-iCMM are also described. Finally, I describe the use of assessment indicators in rating processes.

In chapter 7, I describe some standard process lifecycle models. These models provide the next level of detail and guidance that an organization requires in order to implement a detailed process infrastructure. The German V-Model, the Rational Unified Process are covered.

In chapter 8, I describe the requirements on assessors, specifically competence, both what is needed to gain the standing of competent assessor, as well as training, registration and certification. Finally, the chapter looks at how to assemble an assessment team that meets the assessor competence requirements of the standard.

In chapter 9, I provide a detailed example of assessing a process to capability level 5.

In chapter 10, I summarize the SW CMM® and CMMI® and their relationship to ISO/IEC 15504. The popularity of CMMI® versus ISO/IEC 15504-2 and advantages and disadvantages of each are covered.

In the Annexes, there is a short history of process assessment development and the ISO/IEC 15504-2 harmonization aspects and a Glossary of Acronyms and Terms.

Reader Guidance

The second edition of this book highlights changes in the standard, particularly in Part 5, the exemplar process assessment model and introduction of part 6 for assessing system processes. In addition I have updated the SPICE for SPACE, Automotive SPICE, and the CMMI information describe the latest issued versions. I have also introduced the concept of Enterprise Architecture and its relationship to processes in the first chapter.

The reader should keep in mind that parts of the standards are still evolving and I have written the book against the best available information at the time or writing. The following table suggests the most useful chapters for readers of the reference book and the practical guide.

Table 1. Reader Guidance to Books.

Reader	Reader's interests and expected benefits	Reference Book	Practical Guide
Manager	Benefit from the use of process assessment and process improvement	1	1, 2, 5, 4, 10
Quality Professional	General quality system and process management. Comparing assessment models, and the uses of process assessment.	1, 2, 3, 4, 5, 7, 9, 10, Annex 1	1, 2, 3, 4, 5, 8, 9, 10
Assessors	Conducting a conformant assessment, developing the skills and competencies needed to perform an assessment. In-depth capability rating guidance.	3, 4, 6, 8, 9, Annex 2, Annex 3	2, 6, 7, 8, 9, 10, Annex 1, Annex 2
Assessment Sponsor	How an assessment is conducted, what tools and other support are required, how to initiate an assessment. Various types of uses of assessments, Interpreting the results.	1, 3, 4, 8, Annex 3	1, 2, 3, 4, 5, 6, 8, 11
Process Owner	Design and implementation of processes. Improving processes.	1, 5, 7	1, 5
Process Expert	Provide expertise on process design and applicability of the standard to design and improvement of processes.	2, 4, 5, 6, 7	5, 7, 8
Process Practitioner	Implement a process; participate in design and assessment of processes.		1, 2, 4, 5
Process Improvement Sponsor	Initiating an improvement programme, defining assessment inputs for an assessment for improvement purposes, using assessment results for improvement.	1, 3	1, 2, 5, 8, 9, 10, 11

Process Capability Determination Sponsor	Initiating a programme for the determination of supplier capability, defining a target capability profile, verifying and using assessment results in a capability determination exercise.	1, 3	1, 2, 4, 8, 10, 3 (optional)
Developers of Process Assessment Models	Developing Process Assessment Models for performing assessments against a compliant Process Reference Model and measurement framework of ISO/IEC 15504-2.	1, 2, 3, 4, 5, 6, 7 Annex 2, Annex 5	
Developers of Methods	Developing a method that will support the performance of conformant assessments.	3, 5, 6	
Tool Developers	Developing tools that support assessors by collecting, recording and classifying evidence in assessments.	3	Annex 1, Annex 2
Improvement Team Facilitator	Help teams in a Team Based Business Design Improvement process.		2, 5
Customer	Benefits and use of process assessment from a customer perspective, particularly for setting target profiles, capability determination and improvement.	1	1, 2, 3, 5, 8, 10, 11

An International Standard for Process Assessment

Foundation for success

Yet another Quality Standard?

Over the past three decades, there has been a proliferation of Quality Standards covering products and processes. These products and services are increasingly using software as a fundamental way to create competitive differentiation. The creation and use of software often requires more attention to the processes used to produce the products and services.

There are many organizations that develop these standards, including the International Organization for Standardisation (ISO for short), The International Electrotechnical Commission (IEC), the Institute for Electrical and Electronic Engineers (IEEE), and the United States government through bodies such as the National Institute for Standards and Technology (NIST). In addition, many other organizations are involved in contributing to standards development including the United Kingdom government through the UK Ministry of Defence (MoD) and the Software Engineering Institute (SEI).

There are industry standards both de facto and formalized by industry organizations, formal association driven standards, government standards, national standards and International standards.

There are standards that specify management approaches; standards that specify technical work approaches such as product development and testing; standards that specify safety and security requirements for products, standards that specify product compliance requirements; and standards that specify environmental management aspects.

In this book, I focus on standards related to processes, of which there are more than enough to keep anyone busy staying up to date with their evolution.

There are several standards addressing quality aspects of processes at international and national level.

Perhaps the most well known set of standards in quality are the ISO 9000 series. ISO 9000 provides a general set of International Standards covering an organization's achievement of quality, especially quality from the customer viewpoint. The standard has evolved to focus more on development (ISO 9001), implementation and improvement, in particular how it applies to the organization's processes for developing customer products and services.

When properly applied, standard such as ISO 9001 can help an organization to more efficiently and effectively produce quality products and services. When an organization applies ISO 9001, there is a requirement to assess how they perform. Traditionally ISO 9001 was used to audit an organization's processes for conformance[1].

So why another quality standard?

The international standards community decided that there was a need for a process assessment standard that provides for assessing *how well* processes are performed.

Another principal justification for a new standard was that assessment approaches were multiplying, and they were not consistent and compatible with each other. Process assessment was being widely applied in commercially sensitive areas (supplier selection, supplier management) and incompatible approaches could lead to inconsistent results.

The international standards community therefore proposed a process assessment standard, created with the aim to consistently assess processes.

The standard consists of 3 main elements:

- a measurement framework,
- a set of requirements for defining processes, and
- a set of requirements for how to perform consistent assessments.

In addition, the standard should provide a means of harmonization between various international standards for processes and for professional organization process assessment methods. This would allow an organization to compare results from different conformant assessment methods; it allows them to *"compare apples against apples"*.

This standard is known as ISO/IEC 15504.

ISO/IEC 15504 differs from many preceding standards in two fundamental ways. First, it does not prescribe a way of working (i.e. the processes to be followed). It is important to note that while the standard refers to processes, they are meant to be typical examples for the purpose of assessment, not required processes to run an enterprise! Secondly, it does not focus on

---

[1] In ISO 9004:2000 there has been a move towards assessing more than conformance, expanding it to assessing *how well* processes are performed.

process compliance, but rather on how well processes are performed and managed.

The standard meets the needs of ISO 9001 sub clause 8.2.3 for monitoring and measurement of processes. In fact, ISO/IEC 15504 assessments have no 'pass' or 'fail' criteria (compared to quality audits that traditionally assess for conformance or non conformance). Instead, ISO/IEC 15504 focuses on how well a process is performed, managed, defined, measured and improved.

People-Process-Product

The preceding section emphasizes the existence of a large number of quality standards and this book focuses on process related aspects of these standards. Simply, the fundamental question is "why do we have quality standards?" The basic reason for quality standards is to help organizations to achieve success by meeting their customer's needs, and to assure others that this achievement is as consistent as possible, so that they will benefit as customers (or partners or even suppliers).

So how do organizations achieve success?

Organizations rely on their people, processes and products to achieve success.

However people, processes and products interact in organizations in a variety of ways and no two organizations interact the same way. This is primarily because each organization has different people and groups of people. The people in the organization decide upon the products and processes. In discussing process assessment, it is important to understand what a process is. In ISO/IEC 15504, it uses the following definition:

Process – "*a set of interrelated activities, which transform inputs into outputs.*"

The ISO definition is mechanistic and a bit abstract; after all normally it is people who perform activities. Let's look at another definition. The Cambridge Dictionary of American English definition is:

"*A process is a series of actions that you take in order to achieve a result.*"

This definition encompasses people, actions (processes) and results (outcomes). Furthermore, the results may be product oriented, people oriented or process oriented. I model this interaction in a simple model I call the People-Process-Product model. This is described in detail in the author's book: Reach for the STARS, Leadership and management in the new millennium [1].

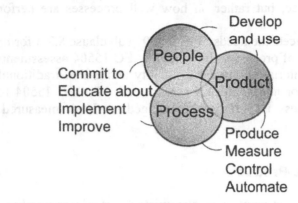

Fig. 1. People-Process-Product model. .

- People develop products (goods and services) for customers.
- People invent, commit to, educate themselves and others, and implement processes in order to produce these products.
- People use products (also often referred to as technology or tools) in their organization/business.
- Processes are used to measure and control the production of products.
- People improve processes as one way to improve products.
- Products can be used to simplify and automate processes.

Each organization can decide the balance between the way people, processes and products interact, the extent that they interact and the extent they rely on each. For example, I can decide upon various ways to achieve success:

- Do I allow people to choose the way they do something (e.g. craftsmanship)?
- Do I automate the way something is done by means of a product (e.g. an automated tool or software)?
- Do I define a standard process?

All three ways may be possible. Naturally, an organization striving for success wants to use the 'best way' (the most efficient and effective) that is available to them. This will normally require the organization to select a particular combination of people, processes and products that reflects the experience and knowledge of their people, the types of products they create and the processes they need to follow.

One important point to keep in mind is that people vary in the way that they perform activities. This variation is a natural phenomenon. Different people can vary in doing the same or similar tasks, and one person can vary depending upon how they feel or think at different times. Sometimes this variation can be positive, for example finding ways to improve a product or service, sometimes this variation can be negative, for example failing to completely test a product due to time constraints. Poor processes can lead to poor or inconsistent quality products and failure. So appropriate processes are one of the 3 important organizational prerequisites to achieve success.

When people define and implement processes, they have an important means to manage achievement of their organizational success, and to manage variation in performance of the activities that achieve successful results.

When these people, processes and products interact together harmoniously and in synergy, they help the organization to achieve success.

A process view of the world

When people define and implement processes, they need to consider several aspects:
- What outcomes do I want to achieve?
- What outputs do I produce that achieve these outcomes?
- What inputs do I need?
- What are the activities I need to perform to create the outputs?
- Who needs to be involved?
- Do I need any other resources to support the activities?
- How do I control the process to make sure any variation does not cause poor quality?
- How do I check that I have achieved the right outcome?
  The following diagram represents a simple process that covers the above.

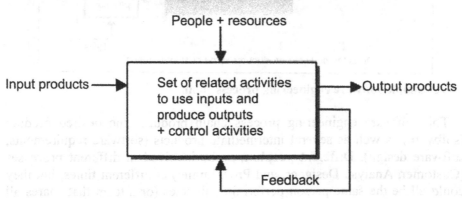

Fig 2. Simple process block diagram.

The process diagram not only has a set of activities focused on producing outputs that meet the desired outcomes, but also has a means to control variation (through use of feedback) that helps to manage the achievement of the desired outcomes.

It is possible to create one process that takes all the required inputs, uses all the people and resources and produces all the required outputs. Generally, though that is not a good idea for the following reasons:

- I may only need some of the people for some of the activities.
- I may not need to do all the activities all the time.
- I may need to look at other products beside the final outputs of a process.
- I may want to better manage a process by having different feedback and control at different times.

Therefore, people design process chains that link a set of processes together The following is a simple example of a set of processes for creating software to meet a customer's needs.

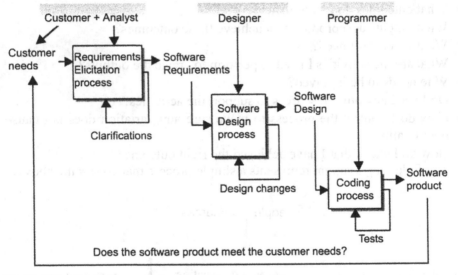

Fig. 3. Simple software engineering process chain

This software engineering process chain produces the desired product (software) as well as several intermediate products (software requirements, software design). Different people may be involved in different processes (Customer, Analyst, Designer, and Programmer) at different times, but they could all be the same person performing all roles (or a team that shares all the roles).

Whether performance is by one person or a team, the people involved still have a vital quality question to resolve:

"Does the software product meet the customer needs?"

If the answer is positive, then it can be said that the above process chain meets its purpose and the desired product outcomes have been achieved.

But is this the only purpose of the process chain?

Here are some other questions to ponder:

- Did I produce the software by the time that the customer wanted it?
- Did I produce the software at a cost that allowed me to make a profit (or at least break even)?
- Did the people involved work efficiently, or were some of them doing nothing some of the time?
- Can I follow the same process again to make another software product for another customer?
- Do I know how well all the activities were performed?
- Could I improve the way I do it next time to be faster and make it cost less?

A good way to answer these questions is by doing process assessment.

Enterprise Architecture

The process view of the world can be extended further. The view can be expanded to cover people and products (technology), at least in part. This is termed an Enterprise Architecture. Enterprise Architecture is a method for describing an organization's processes, information systems, personnel and organizational structure. The aim is to align these elements with the organization's core goals and strategic direction.

Enterprise Architecture started as an information technology (IT) initiative, but IT oriented (consulting) firms are applying it to the practice of business optimization, addressing business architecture, performance management and process architecture. The primary purpose of creating an Enterprise Architecture is to ensure that business strategy and IT investments are aligned.

The practice of Enterprise Architecture involves the creation and application of an architectural framework to describe a current or proposed future architecture for the organization. The framework describes the organization structure, roles, entities and relationships that exist or should exist to perform a set of business processes. The framework specifies a taxonomy and ontology that clearly identifies the business processes and how they are performed. This results in a set of artefacts that describe, in varying degrees of detail, how an enterprise operates and what resources are required.

The enterprise decision makers use the artefacts as a basis to make informed decisions about when and where to invest resources, when and where to realign organizational goals and processes, and what policies and procedures are needed to support core missions or business functions. An Enterprise Architecture process helps to answer the following questions:

- Is the current architecture supporting and adding value to the organization?
- Are parts of the current architecture wasteful (no added value)?
- How could the architecture be modified to add more value to the organization?
- Based on the enterprise vision and mission for the future, will the current architecture support or hinder achieving this?

The first step in implementing an Enterprise Architecture starts with documenting the enterprise's strategy and details such as where and how it operates. The Enterprise Architecture then documents in increasing amount of detail the core competencies, business processes, the enterprise process interactions internally and with external parties such as customers, suppliers, and government entities. These Enterprise Architecture process then flows down into the information technology components, including:

1. Organization charts, activities, and the process flows of the Information Technology Organization.
2. Organization cycles and processes, periods and timing of activities.
3. Applications and software inventories and diagrams.
4. Interfaces between applications such as data flows and relationships, timed and consequential events (one event that triggers another).
5. Suppliers of technology hardware, software, and services.
6. Intranet, Extranet, Internet, eCommerce, and eBusiness within and external to the organization
7. Databases and supporting data models
8. Hardware, platforms, and hosting servers.
9. Connections including local and wide area networks, and Internet connectivity diagrams.

As much as practicable, the above components are related to the organization's strategy, goals, and operations. The intermediate outcome is a comprehensive inventory of business strategy, processes, organizational charts, system and interface diagrams, technical/component inventories, network topologies, and the interrelationships.

The Enterprise Architecture documents the current status, as well as a desired future state (Reference Architecture). The Enterprise Architecture should also document a Target future state. The Target state is a modification of the Reference Architecture, taking account of tradeoffs and compromises. The result is set of models representing the Enterprise Architecture.

In addition to the models, the Enterprise Architecture should document a set of good and best systems engineering practices. These should cover manageability, adaptability, scalability, security, etc. The organization must design and implement a process that ensures continual movement from the current state to the future state. The future state will generally be a combination of one or more:

- Activities to close gaps between the current organization strategy and the ability of the IT organization to support it
- Activities to achieve the desired future organization strategy and the ability of the IT organization to support it
- Necessary upgrades and replacements to the IT architecture based on performance of software and hardware, capacity issues, regulatory requirements, and supplier issues.

Enterprise Architecture is a key component of the IT governance process at any organization of significant size (and hence subject to Sabanes Oxley act in the United States). A formal Enterprise Architecture process supports the governance and management of IT, while relating IT to business optimization.

Because Enterprise Architecture addresses business architecture, performance management and process architecture, it has a need for some form of assessment. Hence, process assessment can assess many of the aspects of Enterprise architecture.

Fundamentals of Process Assessment

The previous sections highlights what an Enterprise Architecture, a process and a process chain can achieve (the purpose and outcomes) to meet the goals of the organization. It poses questions that are related to efficiency and effectiveness of the processes themselves, and the organization implementing these processes.

An organization can use various means to assess its performance. From a business viewpoint, it is important to consider why process assessment is a good means to do this.

To be efficient and effective, organizations need to know how well their current processes help them achieve their goals (amongst other factors). To be competitive, organizations also need to compare their efficiency and effectiveness with their competitors. Competitive forces will often mean that an organization needs to improve various aspects of their activities, including improvement of processes in order to remain competitive.

In addition, if the organization can relate what they used (inputs, resources) to the results they obtain, they can determine their efficiency. If an organization can compare their efficiency and effectiveness (achievement of their goals) to other organizations, they can judge their competitiveness.

When people assess processes, they increase their understanding of their actual performance and management of activities, and the potential for improvement. Following the People-Process-Product model, people performing process assessment are assessing one of the 3 major factors leading to organizational success. Simply stated, process assessment provides an organization with an important means to assess and improve their performance.

What specific aspects of process assessment are important?

In order to effectively and efficiently assess processes, the organization must use a clear and consistent measurement scale. The measurement scale should make clear distinctions between the levels of achievement. These clear levels of achievement not only help the organization understand its current performance, but can also act as guidance to what it should try to achieve in the future (improvement). A simple analogy of this measurement scale might be to compare it to a home:

- Level 0 is like living outdoors on the bare earth under a tree. Not good.
- Level 1 is having a floor, four walls and a roof. Just basic shelter.
- Level 2 means you have doors and windows. Now you have some limited control of the environment inside your home (you can stop the wind and rain blowing in).
- Level 3 means you have basic services such as electricity and plumbing. Now you can better control the environment inside your home.
- Level 4 means that you have all the basic furniture and fittings. You are starting to feel at home and can think about what comforts you want.
- Level 5 means that you have all the desired modern conveniences, perhaps air conditioning, security, the latest home entertainment system, fast internet connection and so on. You are able to optimise your living environment to suit your lifestyle.

Naturally, a real process assessment measurement framework is a bit more complicated than the above analogy, but the principle of clear levels of achievement applies.

Furthermore, if the measurement scale is standardized, organizations that perform process assessment have one indirect form of comparison to competitors (their process capability). In addition to a good measurement scale, process assessment requires a consistent approach (in fact a well defined process). The following diagram illustrates some of the major activities and documented components that need to be addressed to ensure consistent process assessment.

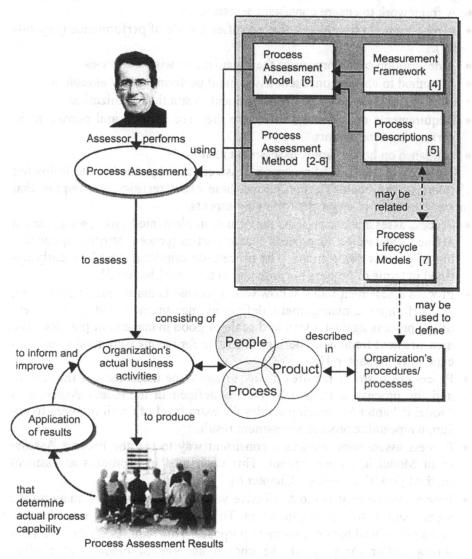

Fig. 4. Process assessment overview.

As illustrated in the diagram, process assessment assesses the organization's actual business activities in terms of one or more implemented processes (process chains) against a (standard) measurement framework. The characteristics of a process assessment approach that make it useful for an organization can be summarized as:

- A framework to ensure consistent assessments.
- A measurement framework that specifies a scale of performance (capability).
- A description of the processes the organization wishes to assess.
- A method to ensure consistent assessment performance by assessors.
- Guidance on how to tailor the assessment to suit the organization.
- Requirements on assessors to ensure they are capable and consistent in performing assessments.
- Guidance on how to apply assessment results.

These characteristics of process assessment are expanded in the following chapters of the book. To summarize these characteristics, we require that process assessment cover the following aspects.

- Process assessment compares the actual, implemented processes against a defined standard set of process characteristics (process attributes) consisting of process descriptions. The process descriptions must be clearly defined in terms of process purpose and outcomes [Chapter 5].
- Process assessment looks at how well a process is managed, by comparing the performance, management, definition, measurement and improvement of the process against a standard scale of good management practice. The measurement framework defines this scale for the measurement of process capability[2] [Chapter 4].
- Process assessment requires a way to apply the measurement framework and the process descriptions. This is defined in a Process Assessment Model [Chapter 6], which provides the extra level of detail required to ensure a repeatable process assessment result.
- Process assessment requires a consistent way to use the Process Assessment Model in an assessment. This is defined in a process assessment method [Practical Guide – Chapter 6].
- Process assessment is most effective when there is a way of adapting the assessment to suit the organization. This is especially important when assessment is used for improvement purposes. This requires guidance on tailoring and/or mapping of the chosen assessment model and method [Chapter 3].
- Consistent process assessment also requires a level of skill, experience and competence of the assessors [Chapter 8].

---

[2] Process capability relates to the organization's ability to deliver specified or desired performance consistently/predictably.

- A comprehensive process assessment approach will also provide guidance on interpretation and application of the assessment results (see the Practical Guide).

When an assessor performs process assessment, he/she will assess whether the organization has adopted some form of consistent approach for its processes. When an organization standardizes not just one or two processes, but defines a complete set of processes (process chains) so their interactions are also defined, they have a coherent process framework that improves their ability to succeed.

To help organizations decide how to define such a process framework, they can look at standards that define such frameworks in Process Reference Model standards [Chapter 5]. They can also look at more detailed implementation guidance contained in process lifecycle models [Chapter 7].

Process Assessment and ISO/IEC 15504

Process assessment can use a variety of approaches to achieve all of the requirements and needs in the previous section. Different models have been developed over time, many of which have been incompatible with each other.

ISO/IEC 15504 is a standard that provides a way to achieve all of the above. It specifies and/or refers to all the process assessment requirements needed to ensure consistent process assessments. ISO/IEC 15504 consists of 5 parts; part 2 is the normative part of the standard.

Many organizations have embraced the standard. They range from the international and national standards setting authorities, through professional organizations such as the Software Engineering Institute in the USA, the European Software Institute and the Software Quality Institute in Australia. They include large multinational and global firms and organizations such as the European Space Agency, France Telecom and automotive manufacturers, and even small and medium enterprises operating within a single country, state or city. The standard provides an ability to tailor it to suit each type and size of organization.

Organizations use the standard as a means to:
- assess the capability of their suppliers;
- provide a means to assure that consistent processes are applied in a manner to produce consistent quality products; and
- help their suppliers to progress to better process management.

Most importantly, many organizations use ISO/IEC 15504 to improve their own business and this is the primary reason that use of the standard is so attractive.

One of the strengths of an ISO/IEC 15504 process assessment is that it defines where you are now and provides direction on how to improve your processes (capability). Improving process capability can help an organization's business aim to improve efficiency and effectiveness.

ISO/IEC 15504 in part 2 provides a complete framework for process assessment. The diagram below illustrates all the basic requirements for process assessment. It describes the four documented components required in the previous section, namely:

- The process assessment model.
- The measurement framework.
- The process descriptions.
- The process assessment method.

The latest revision of ISO/IEC 155504 part 2 specifies requirements on the externally specified process descriptions and process assessment methods.

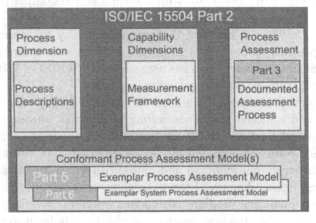

Fig. 5. ISO/IEC 15504 process assessment components.

ISO/IEC 15504 Part 2 is aided by Part 3, which provides informative guidelines for application of the process assessment process (methodology), and by part 5 and 6 that provide exemplar Process Assessment Models meeting the part 2 requirements for a conformant Process Assessment Model.

As shown in the above diagram, ISO/IEC 15504-2 specifies the requirements for process assessment using two complementary orthogonal dimensions:

- Capability dimension.
- Process dimension.

The two dimensions work together to provide complete process assessment ability. The standard specifies the capability dimension as consisting of 6 Capability Levels (CL 0 – CL 5). The standard specifies requirements for the process dimension consisting of a set of process descriptions (P1, ... Pn), which are defined in a Process Reference Model.[3]

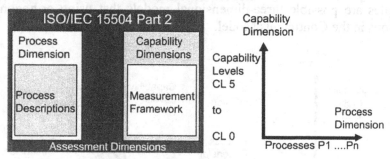

Fig. 6. Two process assessment dimensions – continuous model.

ISO/IEC 15504-2 uses a continuous model representation[4] for the capability and process dimensions. The advantage of this two dimensional continuous model is that it allows for any process to be assessed and rated at any Capability Level, independently of any other process[5].

Therefore, the organization can decide to assess one process or a group of processes. It can select different groups of processes depending upon their importance to specific projects or organizational units (for example a customer help desk uses different processes to a project developing new software). The organization can also decide to which Capability Level it wishes to assess each process, for example the organization may decide to assess all processes to the same Capability Level, or it may decide to assess some processes to a higher Capability Level than others.

---

[3] These processes are normally structured into process categories of related processes but for assessment purposes can also be considered as separate processes.

[4] Note: earlier process assessment methods consisted of a staged model (for example, Software Engineering Institute SW CMM® V1.1) where processes were required to be implemented in a specific order to indicate increasing process maturity. This is in some ways easier to follow, but much less flexible than using a Continuous Model (see the chapter comparing SW CMM® and CMMI® to ISO/IEC 15504 for further discussion of advantages and disadvantages).

[5] We will see later in the book that there are some logical, associated process dependencies.

This level of flexibility is very useful, as the organization may need some processes to be implemented with higher process capability in some projects/units due to their importance (for example in a safety critical development project), while allowing them to run at lower levels of capability in other projects.

The two dimensional model has other advantages compared to a staged model. It allows further orthogonal dimensions to be added. The following examples are possible three-dimensional models that using orthogonal dimensions in the Continuous Model.

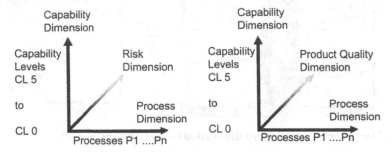

Fig. 7. Three dimensional models using risk and product quality dimensions.

The ability to have additional dimensions allows the organization to compare these additional aspects to the process aspects. For example, if the organization has higher capability processes, how do they affect product quality, risk or the use of technology?

For an organization using an Enterprise Architecture, the third dimension could be related to implementation of information technology. For example, the organization may look at how and where information technology can automate processes or how governance standards translate business process goals into information technology outcomes.

For examples of use of the risk and information technology dimensions, readers should look at the Practical Guide. Further advantages of the continuous two dimensional model are:

• The capability dimension is generally applicable to any process. In other words, any process can be assessed between capability level 0 and capability level 5. This is important when a business needs to determine the most appropriate level of management of various processes in various situations. In single dimension (staged) models, this is not the case, as processes are tied to specific maturity levels. A single dimensional model may suit many businesses but will not suit all businesses.

• An ability to use a variety of Process Reference Models without affecting the Capability dimension.

- An ability to use a variety of Process Assessment Models (and methods) for each Process Reference Model.
- An ability to use the Capability dimension with multiple International Standards (ISO 9000, ISO 12207, ISO 15288).
- There is a clear definition of processes (no mix of process description and how well the process is performed and managed).
- There is a clear definition of the Capability Levels and attributes of process capability.

Part 2 of the standard specifies the requirements for a Process Reference Model if the organization wishes to have an ISO/IEC 15504 conformant process assessment.

With the latest revision of part 2, this model is now specified externally to the standard. This allows an organization to choose and/or design their own Process Reference Model. The organizations may choose an existing model that suits their business (for example an existing software process standard or system engineering process standard), add processes that are unique to their way of doing business, or even create a complete process model. This flexibility also provides organizations that have used older standards a form of backwards compatibility that enables them to migrate to the new standard.

In fact, several industries are creating and using their own Process Reference Model. The automotive industry, space industry and object oriented software development industries have created their own process reference models.

Also, part 2 specifies how an organization can validate the compliance of a conformant Process Assessment Model. One such conformant model is provided in part 5 of the standard as an exemplar. This model in part 5 meets all the requirements of part 2 for a Process Assessment Model for assessing an organization involved in acquiring, developing and/or supporting software oriented products and services. Furthermore, the model in part 5 is based on and compatible with ISO/IEC 12207. Part 5 is not just an exemplar but is also the foundation used for the extended space and automotive industry models.

In addition, the standard now includes another exemplar Process Assessment Model in Part 6, based on ISO/IEC 15288 for system life cycle processes.

The capability dimension has a measurement framework with nine process attributes that is grouped into Capability Levels 1 to 5. These Capability Levels (CL 1 – CL 5) define an ordinal scale of increasing process capability[6]. Note that Capability Level 0 is defined as an incomplete process and indicates a lack of achievement of the Capability Level 1 process attribute.

One of the strengths of this ordinal scale is that there is a clear level of achievement at each Capability Level. At Capability Level 1, the level of achievement is related to the performance of the process.

From Capability Level 2 to Capability Level 5, the level of achievement is related to how well the process is managed, defined, quantitatively controlled, and improved using a standard scale of good management practice. The Capability Levels apply consistently to all processes. This ordinal scale is a differentiating feature compared to most other assessment measurement frameworks.

Table 2. Measurement Framework

	Capability Level	Process Attribute	Rating Scale
ISO/IEC 15504 Part 2 — Capability Dimensions — Measurement Framework	CL 0	None	NPLF
	CL 1	PA 1.1	NPLF
	CL 2	PA 2.1	NPLF
		PA 2.2	NPLF
	CL 3	PA 3.1	NPLF
		PA 3.2	NPLF
	CL 4	PA 4.1	NPLF
		PA 4,2	NPLF
	CL 5	PA 5.1	NPLF
		PA 5.2	NPLF

Rating Scale: N=Not, P=Partially, L=Largely, F=Fully

In the following chapters, I will look at how the process and capability dimensions are further developed into a Process Capability Measurement Framework, a Process Reference Model, and a Process Assessment Model.

In an Annex, I briefly outline the history of the development of process assessment, including ISO/IEC 15504 and also describe one of the other objectives of the standard, which is to act as a means for harmonization for a wide variety of process assessment methods and models, so that assessment results can be exchanged.

---

[6] Another simple analogy is the Star rating of hotels (1 Star to 5 Star hotels). Each hotel offers a room with a bed, but as a hotel receives more stars, the quality and reliability of the accommodation improves.

ISO/IEC 15504 document set

ISO/IEC 15504 document set

In this chapter, I describe the structure, relationships and assessment dimensions of the new standard as guidance to readers who need to understand the relationship between the various parts of the standard.

Assessors, quality professionals and other personnel involved in process design, implementation and assessment need to be aware of the process assessment dimensions and measurement framework so that processes are designed and assessed in a manner consistent with the requirements of the standard.

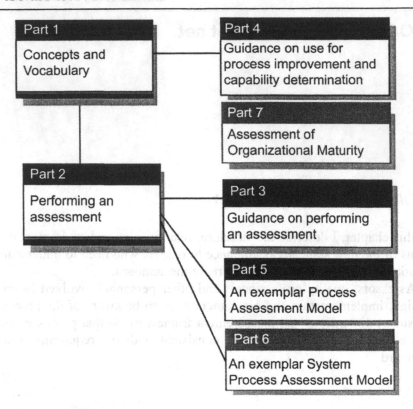

Fig. 8. ISO/IEC 15504 Document set.

ISO/IEC 15504 standard [2] consists of five parts. Part 2 is the normative part of the standard, and parts 1, 3, 4 and 5 are informative only (but provide important guidance and clarification). The document set of the standard is fully approved as a standard. The five parts are titled:

- ISO/IEC 15504-1 Information Technology - Process Assessment - Part 1 - Concepts and vocabulary.
- ISO/IEC 15504-2 Information Technology - Process Assessment - Part 2 - Performing an assessment.
- ISO/IEC 15504-3 Information Technology - Process Assessment - Part 3 - Guidance on performing an assessment.
- ISO/IEC 15504-4 Information Technology - Process Assessment - Part 4 - Guidance on use for process improvement and process capability determination.
- ISO/IEC 15504-5 Information Technology - Process Assessment - Part 5 - An exemplar Process Assessment Model.

In addition to the standard parts, there are two additional parts under development and review. These are:

- ISO/IEC TR 15504-6 Information Technology - Process Assessment - Part 6: An Exemplar System Life Cycle Process Assessment Model.
- ISO/IEC TR 15504-7 Information Technology – Process Assessment Part 7: Assessment of Organizational Maturity[7].

Part 1 of ISO/IEC 15504 provides a general entry point to readers of the standard. It describes how the parts of the document suite fit together, and provides guidance for their selection and use.

Part 2 is the normative part of ISO/IEC 15504 (i.e. the actual standard). ISO/IEC 15504-2 defines the 2-dimensional assessment model; consisting of a process dimension and a capability dimension. The process dimension refers to an external Process Reference Model (e.g. ISO/IEC 12207 [3]). A compliant model must provide a statement of process purpose and process outcome. Part 2 sets requirements for verification of model compliance.

The capability dimension in part 2 has nine process attributes. The process attributes are grouped into five process Capability Levels (there are none at Capability Level 0), defining an ordinal scale of capability, which is applicable across all processes. It also sets requirements for performing conformant assessments and assessment models.

The third part of ISO/IEC 15504 provides an overview of process assessment with guidance on meeting the requirements for performing an assessment, including:

- An assessment process.
- Guidance on the measurement framework for the process capability dimension.
- The requirements on the Process Reference Model and on process assessment methods.
- Guidance on competency of assessors

Readers with specific interest in either process improvement or supplier capability determination should read Part 4 for detailed guidance on these contexts of use. The concepts and principles of process improvement are generic and applicable to any type of organization or business. The guidance for process capability determination can be applied to any customer-supplier relationship. This part will enable the user to identify the appropriate usage of the normative components of ISO/IEC 15504 (part 2).

The seventh part extends the concept of process capability determination to apply it to an organizational maturity level determination. This part provides a concept and approach to determining the overall maturity of the or-

---

[7] At the time of writing the second edition, this was a working draft (WD) document.

ganization, based upon assessment of the process capability levels in several organizational units. The current version of part 7 is in response to user requests to have an organization wide assessment result in a manner similar to that possible using SEI CMMI. ®.[8]

The fifth part of ISO/IEC 15504 provides an exemplar model compatible with the reference model in ISO/IEC 12207 AMD 1 & 2. This extends the reference model required in part two with a comprehensive set of indicators of process performance and capability for organizations that acquire, develop and operate software products. The sixth part of ISO/IEC 15504 is released as a Technical Report (TR) in a similar manner to the way that part 5 was also initially issued. It provides another exemplar model that covers system life cycle processes. It is compatible with the reference model developed in ISO/IEC 15288[4]

Note that Part 5 and 6 are provided as part of the standard, and that they are examples of Conformant Process Assessment Models.

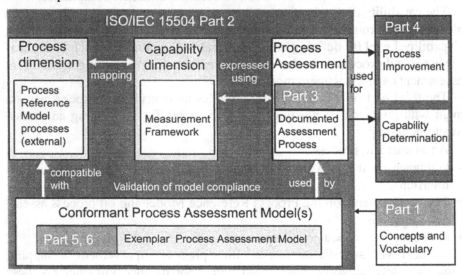

Fig. 9. ISO/IEC 15504 relationship of parts.

The diagram illustrates that the standard not only provides all the requirements for process assessment, but also provides guidance on how to use the results of process assessment (Part 4 and eventually part 7), and requirements on validation of Process Assessment Models.

As various stakeholders in a process assessment need to use the standard, it is possible to guide readers. Table 1 identifies the principal readers for

---

[8] The approach is not exactly the same as SEI CMMI and will be described in more detail later in this book.

ISO/IEC 15504 and shows where their primary areas of interest are addressed within the document set.

Table 3. Readership of parts of ISO/IEC 15504.

Reader	Reader's Interests	Suggested parts
Assessment Sponsor	How an assessment is conducted, what tools and other support are required, how to initiate an assessment.	1, 2, 3
Process Improvement Sponsor	Initiating an improvement programme, defining assessment inputs for an assessment for improvement purposes, using assessment results for improvement.	4
Process Capability Determination Sponsor	Initiating a programme for the determination of supplier capability, defining a target capability profile, verifying and using assessment results in a capability determination exercise.	4
Assessors	Conducting a conformant assessment, developing the skills and competencies needed to perform an assessment.	2, 3, 4, 5, 6
Developers of Process Assessment Models	Developing Process Assessment Models for performing assessments based on a compliant Process Reference Model and the measurement framework as defined in ISO/IEC 15504-2	2, 3, 5, 6
Developers of Assessment Methods	Developing a method that will support the performance of conformant assessments.	2, 3, 5, 6
Tool Developers	Developing tools that will support assessors by collecting, recording and classifying evidence in the performance of assessments.	2, 3, 5, 6

As the documentation set is quite large, it is inappropriate (and too time consuming) for everyone in the organization to read all parts of the standard. Therefore, the reading guide should be used to guide persons having various roles within the organization being assessed.

If an organization is preparing an assessment, the persons (normally the assessors) involved should consider creating a presentation that covers the main aspects of the assessment process and the improvement process for the sponsors, rather than relying on the sponsors to read the relevant sections of the standard.

ISO/IEC 15504 and shows where their primary areas of interest are addressed within the document set.

Table 3: Readership of parts of ISO/IEC 15504

ISO/IEC 15504 Requirements

Meeting the requirements of ISO/IEC 15504

ISO/IEC 15504 has a requirement to harmonize various Process Assessment Models and methods to ensure that assessment results are compatible and can be used in a variety of organizations. This affects the various assessment models, assessment methods and certification aspects and in this chapter, I describe how the harmonization requirements set explicit requirements for conformance for these aspects. This chapter will be of interest to assessment model developers, assessors and assessment sponsors.

The ISO/IEC 15504-2 requirements for conformance specify relationships between a Process Reference Model, a Process Assessment Model and a Conformant Assessment process.

Since the standard is a process assessment standard, from a practical viewpoint, businesses and assessors are primarily interested in how to make conformant assessments. The standard requires five elements to be defined:

1. A conformant assessment process.
2. A conformant Process Assessment Model.
3. Specified roles and responsibilities, particularly for qualified assessors.
4. Specific assessment inputs.
5. Specific assessment output.

There are several defined roles in assessments beside the competent (qualified) assessor. They include the assessment sponsor who defines the need for an assessment and the desired outcomes. There should be a coordinator who organises the personnel and interview time and place. There often will be additional assessors, some of whom are in training or qualification to become competent assessors. Finally, there are the assessment participants, who are interviewed.

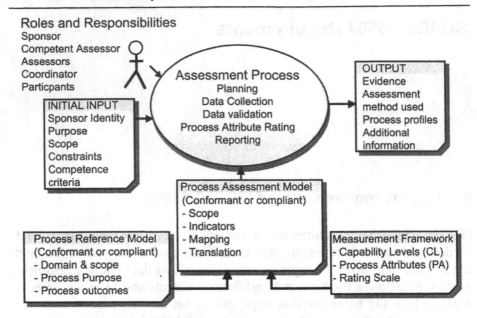

Fig. 10. Process Reference/Assessment Model and Assessment relationships.

The standard requires that the conformant Process Assessment Model has a defined relationship to the required Measurement Framework (in part 2) and a Process Reference Model. The diagram illustrates that the process reference model provides domain, scope, process purpose and outcomes. The measurement framework provides the capability levels, process attributes and rating scale.

ISO/IEC 15504-2 (part 2) specifies the Process Capability Measurement Framework. All assessments must use this measurement framework or map their results to this framework in order to be conformant[9].

ISO/IEC 15504-2 specifies the need for a Process Reference Model. The Process Reference Model specifies the processes to be assessed, and hence provides the mechanism whereby a Process Assessment Model(s) is related to the measurement framework defined by ISO/IEC 15504-2.

The Process Reference Model is defined external to ISO/IEC 15504-2 (see the Process Reference Model chapter for examples), so that it can be changed to suit the organization. Not all reference models are relevant to an organization; in addition some organizations will require specific processes that do not exist in standard models.

---

[9] The FAA iCMM and SEI CMMI need to map their results to the measurement framework, since parts of their primary measurement framework differ to the ISO/IEC 15504 capability levels.

The Process Assessment Model is based on the process descriptions provided in Process Reference Models (see the Process Assessment Model chapter for examples). It expands the level of detail so that sufficient indicators are provided to enable an assessor to effectively assess a process.

ISO/IEC 15504-2 specifies the requirements for a conformant assessment process using the selected Process Assessment Model. It specifies the required roles, skills and experience of assessors and the required inputs and outputs.

Conformant Process Reference Model

An ISO/IEC 15504 conformant Process Reference Model shall adhere to certain requirements to assure that assessment results are translatable into an ISO/IEC 15504 process profile in a repeatable and reliable manner. The model shall fulfil the following requirements:

- A declaration of the domain of application (for example, software development, space software, automotive).
- Description of the processes[10] shall include:
  - Purpose and outcomes.
  - The set of process outcomes shall be necessary and sufficient to achieve the process purpose. This could be production of an artefact, a significant change of state or meeting specified constraints such as requirements or goals.
  - Unique process descriptions and identification for each process.
- Process descriptions shall not contain or imply aspects of the measurement framework beyond Capability Level 1.
- A description of the relationship between the Process Reference Model and its intended context of use within its domain of application.
- A description of the relationship between the processes defined within the Process Reference Model.
- The Process Reference Model shall document the community of interest of the model. In addition, it shall describe the actions taken to achieve consensus within that community of interest.
  - The relevant community of interest will be characterized or specified.
  - The extent of achievement of consensus shall be documented, or if no consensus actions are taken, a statement to this effect.

---

[10] See clause 6.2.4 of ISO/IEC 15504-2

- Verification of the extent to which the model meets the requirements of ISO/IEC 15504 may be through either demonstration of conformity or demonstration of compliance[11].

Conformant Process Assessment Model

ISO/IEC 15504-2 specifies that a conformant Process Assessment Model shall be based upon a suitable reference source of process definitions, which is called a Process Reference Model.

It is feasible to have different Process Assessment Models using the same Process Reference Model basis, as long as they meet the conformance requirements through their relationship with the specified Process Reference Model.

It is also feasible to have one Process Assessment Model using several Process Reference Models for its basis, but this is more difficult to achieve (and the author has yet to see one in practice). However, one Process Assessment Model has industry specific extensions in addition to a standard Process Reference Model[12]. There is also a discussion in the user group about creating an enterprise architecture scoped Process reference Model.

A conformant Process Assessment Model provides a two-dimensional view of process capability[13].

In order to ensure consistency and repeatability of assessments, a conformant Process Assessment Model shall contain:

- A definition of its purpose, scope, elements and indicators.
- A mechanism for consistent expression of results.
- The mapping to the ISO/IEC 15504 Measurement Framework and the specified Process Reference Model(s).

The Process Assessment Model shall be based on process management principles and designed for assessing process capability, addressing all of the Capability Levels of the measurement framework for each of the processes within its scope. Note: the standard allows for the possibility that models

---

[11] The party performing verification shall obtain objective evidence that the Process Reference Model fulfils the requirements set forth in ISO/IEC 15504-2 clause 6.2. Objective evidence of conformance or compliance shall be retained.

[12] SPiCE for SPACE used ISO/IEC TR 15504-2:1998 Process Reference Model the ISO/IEC 12207 Process Reference Model as inputs, and added space industry specific extensions.

[13] The model must provide at least a process and a capability dimension, it may optionally provide more (e.g. risk, product quality, information technology implementation).

may only address a continuous subset of the Capability Levels starting at level 1 (but model developers are unlikely to use this option).

The Process Assessment Model shall declare its scope of coverage in the terms of:

• The selected Process Reference Model (s);
• The selected processes from the Process Reference Model (s);
• The Capability Levels selected from the measurement framework.

The conformant Process Assessment Model shall use a set of process capability indicators (PCI). The process capability indicators shall explicitly address the process purpose(s) of the selected processes from the selected Process Reference Model(s). They will demonstrate the achievement of the process attributes within the selected Capability Levels.

The Process Assessment Model shall provide a formal and verifiable rating mechanism for representing the assessment results as a set of process attribute ratings for each (assessed) process. The representation of results may involve a direct translation of Process Attribute ratings into a process profile[14] as defined in ISO/IEC 15504. Alternately, it may use the conversion of the data collected during the assessment (and any additional information collected) through further judgment on the part of the assessor.

Conformant Process Assessment Models shall enable comparison of outputs from assessments based upon the same Process Reference Model, using different Process Assessment Models.

Mapping Process Assessment Models to Process Reference Models

ISO/IEC 15504-2 specifies the need for mapping between the various models. The mapping must provide a way to relate the assessment model process attributes to the reference model process purpose and outcomes[15]. In practice the simplest way to do this is to use the same reference model components and repeat them as part of the process attributes. This is the way it is done between part 5 of the standard and ISO/IEC 12207[16].

There is one known partial exception to this approach. In the US Federal Aviation Administration iCMM model (FAA iCMM), the mapping is explicitly shown in extensive mapping tables, because their model is structurally different to the reference models.

---

[14] Process profile = set of process attribute ratings for a process
[15] See ISO/IEC 15504-2, 6.3.4
[16] After ISO/IEC 12207 was rewritten to meet this need!

The mapping provides the way to translate ratings from an ISO/IEC 15504 conformant assessment into a common format, which makes it possible to compare assessment ratings (from different assessments and from different Process Assessment Models).

The mapping requirements in the standard specify that the Process Assessment Model be accompanied by a detailed set of mappings, which demonstrate:

- How the indicators of process performance provide coverage for the purposes and outcomes of the processes in the specified Process Reference Model.
- How the indicators of process capability within the model provide coverage for the process attributes (including all of the results of achievement of the process attributes) in the measurement framework.

In the following diagram, the mapping requirements for the process capability are shown.

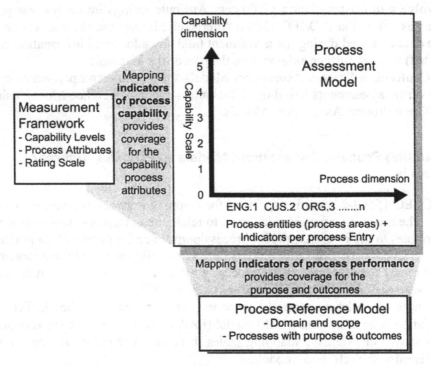

Fig. 11. Mapping of Process Assessment Model.

For an assessment to be considered conformant, it is essential that the assessor has access to the details of the mapping of the elements of the assessment model to the Process Reference Model.

The mapping may be straightforward, for example, the earlier model defined in technical report version of the standard (ISO/IEC TR 15504-5) used the processes of the Process Reference Model directly as the basis for its definition of the processes (one to one process mapping)[17]. The model defined in ISO/IEC 15504-5 (issued as the standard) maps to ISO/IEC 12207 (and its amendments). In addition, the ISO/IEC 15504-5 Process Assessment Model employs a continuous model architecture (one to one capability dimension mapping). A similar approach is used for part 6, which maps to ISO/IEC 15288.

Where the structure of the model is significantly different from the Process Reference Model, as could be the case of a Process Assessment Model employing other architectures[18], the mapping will likely be more complex.

In the early development of the standard (ISO/IEC PDTR 15504-5, the preliminary draft technical report version of the standard), the assessment trials indicated several instances where elements were components of more than one process attribute. This required modification to the model which was incorporated in the draft technical report and in the technical report version and in the standard version: ISO/IEC 15504-5.

Mappings that result in elements being identified as components of more than one Process Attribute may indicate problems with the model structure, which could result in ambiguous translation of results. This is also an issue when models are created using a single dimensional form[19].

Therefore, a Process Assessment Model developer should ensure that the mapping is clear and unambiguous. The standard requires that the model developer provide proof that the model conforms to the requirements for mapping clarity and translation of results.

An assessor should confirm that the mapping is meaningful – especially when trying a new model or when the model developers indicate that the model is not yet fully proven. One way to confirm that the mapping is meaningful is to sample some of the lowest level components in the model, and locate them in the Process Reference Model, either as elements of a process or as contributors to a process attribute.

The mapping also allows for an enterprise to create its own business process assessment model. In the simplest situation, this may be a mapping between existing process elements or business activities and one or more parts

---

[17] The Process Reference Model was contained in the earlier ISO/IEC TR 15504-2:1998 version of the standard, but has been removed in the issued version of the standard ISO/IEC 15504-2:2003. It is based upon ISO/IEC 12207 and its amendments.

[18] An example is the staged representation of the SEI CMMI®.

[19] Such as SEI SW CMM®

of a process reference or assessment model. This allows unique business processes that create competitive advantages, to still be assessed. I called this Business Process Mapping and it is described in more detail in the Practical Guide book [5].

Conformant Assessments

ISO/IEC 15504 defines the requirements for a conformant assessment. The requirements can be summarized as follows:

- Use a documented assessment process, which must be capable of meeting the assessment purpose[20].
- Define roles and responsibilities of the sponsor, the competent (qualified) assessor and assessors.
- Define the assessment inputs for each assessment.
- Conduct the assessment according to the documented assessment process.
- Record the assessment output according to the standard.

Some clarification of the requirements of the standard is provided in the following text, including guidance on practical aspects associated with process assessments.

Planning

Planning depends in the first place on the assessment purpose (e.g. capability determination or improvement) and scope. The purpose and scope influence the processes to be assessed, the activities to be performed, the resources required (people, places and tools) and the schedule proposed.

In addition, the rigour required for the assessment varies depending upon whether the assessment is a formal assessment of capability levels or a check that defines improvement appears to be being correctly implemented.

The scope needs to specify the parts of the organization, i.e. the organizational unit(s), to be assessed. An organizational unit may be a project team, a department, a business unit or some other form of organizational entity.

It is preferable that the assessors work with the sponsor and the organizational unit(s) representative when planning the assessment(s).

An assessment consumes organizational resources. Therefore, it is important that the planning are clearly defines the roles and responsibilities for the main assessment participants in order to help maximize the efficiency and effectiveness of the assessment process. As most assessment methods rely

---

[20] ISO/IEC 15504 defines assessment purpose as a statement which defines the reason for performing the assessment. It is part of the assessment inputs.

substantially on interviews with people executing the process, it is important to carefully select who to interview, and arrange the interview times and facilities in the planning stage. People interviewed should be able to describe the processes and access/provide needed data to illustrate the process implementation.

In addition, during planning, the assessment inputs and outputs need to be stated and agreed. These may include project documents, organizational unit process descriptions and process implementation data, and outputs may include preliminary and final reports, planned discussion sessions on the results with participants, the sponsor and management.

The planning should also refer to the Process Assessment Model being used, any mapping between the organization's processes and those of the model, and any tailoring or criteria applied that demonstrate compliance to the requirements of ISO/IEC 15504.

Data Collection

Before the assessment starts within the organization, there is a need to collect some data about the organizational unit, its processes and those in an assessment model used to assess them. Hence the assessment team needs to establish a correspondence between the actual business processes and the model.

During the assessment, the assessors need to collect evidence to support the assessment scope and purpose. The assessors need to collect data for each process assessed. This may be collected in a variety of ways including interviews, questionnaires, general discussions and data/document review. The strategy and techniques should support the assessment purpose and be explicitly documented.

The organizational unit may need to illustrate how they have implemented the process and whether it is an existing standard process or a modified or unique process implementation (objective evidence).

In the case of a modified implementation, the assessor should try to determine how the information provided by the organizational unit illustrates this modified/tailored process implementation. This explicit step should also check the relationship to the Process Assessment Model. It is preferable that any such checking occurs before the assessment, but assessors may often only become aware of this during the data collection. In some cases, there may be an explicit mapping of the implemented (defined) process.

There may also be iteration of which processes are sampled (for example, the same process may be sampled in several projects). The decisions on selection and sampling should be noted to guide other personnel (and can be useful for repeating assessments later).

The data may be manually or automatically collected and reported (e.g. project dashboard type data collection at defined project milestones). In both cases, the evidence collected needs to be retained to allow data validation and later verification of the assessment ratings.

Data Validation

This activity in the assessment is concerned with checking that the data collected is representative of the processes assessed, both in terms of sampling (organizational units, data types and processes) and in meeting the assessment purpose and scope. Furthermore, the assessors need to check that the data collected across processes (especially related or connected processes) is consistent (for example, document and configuration management).

In cases where the assessment is a repeat assessment used to confirm process improvements, the assessor may compare the data against that collected in prior assessment to confirm the improvements.

The assessors should use the preliminary results presentation to the organization as another basis for validating that the data represents the organizational unit assessed. When the preliminary results are in dispute, the assessors need to collect new or more data to validate their findings. If this proves impossible, then the assessors need to clearly state this in the assessment report together with an analysis of what this means in terms of rating, improvement opportunities and risks of misinterpretation of the results.

Process attribute rating

The assessors need to use their expertise when performing the Process Attribute rating. The rating is based upon the evidence (data) collected as much as possible, measured against the assessment indicator(s), but may still require some expert judgment and interpretation by the assessors.

The judgment should explicitly refer to sufficient evidence so that other organizational personnel (or subsequent assessments) are able to conclude that the ratings are valid for each Process Attribute assessed. In the simplest case, the rating components should accurately reflect the Process Assessment Model, the Process Reference Model (i.e. process purpose) and have a clear traceability to ISO/IEC 15504 process attributes.

Normally the assessors should agree on the rating (or use some documented rule in the case that agreement is not unanimous).

Note: In the author's experience, when assessments are performed for internal improvement purposes, it is preferable to also involve the organizational unit personnel in the rating. The reason to do this is that the personnel are more likely to adopt a positive attitude to the assessment and subsequently be more willing to perform improvements.

The set of Process Attribute ratings constitutes the process profile for the assessed organizational unit. This process profile should be presented in a manner that allows straightforward interpretation of meaning and value.

Reporting

Assessment reporting can focus on two types of detail:
- Capability determination and associated risks of capability target gaps.
- Improvement opportunities.

Normally the assessors should make a preliminary presentation of the results as part of the data validation to ensure that their final report reflects the assessed organizational unit performance, any feedback from the unit, and provides a clear and easy way to interpret the result.

The final reporting should also reflect the assessment purpose (for example, improvement and/or capability determination focus), together with agreed supplementary information (for example, improvement opportunities, action plans, benchmarks, comparison to prior assessment results or against other organizational units – see the Practical Guide for templates).

The introduction of an organizational maturity level determination will result in an extension to the capability determination. In this case, the capability determinations will be aggregated into an organization maturity level.

Roles and responsibilities of involved personnel

The roles and responsibilities for the key personnel in assessments must be defined, including:
- The assessment sponsor, who:
  - should verify that the assessment has a competent assessor with the necessary competence and skills;
  - ensures that adequate resources are available to conduct the assessment, including key personnel for interviews, infrastructure, and documents to be examined; and
  - ensures that the assessment team has access to the relevant resources, including the assessed organizational unit management as needed.
- The competent assessor, who
  - shall confirm the sponsor's commitment to proceed with the assessment;
  - ensures that the assessment meets the agreed purpose;

- ensures (and verifies) that the assessment is conformant to ISO/IEC 15504;
- ensures that participants are briefed on the purpose, scope and approach at the start or during the assessment (normally there should be an introductory briefing for the main personnel, with shorter briefings for interviewed personnel who did not attend the introductory briefing);
- ensures that the assessment team members have appropriate knowledge and skills, including use of any assessment tools;
- ensures that the assessment team members have access to appropriate documented assessment activities guidance; and
- confirms that the sponsor receives the assessment result deliverables.

In addition, the role and responsibilities of assessors and assessment coordinators (for example the assessed organizational unit coordinator) should be clearly defined and documented.

The assessors shall:
- carry out assigned activities including planning, data collection, data validation and reporting; and
- rate the process attributes.

In summary, ISO/IEC 15504 requires the combination of a documented assessment process and competent personnel for a conformant assessment.

Opportunities for Certification

There are several areas in which certification are relevant. They include:
- Certification of Assessors.
- Certification of Assessment Results.
- Certification of conformance of a Process Reference Model.
- Certification of conformance of a Process Assessment Model.

In the standard, there are several mechanisms for verification of conformity to verify that the requirements of ISO/IEC 15504-2 have been fulfilled.

The conformity to the requirements of ISO/IEC 15504 may be verified by self-declaration (first party), by a second party, or by a third party. A first party could be a model developer or user. A second party could be a community of interest, for example, the group of automotive manufacturers involved in defining Automotive SPICE or the European Space industry for SPiCE for SPACE. A third party could be the national standards body, an independent certification body, or potentially ISO or the IEC.

In essence, if a Process Reference Model meets the requirements of clause 6.2 in ISO/IEC 15504-2:2003 it can be verified by those involved in its development and use, and submitted for conformity to the relevant community of interest. If a Process Assessment Model meets the requirements of clause 6.3 in ISO/IEC 15504-2:2003 it can be verified by those involved in its development and use and submitted for conformity to the relevant community of interest.

If a process assessment result meets the requirements of clause 4 in ISO/IEC 15504-2:2003 (see section 5.4 above) and it is verified by a competent assessor, it can be submitted to the community of interest. In general, the community of interest responsible for a particular assessment model will only certify that the assessment was conducted in conformance with the requirements and not certify the assessment result (for example the Software Engineering Institute will register assessment results for SW CMM® and CMMI® assessments, but not certify that the organization assessed is at a particular maturity Level). There is work in progress to create a Certification scheme for ISO/IEC 15504 assessments and this is being documented in a new part 7 to the standard.

It is important that readers recognize the difference between certification of an assessment result and certification of performance of an assessment.

In the former case, the organization could claim certification that it performs at an internationally recognized standard of process performance and this places a liability on the certifying authority. In the latter case, the liability is removed from the certifying authority and the assessment result becomes the responsibility (with any resultant liability) of the competent assessor.

Hence, it is common practice for the competent assessor to explicitly state that the assessment was properly performed and applies only to the organizational instance(s) assessed. For example, in Organization 1, for project XYZ the processes A, B, C were assessed at a particular Capability Level.

Therefore when reviewing organizational capability or maturity level claims, readers should not just note the claimed performance, but also the scope of the assessments performed (and by whom) in order to decide how well the claimed performance will reflect performance for their specific needs.

Certification of Assessors also requires achievement of particular ISO/IEC 15504 requirements, including the assessors:

- general level of education;
- experience;
- assessor training by a recognized training provider (e.g. SQI, iSQI, SYNSPACE, Software Engineering Institute);
- performance of assessments under the guidance of a recognized competent assessor; and

- leading an assessment(s) under the guidance of a recognized competent assessor.

The chapter on **Assessor Competence** describes the guidance on competence of assessors in more detail.

The Measurement Framework

The Measurement Framework

The measurement framework of the standard is focused on the capability dimension as described in chapter 3.

In this chapter, I describe the measurement framework at the overall Capability Level, then in more detail for each process attribute for each Capability Level. I provide further information for each Process Attribute under the headings: clarification, state of practice experience, and guidance to users on changes to the standard. The rating scale, known as NPLF (meaning Not, Partially, Largely, Fully achieved) is described. The next section in the chapter describes the way the process attributes map upwards to the Capability Levels. Finally I make a comparison between ISO/IEC 15504 and ISO 9004:2000, which also has a (different) maturity dimension and provide a mapping of the process and capability dimensions derived in the European Space Agency S9KS study project.

This chapter will be of interest to anyone designing or assessing processes, including assessors, process owners, process experts, and developers of assessment models.

Capability Levels ISO/IEC 15504

In part 2 of the standard, ISO/IEC 15504 defines a measurement framework for the assessment of process capability. The measurement framework provides a mechanism for evaluating the capability of an implemented process with respect to a Process Assessment Model.

The Capability dimension of ISO/IEC 15504 consists of 6 Capability Levels. This process capability is defined on a six point ordinal scale that enables capability to be assessed and expressed on a scale ranging from **In-**

complete at the bottom of the scale to **Optimising** at the top end of the scale.

At **Incomplete,** the basic purpose of the process is not achieved. At **Optimising,** the process meets current and projected (expected future) business goals. The scale therefore represents increasing process capability of the implemented process. It thereby also defines a possible route for improvement for each process.

In brief, the Capability levels are:

* Incomplete: The process is not implemented, or fails to achieve its process purpose.
* Performed: The implemented process achieves its process purpose.
* Managed: The process is now implemented in a managed fashion.
* Established: The process is now implemented using a defined process that is based upon a standard process and that is capable of achieving its process outcomes.
* Predictable: The process now operates within defined limits to achieve its process outcomes.
* Optimising: The process is continuously improved to meet relevant current and projected business goals.

The Capability Levels are dependent and cumulative. The higher Capability Levels are dependent upon meeting the lower Capability Levels first, and the assessment rating accumulates as each level is attained. This means that during an assessment the process capability must first meet the requirements of Capability Level 1 (CL 1), before it can be rated at Capability Level 2 (CL 2), and so on.

The Capability Levels are further divided into Process Attributes (and management indicators). These aid assessors to ensure that reliable and sufficient evidence is available that a process achieves (or does not achieve) a Capability Level.

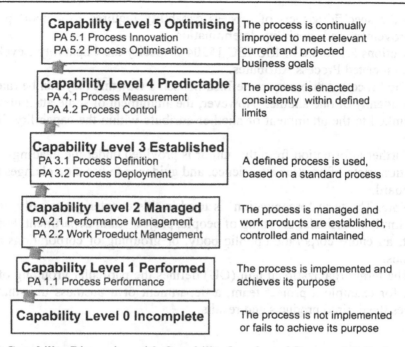

Fig. 12 Capability Dimension with Capability Levels and Process Attributes.

The Capability levels have been refined in successive versions in the development of ISO/IEC 15504. In brief, the latest version of the standard contains redrafting to remove ambiguity and increase consistency with ISO 9001:2000. This resulted in Capability Level three (CL 3) being restructured into definition and deployment. At Capability Level four (CL 4), the definitions have been clarified to make the concept of "quantitative understanding" clearer, and at Capability Level five (CL 5), there have been significant changes in the names and descriptions of the attributes of process capability, although the capability issues addressed substantially the same purpose.

The latest version aids clarity and ensures consistent interpretation of the various Capability Levels.

Process Attributes

Within the measurement framework, the measure of capability is based upon a set of Process Attributes (PA). Process attributes are used to determine whether a process has reached a given capability. Each attribute measures a particular aspect of the process capability. The attributes are themselves measured on a defined scale and therefore provide a more detailed insight into the specific aspects of process capability required to support process improvement and capability determination.

Sections 5.1 to 5.6 of ISO/IEC 15504-2 specify the Capability Levels and the associated Process Attributes.

The Process Attributes are defined in such a way that they can be rated independently of one another. However, the attainment of some attributes may be linked to the attainment of another attribute within the capability dimension.

Further information from the author is provided under the headings: clarification, state of practice experience, and guidance to users on changes to the standard.

Note. The term 'organization' is used in this chapter generically; it does not imply a particular grouping of people, project team, department, business unit, an entire corporation/public body, or grouping of corporations/public bodies.

The term organizational unit (OU) defines the particular grouping of people, for example a project team, a department or a business unit that produces the desired products and results.

Level 0: Incomplete process

Capability Level 0 (zero) states that a process is not implemented or does not systematically achieve its purpose. [See section 5.1 ISO/IEC 15504-2]

Clarification

First, it is assumed that the process is needed (it has a purpose). The emphasis is on whether a process is performed to achieve its **purpose**, or not.

This Capability Level may appear to be superfluous, but in fact, the amount of activity may vary from 'not performed at all' to performed but does not achieve the complete process purpose. Secondly, it is possible that the process is performed, but so inconsistently or irregularly over time or in different organizational units (i.e. projects, sections, departments, business units) to be considered not systematic. There is also no systematic evidence (work products) that demonstrates that the process is performed. Work products are artefacts associated with the execution of a process.

An example could be testing. On some occasions testing is performed, on others it is not performed, or only partially or poorly performed. This may be due to schedule pressure, disinterest, or a lack of prepared manual tests, or no automated testing. The result is that faults that would normally be found in testing are not found.

State of Practice Experience

In the author's experience organizations are sometimes rated at level 0 due to a failure to understand some fundamental aspect of the purpose of the process and hence implement an activity to achieve this aspect. For some technical disciplines in software development, there may be 6 to 10 fundamental activities to perform. This level also quickly illustrates to management the missing fundamentals in their organization's processes.

Level 1: Performed process

Capability Level 1 (one) states that process does achieve its purpose. There is one Process Attribute (PA 1.1) which defines Process Performance as a measure of the extent that the process purpose is achieved. This is measured by achieving the defined outcomes of the process. [See clause 5.2 ISO/IEC 15504-2]

Clarification

First, the purpose of the process implemented within the organization is understood. This means that the organization can state the purpose of their process (the 'why') in terms of the outcomes it should achieve. This statement of purpose and the desired outcomes may be documented or may be the common view of the persons implementing the process.

Secondly, the organization routinely performs the fundamental activities needed to achieve the purpose and create the desired outcomes to a greater (or lesser) extent. This performance is demonstrated by some form of process outcome, which could be:

- Production of an artefact (document, product);
- A significant change of state (team understands product requirements); or
- Meeting a specified constraint (goal, requirement, etc.).

The organization's fundamental activities and the outcomes will naturally vary for each process. These are defined in the relevant process reference model.

Assessors will try to verify that the people performing the process understand the purpose of the process itself and perform the necessary activities. The assessors determine if these practices have been performed in a systematic and (fairly) consistent manner.

If necessary, the assessor may refer to the applicable Process Reference Model to determine the types of fundamental activities that are relevant to indicators. These are termed Base Practices in the Process Assessment

Model. This will help determine whether these indicators show that the process outcomes are achieved. The assessors will look for process performance indicators that meet the requirements of Process Attribute [PA 1.1]. These may consist of the following types of indicators:

- identified work products that are input to the process; and/or
- identified work products that are produced by the process; and/or
- actions taken to transform the input work products into output products.

The work products resulting from performing the activities, together with input work products, are evidence of process performance when they contribute to achieving the process purpose. If they do not contribute to achieving the process purpose, they are not considered relevant process performance indicators. Note that processes performed at this level are not *assumed* to be meeting time, budget or other management restraints. Hence, they could be performed but too slowly to be efficient and effective.

State of Practice Experience

In the author's experience, most organizations that understand the purpose of the process have also researched the required fundamental activities and outcomes in order to achieve the process purpose.

Organizations that do not fully achieve level 1 generally miss one activity equivalent to a base practice or cannot show evidence of achievement.

This is especially true in organizations that have evolved their practices over time into new areas of application and have not accordingly adapted their processes.

More often, the organization produces artefacts based on templates that may not take into account the new application and thereby miss some important evidence of process performance. In most cases, the assessed organization can relatively simply complete the missing evidence.

A note to assessors: the indicators of process performance listed above are complementary – any one of them may be sufficient evidence of performance. Achievement at level 1 does not necessarily require all indicators. Assessors need to consider whether all the Base Practices are needed and sometimes their relative importance. It is not mandatory that all Base Practices are performed, although in many cases they should all be performed.

Also, the Process Reference Models and Process Assessment Models will list many work products. Only some of these may be relevant and needed by the organization and therefore be relevant indicators of process performance.

Guidance to users of earlier versions of ISO/IEC 15504 Technical Reports

The Capability Level remains basically unaltered from earlier versions of the standard, although the earlier technical report version explicitly required identifying the scope of work, which is assumed to be in the defined outcome achievement.

Level 2: Managed process

Capability Level 2 (two) specifies that the performed process (at Capability Level 1) is managed. This means it is planned, monitored and adjusted. It also requires the work products to be established, controlled and maintained. [See clause 5.3 ISO/IEC 15504-2]

Clarification

At level 2, the organization manages the performance of the processes. This is the first Capability Level at which explicit management of the process occurs. This means that the performance of the process is planned, monitored and adjusted to meet organization needs and objectives. The process performance is adjusted as necessary if it does not meet the planned needs and objectives. This adjustment is not assumed to be predictive; it is more likely to be reactive (in response to negative events or performance).

When work products are established, it means that specific work products are expected to be created and used in the process. The organization selects and uses work products that help them meet the objectives of the process and demonstrate achievement of the process outcomes. These work products are appropriately identified, documented and controlled.

The management of the process is focused on ensuring that the organization knows what to produce (work products), by when it needs to be produced (plan, schedule), that the outputs meets the organization needs, and that the process more reliably meets the planned performance.

The management of the process will result in artefacts and/or activities, which are verifiable (e.g. planning and/or plans, monitoring mechanisms, and/or process control mechanisms, and/or adjustments to the process based upon the results of comparison of the planned versus actual performance of the process.)

PA2.1 Performance Management attribute

The performance management attribute is concerned with the application of management techniques to provide reasonable assurance that process performance objectives are met.

The organization must first identify the process performance objectives, which could include one or more of the following:
- time planned and taken for the process (i.e. process cycle time);
- resources used in the process (e.g. people, products, finances, time);
- quality of the outputs/artefacts produced (e.g. performance, reliability, usability).

The organization also sets the objectives for process performance based on a set of internal and external considerations, including:
- organizational unit constraints (e.g. deadlines) and characteristics (e.g. research and development, maintenance projects);
- product constraints (e.g. cost) and characteristics (e.g. innovative technology, quality robustness);
- process inputs from another process or external source (e.g. client); and/or
- personnel constraints (e.g. availability of required personnel, training needs).

At level 2, the process performance objectives may be either qualitative terms (e.g. tests will be easy to understand and to conduct) or quantitative terms (e.g. tests will detect at least 90% of the defects in the product). The organization's process performance objectives allow the personnel to apply management techniques to provide reasonable assurance that process performance objectives are met.

For a process to be effectively performed, the organization must ensure that the personnel are empowered (have clear lines of authority) to perform the activities. They must also have a clear commitment to be responsible for the performance desired. Without this authority, commitment and responsibility, the performance of the process may fail to achieve the purpose. Hence, the organization must ensure explicit assignment of responsibility and authority for performing the process ('who does what'). The essential aspects to be addressed are the identification, assignment and communication of responsibilities and authorities for performing the process and the commitment of the persons involved. The organization needs to ensure that all stakeholders in the process (e.g. process owner, process implementers, etc) are informed of these activities.

The organization must identify the resources and information needed to implement the process (in accordance with the identified process performance objectives). They must also ensure the resources and information are made available, allocated and used. The organization must be prepared to adjust the resources and information as part of the management of the process performance in response to deviations from the planned performance.

In the (normal) situation that the process involves different parties or teams within an organization or in external organizations, it is important that the interfaces are clearly defined and managed between the involved parties. This must ensure effective communication and clear assignment of responsibility. There are typically several types of stakeholders to consider:

- the process owner(s),
- the process implementer(s),
- the process resource provider(s) who provide the necessary resources and information,
- the clients who are involved downstream of the process,
- the suppliers who are involved upstream of the process, and
- potential other stakeholders (e.g. governance bodies, regulators).

Organizations mostly perform the interface definition activity in the initial planning but often fail to manage the effect of changes in the interfaces due to changes in process performance (different people and stakeholder involvement). Therefore it is important that the interfaces between these parties be planned, monitored and adjusted as appropriate and that these be communicated in a clear and timely manner.

PA 2.2 Work product management attribute

Work products are artefacts associated with the execution of a process and hence the nature of the work product will vary depending on the purpose of the process and may be a part of the deliverable product or not (e.g. quality records).

The organization must manage the work products of the process (produced by the Capability Level 1 process) to provide reasonable assurance that they are appropriately identified, documented, and controlled.

This starts by identifying the requirements for the process work products to provide a basis for their production (as well as verification). These requirements can have a significant influence on the performance requirements for the process (e.g. the type and level of detail required to specify a web page is very different to specifying a Customer Relationship Management system). This simple example illustrates how the two process attributes at Capability Level 2 are interdependent.

The organization needs to cover both functional and non-functional requirements involved in managing work products. Functional requirements pertain to attributes of the work product (performance, size, etc.). Non-functional requirements pertain to agreements or constraints (e.g. delivery dates, packaging, etc.), which are not directly related to work product but to their production. Some requirements may be a combination of both functional and non-functional requirements. The requirements may be incorporated within a work product (for example in a template) or may be separate, for example in a checklist.

The organization must also define requirements for the documentation and control of the process work products, which are distinct from the requirements for the work products themselves. Depending upon the complexity of the work products, the complexity of the inter-relationships to other work products, the organizational unit specific or customer mandated needs; the organization must apply various degrees of change control or even configuration management.

The organization applies the defined requirements for the identification, documentation and control of the process work products.

To provide adequate product assurance, the organization must review the process work products resulting from implementation of the process, in accordance with the planned arrangements and adjusted as necessary to meet (changing) requirements. The extent and nature of the review will depend upon many factors (e.g. work product criticality and complexity, balancing resource use in review against production, balancing effort versus work product quality improvement, etc.) all of which should be considered as part of the planning for work product management.

State of Practice Experience

In the author's experience, organizations more often meet the performance management attribute than the work product management attribute. In cases of poor work product management, the work product requirements are often well defined but problems occur due to the lack of update, change control and review.

Organizations with strong review and configuration management processes often successfully fulfil the requirements of PA2.2.

Another interesting point to note is that many ISO 9000 organizations that met many of the Capability Level 3 requirements do not always achieve a corresponding level of performance management of processes at level 2. This is sometimes due to inadequate education of those persons responsible for implementing and managing the processes (a lack of consistency), and is more evident in organizations without strong project management and review processes.

In addition, the organizational structure involved in the performance management of processes varies according to the types of processes being performed. For example, engineering and support processes are often performed and managed within a project team. Organizational and the more general management processes (e.g. Human Resource Management, Quality Management, and Improvement) may be performed and managed across an entire corporation or public body. When larger numbers of personnel are involved in a process, the way the process is defined, performed and managed often needs to be different to the way it is defined, performed and managed in a small group or project team.

In general the organizational and general management processes are less well performed than engineering and support processes. This is due to the number of people involved across an organization. It is sometimes due to a clear lack of line management involvement and responsibility, and unclear lines of authority.

Assessors need to consider consistency (or inconsistency) of process performance as the organizational scope changes (small to large number of people, number of organizational units involved, etc.).

Finally, on the positive side, PA2.1 is often fulfilled for processes in a project via regular progress reporting by the Project/Team Manager to their management.

Guidance to users of earlier versions of ISO/IEC 15504 Technical Reports

The description has been redrafted to better align with ISO 9000. The changes include
- adjusting the performance of the process to meet plans,
- resources and information are identified, made available and used (now part of PA 2.1 for specific project/instances whereas this was formerly specified explicitly only in PA 3.2),
- interfaces between involved parties are managed, and
- inclusion of qualitative and quantitative data for management purposes at level 2.

It was previously unclear whether quantitative data was a requirement for Capability Level 2 or was an indicator for Capability Level 4. The new version makes it clear that this quantitative data should be used, if appropriate, at Capability Level 2 and could include basic metrics covering cost and schedule tracking of the use of resources in a particular project/instance. Qualitative measures will still dominate and may be considered sufficient at this level (e.g. lessons learnt reports, ease of use feedback reports) for many processes. The use of quantitative data is considered project or instance specific at Capability Level 2, not institutionalised at a broader organization level, which is the intent at Capability Level 4.

There is now explicit allocation of resources, and the definition of responsibilities and authority for personnel allocated to projects/instances. This was previously only explicitly stated in PA 3.2 where it applies for defining and deploying processes throughout the organization.

Level 3: Established process

Capability Level 3 specifies that the managed process (at Capability Level 2) uses a defined process. This defined process is based upon a standard process that is tailored as needed and deployed to the relevant organizational units. [See clause 5.4 ISO/IEC 15504-2]

Clarification

At Capability Level 3, the organization has established and maintains a standard process. This should be familiar to organizations that follow ISO 9000, which requires documented processes.

The organization then establishes a defined process, which is an instantiation of the standard process. The defined process achieves the process outcomes in a particular context (for example in a project or in a department). The defined process may be a tailoring from the standard process to suit the requirements of the particular context (e.g. a simple or a complex project) or may use the standard process when this is suitable to use without change.

The definition and use of standard and defined processes is the primary distinction from the Managed Level (level 2).

The organization identifies resources, both human and infrastructure, needed for performance of the standard process. The resources are incorporated into the defined process. The organization collects appropriate data (qualitative and/or quantitative) on the performance of the defined process to identify opportunities for understanding and improving both the defined process and consequently the standard process.

The standard process which is tailored and effectively deployed along with the infrastructure needed to provide the basis for a closed loop feedback cycle for process improvement is the foundation required for effective application of process measurement at Capability Level 4.

PA 3.1 Process definition attribute

The process definition attribute is concerned with establishment of a standard process. Process definition needs to cover:

- the process usage as the basis for performance of the defined process,
- roles and competencies,
- the collection and evaluation of process performance data as the basis for understanding and improvement of the standard process, and
- relationship to other processes.

There is an increase in the scope of this process attribute, in that the definition of the process must also consider the sequence and interaction with other processes.

In addition, the roles and competencies must be identified for the standard process ('who does what' and 'the skills and competencies they need to have').

There must also be a monitoring of process effectiveness and suitability. This creates a feedback loop to correct unwanted deviations and identify potential improvements.

The organization must document the standard process and associated tailoring guidelines and make these available and known to those implementing the process.

The organization's standard processes may be described at a general level that may not be directly usable to perform the activities. This is not mandatory; it is possible for the standard process to be directly useable as a defined process. This normally requires a high level of organizational discipline to ensure it is accurately implemented and no informal, unauthorized changes are implemented. Not all organizational cultures are suited to this discipline, and may in fact see this as too rigid or bureaucratic.

The tailoring guidelines need to provide clear direction regarding appropriate adaptation of the standard process. This needs to cover the range of applications for which the standard process is intended to apply. This should take into account the objectives, constraints and conditions that constitute the environment in which the process will be deployed (e.g. work scope, number of persons in the team). The guidelines should describe what can and cannot be modified and identify process components that are candidates for modification.

The resultant defined process is a maintained process description and provides a basis for planning, performing, and improving the organization unit's tasks and activities.

In addition, the defined process should contribute work products, measures, and other process improvement information to the organization's process assets (i.e. provide feedback to the standard processes). It can only do this if a mechanism is established in which the persons implementing the process act in accordance in the defined process (i.e. they implement the process with fidelity). As process usage data (qualitative and/or quantitative) are collected, the organization is able to create a basis for evaluating the behaviour of the standard process. This repository of knowledge provides the basis for understanding and (continual) improvement of the standard process.

PA 3.2 Process deployment attribute

The process deployment attribute is concerned with the effective deployment of a defined (and tailored as appropriate) process within an organizational unit.

When an organization achieves the process deployment attribute, the defined process as implemented retains fidelity to the standard process, so that the data on the deployment provides applicable feedback to the standard process.

The organization must ensure that enabling conditions for successful deployment (implementation) of the defined process are present. Enabling conditions include:

- Ensuring the people who implement the process have the required specific competencies. These competencies are normally based on appropriate education, training, skills and/or experience. If necessary, personnel are provided with appropriate training (and assistance) to obtain such competency.
- Understanding the process infrastructure required for performing the defined process.
- Successful allocation and deployment of the required human resources and process infrastructures.
- The people understand the roles, responsibilities and competencies for performing the defined process. They are given the appropriate authority to perform, manage and take on the responsibilities of the required tasks and outcomes. The management obtains their commitment to their assignment.
- The organization must also effectively deploy the resources and information required to implement the defined process and ensure that these are used.

The organization must deploy an appropriate process infrastructure, which encompasses tools, methods and special facilities that are required for performance of the defined process.

The organization must determine, collect and evaluate appropriate data relating to implementation of the defined process in order to provide a basis for understanding the behaviour of the defined process as well as demonstrating the suitability and effectiveness of the defined process. This, in turn, contributes to the ongoing improvement of the standard process elements upon which the defined process is based.

State of Practice Experience

In the author's experience, ISO 9000 certified organizations often meet the process definition attribute but fail to meet the process deployment attribute. This was evidenced in several ways:
- there were inadequate resources,
- the people were not always sufficiently competent (due to lack of appropriate training),
- infrastructure and information was missing or never properly communicated,
- the defined process was not checked to ensure it was properly deployed and in use, and
- due to changing organizational or customer requirements, the deployed (implemented) processes were no longer appropriate.

Tailoring of processes is often poorly performed and feedback from the (tailored) defined process to the standard process is sometimes not evident.

On the positive side, organizations with strong quality assurance involvement in project teams and quality management involvement in project reviews collect feedback from the defined processes and use this to improve the standard processes and thereby achieve the requirements of PA3.1.

Guidance to users of earlier versions of ISO/IEC 15504 Technical Reports

The new version changes the attributes into process definition and process deployment as two integral aspects of the same overall management capability for processes. In simple terms, the former defines the (standard) process and the latter implements this as a defined process. This is more consistent than the previous version and clarifies the conflict that existed with the need for resources to be available and managed at level 2. Now these resources shall be defined for the standard and implemented processes and deployed in the controlled manner as defined.

The earlier version of ISO/IEC 15504 PA3.2 described a process resource attribute. This has been realigned in the new version of ISO/IEC 15504 into level 2 and level 3 as outcomes of their process attributes.

Other important additions include:

- the sequence and interaction of the standard process with other processes is determined,
- the required competencies, roles, responsibilities and authorities for performing a defined process are now also identified explicitly as part of the standard process,
- there must also be a monitoring of process effectiveness and suitability, and
- the required infrastructure and work environment for performing a defined process are explicitly identified as part of the standard process.

These additions strengthen the importance of the organization having standard processes (this also strengthens the need to handle process establishment and maintenance as an organizational process).

Part of the weakness of the precise definition of the prior process outcomes has been addressed in the new version, which will hopefully enable organizations to better meet the Capability Level 3 outcomes.

The basis for competence is explained further, the inclusion of information as a particular form of resource is described, and the definition of appropriate data to demonstrate suitability and effectiveness of the processes is emphasized.

The process deployment outcomes reflect the implementation of the process definition outcomes, emphasizing that defining these outcomes is not sufficient in itself; they must be put into practice (something that does not always occur as planned).

Level 4: Predictable process

Capability Level 4 specifies that the established process (at Capability Level 3) operates within defined limits. This predictable process uses quantitative measurement and management to operate the process within the defined limits. [See clause 5.5 ISO/IEC 15504-2]

Clarification

At level 4, the organization consistently operates its processes within defined process control limits that aid the predictability of achievement of the process outcomes. The organization must use quantitative measurement (of both process and related product measures) to manage (control), monitor and set performance criteria for deployment (implementation) of defined processes. The quantitative management of the process supports the overall business goals.

Process measurement and control now occur at wider organizational levels, for example a division running multiple projects would collect and use measurements across several related projects or maybe even all its projects as a means to assess the capability of processes to support the overall business goals of that division.

When performance falls outside the defined limits, the reasons must be investigated and assigned to special causes[21]. The causes of variation in performance must be addressed and actions taken to adjust process performance back to the defined limits. Both the standard and the defined process may be affected by the actions.

PA 4.1 Process measurement attribute

The organization must implement an effective system for the collection of measures relevant to the performance of the process and the quality of the work products.

In order to do this, the organization must clearly identify and describe the overall business goals and then the corresponding organizational unit's specific goals and measures for product and process. This requires the organization to identify suitable quantitative process performance objectives and related quantitative product and process measures that measure the extent of achievement of the organization's business goals.

The organization applies and evaluates the quantitative measures to the performance of the process to determine the extent of achievement of the organization's business goals. Measures of process performance can include cost and schedule, as well as product quality and productivity.

The organization performs measurement of the implemented processes and relates this to the standard processes. This may include capability determination using process assessment, for example, by use of this standard. It may also use evaluation of the consistency of performance be measuring process performance parameters and outcomes. The process measurement must be active, in other words, the measurements provide an ability to control performance within defined limits.

---

[21] Special causes of variation refer to defects in a process, which are not inherent to the process but rather are incidental; these typically stem from implementation problems.

The organization maintains records of measurements of processes, both for historical comparison and for ongoing management and improvement of the process.

The organization may evaluate trends in performance as a form of analysis with the aim to confirm the adequacy and suitability of measures, and to help identify common and special causes of process variation. Trends allow predictive adjustment of processes. For example, a negative trend measurement can allow the process performance to be corrected before causing unacceptable performance and outcomes.

PA 4.2 Process control attribute

The organization must choose and identify analysis and control techniques that are relevant to the nature of the process as well as the overall context of the organizational unit being assessed. This must also include the requirements for the frequency of measurements.

The organization must define acceptable control limits for process performance (based on business goals and the related organizational unit goals). In general, processes vary in performance and this variation is called common cause variation[22]. This variation may be caused by people or defined process variations (different process implementations to suit different circumstances). The control limits can be defined either based on experience (these may initially be estimated or based on past data), or defined in terms of establishing targets for performance. The control limits must recognise that common cause variations occur and be realistic in what is the amount of controllable variation. It does not make sense to set control limits that are impossible to meet due to process variation.

The organization applies the analysis techniques that have been identified for identifying the root causes of variation in process performance (and whether they are common or special causes).

Where the root causes of variations create process instability beyond the acceptable control limits, the organization must implement effective corrective action(s) designed to address the identified root causes of variation. The organization must use measurement and analysis to justify decisions taken, based on their impact on delivery of benefit to the business.

The organization must re-establish process control limits after taking corrective action. The control limits may be different to those before the corrective action was taken.

---

[22] Common causes of variation refer to normal ongoing process variations that are inherent to the process as defined.

Note: not all processes are equally suited to statistical control, and alternative techniques may need to be selected that demonstrate a qualitative understanding of the process.

State of Practice Experience

In the author's experience, organizations that were fully achieving Capability Level 3 and attempting to fully achieve Capability Level 4 were good on establishing process measurement programs, but less frequently controlled the processes quantitatively.

Some organizational cultures see any form of measurement as too restrictive or personally challenging and require cultural education in order to overcome the negative opinions of its members.

The main shortcomings involved:
* relating the overall business goals to the organizational unit goals,
* setting acceptable process control limits,
* using control charts or other techniques to systematically analyze process capability in a way that leads to detection of unacceptable process variation, and
* using the resultant quantitative data for corrective actions.

In general, organizations with strong project management methodologies complemented by formal cost and schedule control systems were able to fully achieve the outcomes of the process attributes PA4.1 and PA4.2 for their project based processes and the related metrics of achievement of their business goals. Organizations using statistical measurement based control systems also find it easier to achieve the process attributes PA4.1 and PA4.2. Most of these organizations have measurement databases and provide incentives for superior performance.

Guidance to users of earlier versions of ISO/IEC 15504 Technical Reports

The new version of the process outcomes of the process attributes clarifies the intent of the earlier versions of the standard. In particular, under process measurement, it first requires the organization to establish quantitative objectives for process performance in support of the defined business goals. These objectives then lead to quantitative objectives and identification of measurements. PA 4.1 also explicitly requires establishment of measurement infrastructure and assignment of responsibilities for this outcome. Process capability measurement is assumed to be one applicable form of process measurement.

For process control, the new version of the standard explicitly requires control limits of variation, control parameters for process performance, and frequency of measurements to be defined. In addition, it explicitly requires corrective actions to be taken in response to variations caused by special causes.

Level 5: Optimising process

Capability Level 5 specifies that the predictable process (at Capability Level 4) is continually improved to meet current and project business goals. This optimising process uses both process innovation and process optimization to make improvements. [See clause 5.6 ISO/IEC 15504-2]

Clarification

When the organization achieves the optimising process Capability Level, it continually changes and adapts its processes in an orderly and intentional manner to effectively respond to changing business goals.

This level of process capability fundamentally depends on the quantitative understanding of process behaviour derived through a predictable process capability.

An organization operating an optimising process (Capability Level 5) has the following critical behaviours. First, the organization has a proactive focus on continuous (continual) improvement in the way that it fulfils current and projected business goals. The improvement efforts are both intentional and planned in order to improve the effectiveness and efficiency of the existing processes (process optimisation of the predictable, defined processes and standard processes).

Second, the organization has an orderly and planned approach to identifying appropriate changes to the existing process and for new processes (process innovation). The organization introduces them in a manner that minimizes undesired disruption to the operation of the process itself and/or the sequence and interaction with other processes. See the Practical Guide for methods to do this.

Third, the organization evaluates the effectiveness of the changes against actual results achieved, and makes further adjustments as necessary to achieve desired product and process goals.

The organization establishes quantitative objectives (based on the relevant business goals of the organization) for improvement of process performance. It collects and analyses data to identify common causes of variation in performance and to identify opportunities for best practice and innovation. The organization pilot innovative ideas and technologies in processes in order to meet defined business and improvement goals or objectives.

PA 5.1 Process innovation attribute

The process innovation attribute is concerned with the existence of the organization's proactive focus on improvement in the fulfilment of both current and projected (relevant) business goals of the organization. These goals must lead to explicit defined process improvement goals.

The relevant business goals and process improvement goals are the drivers for all of the level 5 outcomes.

The organization must:

- strive to understanding the source of existing process problems and variations (common cause variation),
- any potential process problems induced by process improvement goals,
- use this understanding as a source of proposed process changes.

The organization assesses the proposed process changes to existing processes with respect to the current and projected (relevant) business goals in order to select the most appropriate changes to implement.

The organization needs to have a top-level strategy to ensure successful achievement of process innovation due to the inherent complexity of organizational deployment, the long-term nature of improvement and the situation that results often rely upon aggregate changes.

PA 5.2 Process optimisation attribute

The process optimisation attribute is concerned with an orderly and proactive approach to identifying appropriate changes to improve an existing process or set of related processes.

The organization should consider how best to optimise its use of resources in order to achieve the best improvements possible with available resources. It should estimate the impact of proposed changes based in part on the quantitative understanding of the predictable process (from Capability Level 4).

The organization must ensure that introduction of changes minimizes undesired disruption to the operation of the process. This involves the timing and sequencing of agreed changes, the organizational unit activity criticality and status, process change effectiveness evaluation and new business generation. One good way to do this is through pilot or project trials.

The organization must evaluate the effectiveness of changes against actual results and make adjustments as necessary to achieve the relevant process improvement objectives.

Finally, the organization must use the evaluation of the effectiveness of changes as the basis for continuous learning and ongoing process knowledge acquisition and management.

State of Practice Experience

In the author's experience, very few organizations have implemented effective Capability Level 5 processes. To implement processes at this level requires a high degree of ongoing organizational commitment (over a long period of time) to provide resources and promote process innovation and optimisation. In other words, it requires an organizational culture that aims for high quality processes, high quality people to implement and improve them, and appropriate resources (products) to support the people implementing the processes.

In few cases has the author seen truly effective level 5 processes sustained over long periods, even in organizations claiming to be at level 5. The problem lies primarily in the focus and attention of management. When management feels the need for cost cutting or a change of direction, it may abandon or diminish the emphasis on process optimisation. There may also be a significant lag between changes due to business innovation and changes to the processes.

On the other hand, those organizations that have achieved level 5 in at least some of their processes are often better able to adapt to changes in their competitive environment. Some of these organizations operate in special customer-supplier relationships that promote long term quality over short term price/cost saving.

In situations that organizations have designed processes to be at Capability Level 5, the main problems have been demonstrating effective process improvements that continually improve the achievement of business goals. Process innovation and optimisation needs to result in quantitative cost, time-to-market, product quality and/or customer satisfaction improvements. When the demonstration of the improvements does not positively impact on the bottom line of the business, then top level organization management support can be easily lost, especially from managers not totally committed to quality improvement and driven by short term business profitability objectives.

All change requires additional effort and commitment. Therefore, another critical challenge is to minimize the undesired interruption caused by change, otherwise the persons (and especially managers) involved quickly lose a desire to make further changes.

Guidance to users of earlier versions of ISO/IEC 15504 Technical Reports

The process attributes have been completely renamed and the emphasis changed to reflect best practice management thinking and approaches. Overall, the goals are the same, but the outcomes are expanded.

The process innovation attribute was formerly called the process change attribute. The main changes here are to re-emphasize that innovations are related to process improvement objectives (which support the business goals); the data from the predictable processes is analysed (including the process variation data) in order to identify best practice within the organization as well as opportunities for process innovation; the impact of technology is assessed for potential process innovations; and an implementation strategy is established.

The process optimisation attribute was formerly called the continuous improvement attribute (the former PA 5.1 is substantially now PA 5.2). The main changes here are:

- to assess improvements against business goals and not just the objectives of the defined and standard processes;
- the implementation is managed to minimize disruption; and
- evaluation of process change assesses whether results are due to common or special causes.

Rating process attributes

In addition to the ordinal scale for measuring process capability, there is a scale for rating the extent of achievement of the process attributes. The scale applies to each attribute separately. The process rating scale is:

- N - Not achieved. There is no evidence or very little to show that an attribute is achieved. [0 to 15%]
- P - Partially achieved. There is some evidence that an attribute is achieved, but the extent of achievement may be unpredictable. [16 to 50%].
- L - Largely achieved. There is significant evidence of achievement of the attribute in a systematic manner, but it is not complete. [51 to 85%]
- F - Fully achieved. There is evidence of a systematic and complete achievement of the attribute [86 to 100%]

The [percentages] are assigned to the ordinal scale (NPLF) to provide both an indication of the level of achievement as well as the allowable range. [See clauses 5.7.1-5.7.2 ISO/IEC 15504-2]

The assessors must use some expert judgment in rating the extent of process capability and the extent of fulfilment of a process attribute. As such, the above numerical values of the rating levels (anchor points) are intended to provide guidance to assessors rather than be explicitly recorded. The non-linear anchor point placement in the scale is intended to guide the assessor's discriminatory judgment when rating the process attribute.

The assessors also need to consider the relative importance of each of the outcomes of the process attributes for the organizational unit assessed. Not all outcomes may be of equal importance and this may also vary according to the environment in which the process is used. This expert judgment should be considered against the ordinal anchor points in rating the Process Attribute fulfilment. Similarly, the assessed organization should not only consider the rating, but also what outcomes were/were not achieved in order to assess their importance to the business goals. Hence, it is not always correct to state that if 55% of the outcomes and practices are achieved, then the Process Attribute is Largely (55%) fulfilled. It may be that one particular practice that must be achieved is not achieved and this results in a lower rating.

In sections 5.7.3 and 5.7.4 the standard describe the requirement to rate the process attributes. An assessor rates each Process Attribute using the NPLF scale at each Capability Level specified in the assessment scope. For example, the scope may require rating all processes up to Capability Level 5 or may require rating at a lower level for some processes.

The assessors must follow a formalized Process Assessment Model in order to assure that the Process Attribute ratings are verifiable.

The assessors need to present the Process Attribute ratings for each assessed instance of a process. The resultant set of ratings of the process attributes is termed the process profile for that process (i.e. the measurement of capability). The process profile may contain up to nine ratings (one for each process attribute) depending on the Capability Level assessed. The process profile must clearly identify each process and process attribute.

Any Process Assessment Model used for assessment should provide a mechanism for expressing the evaluation of process capability as a series of process profiles.

Process Capability Level model

The assessor shall derive the Capability Level of a process from the Process Attribute ratings according to the Process Capability Level model defined in the Capability Level-rating table. [See section 6.2.1, ISO/IEC 15504-2]

In brief, this means that for a process to be rated at a particular Capability Level, it must be largely or fully achieved at that level and all lower Capability Levels must be fully achieved. This means that all Process Attributes at the highest rated level are largely or fully achieved, and all Process Attributes at lower levels are fully achieved.

For example, a process rated at Capability Level 3 can have both process attributes: Process Definition and Process Deployment only rated as largely achieved (51 to 85% achievement). However, if this process is to be rated at Capability Level 4, then the process attributes: Process Definition and Process Deployment must be rated as fully achieved (86 to 100% achievement).

The reason to require all lower levels to be fully achieved in order to rate at a higher level is that the design of the Capability Levels is accumulative and sustaining. The lower level practices need to be present to ensure that the organization consistently implements, manages and applies the practices. The result is that the cumulative practice achieves better results for the organization.

Theoretically, at the higher Capability Levels, it is still possible to have several small weaknesses at each of the lower Capability Levels. In many cases, too many small weaknesses at lower Capability Levels tend to lead to (or reflect) more important management weaknesses at the higher Capability Levels due to the cumulative nature of the practices. However, it is possible to have some minor weaknesses at the lower Capability Levels and assessors need to take note of these in an assessment and use their expert judgment when rating the processes at the higher Capability Levels.

The following diagram illustrates graphically an example assessment result. The assessed processes are listed on the left hand side, for example, ACQ.1 Acquisition Preparation. The 9 process attributes are shown at the top in order from PA1.1 to PA 5.2[23].

---

[23] This representation is used by SPICE 1-2-1. Other representations are possible.

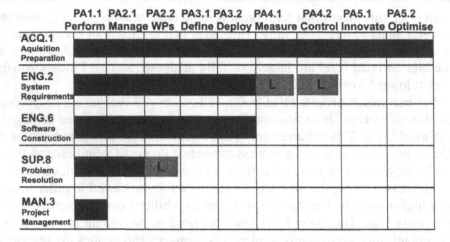

Fig. 13. Example Capability Level ratings – SPICE 1-2-1 representation.

Using the interpretation from the Capability Level ratings, the example Capability Level ratings as shown using SPICE 1-2-1 are:

- ACQ.1 is Capability Level 5 (all process attributes from PA1.1 to PA5.2 are fully achieved).
- ENG.2 is Capability Level 4 (PA1.1 to PA3.2 are fully achieved and PA 4.1 and PA 4.2 are largely achieved).
- ENG.6 is Capability Level 3 (PA 1.1 to PA3.2 are fully achieved).
- SUP.8 is Capability Level 2 (PA1.1 and PA2.1 are fully achieved and PA2.2 is largely achieved).
- MAN.3 is Capability Level 1 (only PA1.1 is fully achieved, no other PA is largely achieved).

Compatibility with ISO 9000:2000 Requirements

The ISO 9000 family of standards [6] has advocated quality management systems in organizations in a wide range of industries with a focus on customer satisfaction. The first release of ISO 9001 was in 1994 [7].

ISO 9001 specifies requirements on quality management systems including requirements for quality assurance and quality control. The way these have been specified has evolved over time. The ISO 9000 standards have been influenced by the development of process-related standards such as ISO/IEC TR 15504:1998, ISO/IEC 12207:1995 and ISO/IEC 15288:2001. As a result, ISO 9001:2000 has adopted a process oriented approach to product development and service delivery. This is expressed in ISO 9001:2000 as: *"promotes the adoption of a process approach when developing, implementing and improving the effectiveness of a quality management system, to enhance customer satisfaction by meeting customer requirements."*

ISO 9001 is a small document, using an abstract model focused on certification. In ISO 9001, the process-oriented approach requires only 6 documented procedures and it focuses on quality records.

ISO 9004 provides further guidance for an organization's quality management system objectives: *"particularly for the continual improvement of an organization's overall performance and efficiency, as well as its effectiveness"*.

It is an informative part of the standard, and provides guidelines for improvement and self assessment that allow:

- application to the entire quality management system, or to a part, or to any process,
- application to the entire or part of the organization,
- identification and prioritisation of opportunities for improvement, and
- facilitation towards **maturing**[24] of the quality management system towards world-class performance.

In Annex A of ISO 9004:2000, it specifies a five performance maturity levels, different to those in ISO/IEC 15504. It is clear that ISO 9000 in the ISO 9004 guidelines recognizes and promotes organizations to embrace an approach that recognizes a performance dimension to its process performance, even if the described levels are formulated differently to ISO/IEC 15504. These were taken into account in the latest revision, although they are still not compatible[25].

---

[24] Author's emphasis.

[25] There are ongoing discussions on what are the best capability or maturity level definitions. The definition – 'world's best practice' would probably be difficult to rate as it is almost impossible to define what is the best practice in the world, it varies over time and industry/regional/national cultures affect the way practices are implemented.

Table 4. ISO 9004 Performance Maturity Levels and ISO/IEC 15504-2:2003.

Maturity Level	Performance Level	Capability Level	Performance Level
		0	Incomplete The process is not implemented, or fails to achieve its process purpose.
1	No formal approach No systematic approach evident, no results, poor results or unpredictable results.	1	Performed The implemented process achieves its process purpose.
2	Reactive Approach Problem or corrective-based systematic approach; minimum data on improvement results available.	2	Managed The process is now implemented in a managed fashion.
3	Stable Formal System Approach Systematic process-based approach, early stage of systematic improvements; data available on conformance to objectives and existence of improvement trends.	3	Established The process is now implemented using a defined process that is based upon a standard process and that is capable of achieving its process outcomes.
4	Continual improvement emphasized Improvement process in use; good results and sustained improvement trends.	4	Predictable The process now operates within defined limits to achieve its process outcomes.
5	Best-in-class performance Strongly integrated improvement process; Best-in-class benchmarked results demonstrated.	5	Optimising The process is continuously improved to meet relevant current and projected business goals.

As can be seen in the comparison table [8], the levels are not directly compatible but in general are focused on demonstrable improved levels of capability from levels 1 to 5. The level scale in ISO/IEC 15504 is of finer granularity than ISO 9004 (6 levels instead of 5) and does not prescribe the ultimate 'Best-in-class' performance maturity level of ISO 9004. In very general terms:

- Level 1 in ISO 9004 is broadly equivalent to level 0 in ISO/IEC 15504,
- Level 2 in ISO 9004 is between level 1 and 2 in ISO/IEC 15504, and
- Level 3 is broadly equivalent in both.
- Level 4 and level 5 allocate the use of statistical process control, metrics and improvement practices differently and are hard to correlate to each other.

Note that the normative part of the standard, ISO 9001:2000 primarily focuses on performance maturity levels 1 to 3 – we will see how that translates later in this section.

Despite the differences in the informative ISO 9004, the widespread acceptance of ISO 9001 and its process orientation provides a natural candidate architecture for defining a Process Assessment Model.

A project sponsored by the European Space Agency has developed a quality management assessment model based on the quality management system requirements of ISO 9001, the guidelines in ISO 9004 in part, and the capability requirements of ISO/IEC 15504.

The process dimension of this overall Quality Management standard includes quality assurance and quality control requirements with an objective to provide adequate confidence to the customer that the end product or service satisfies the requirements. This can comprise activities covering adequate specification and fulfilment of product requirements including controls for the procurement, design, fabrication, integration, test and maintenance of products, maintenance of quality records and non-conformances. It also comprises activities related to interfaces with customers as well as suppliers.

In order to establish an assessment model, all the requirements from ISO 9001 were translated into practices. Practices are categorized as *generic practices*, i.e. those applicable to all processes, or *process-specific practices*, those practices only applicable to a particular process.

For creation of a conformant process reference and assessment model, the generic and process-specific practices were systematically associated with the appropriate process attributes. Process specific practices associated with performance of a process are indicators of process performance for the process dimension and can be considered as (mandatory) base practices. In addition, indicators include work products and work product characteristics. These indicators were assigned as the inputs or outputs of the processes.

It is possible to do the translation from requirements to processes and process practices. One possible translation into a Process Reference Model includes the following process categories and processes.

Customer Focus Requirements Determination Customer Communication Customer Property Product Acceptance and Delivery	**Organisation** Management Direction Quality establishment Management Review Document Control Record Control

Core Processes
Design & Development Management
Design & Development Control
Technical Review
Production & Service Provision
  Control
Product Preservation
Design & Development
Change management
Product Identification
	Resource and Facilities
	Management
	Infrastructure Management
	Work Environment Management
	Human Resource Management
	Control and Monitoring of
	  Measuring Devices

Purchasing Assurance Supplier Selection Purchasing Requirements Supplier Monitoring Incoming Inspection	**Measurement, Analysis and** **Improvement** Internal Audit Process Monitoring & Measurement Product Monitoring & Measurement Non conforming Product Control Corrective Action Preventive Action Continual Improvement

Fig. 14. Compatible ISO 9000 process categories and processes.

The resultant Process Reference Model is compatible with the requirements of ISO/IEC 15504.

The generic practices derived from ISO 9001:2000 associated with different process attributes support the revised definition of the ISO/IEC 15504 process attributes. Since ISO 9001:2000 does not specify the performance maturity (capability) dimension (rather only the informative ISO 9004 does); it is valid to consider the use of the ISO/IEC 15504 capability dimension. Therefore using the ISO/IEC 15504 capability dimension, the normative parts of the standard in ISO 9001:2000 can be represented as follows.

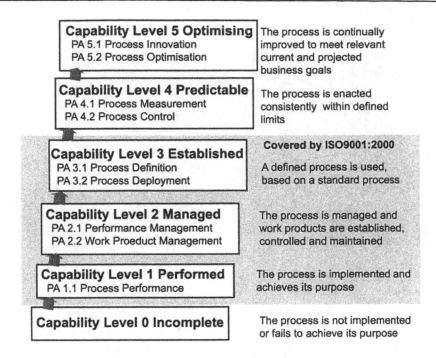

Fig. 15. ISO 9001:2000 and ISO/IEC 15504 Capability dimensions.

Using the developed model and a compliant assessment method allows organizations to perform assessments to determine their capability of quality management processes (thereby verifying compliance with ISO 9001). The use of assessment, rather than audit, for determining the capability of the processes of a quality management system provides a valuable tool to all organizations interested in implementing, maintaining and improving a quality management system based on ISO 9001.

In summary, it is possible to have a conformant assessment model for ISO 9001:2000 using the ISO/IEC 15504 capability dimension (rather than the informative ISO 9004 performance maturity levels). Naturally, the proposed model and the capability dimension will be subject to further discussion and evolution within the communities of interest.

Process Reference Models

Process Reference Models

In this chapter, the process dimension of the standard is described. This is defined in Process Reference Models. In the latest version of the standard, these models are external to the standard so that an organization can choose the most appropriate model to use.

The chapter provides an overview of the generic requirements and then illustrates this with several examples of conformant models in international standards, and some industry specific models.

It is important to note that Process Reference Models are primarily designed to guide users in what processes to define and implement (rather than assess). The actual implementation is described in a process life cycle. The models often provide a framework with implied process relationships. For example, software design may be related to software requirements analysis and software coding. The models often group processes into categories, such as development, management, and support categories as a guide to users about potentially related processes (process chains). These can be useful from the viewpoint of the person/team interested in implementing these processes.

Some models describe the framework in terms of activities and tasks, rather than process purpose and outcomes. Therefore, not all Process Reference Models may be compatible with the needs of process assessment, and may require translation/mapping. For ISO standards, this is part of the work of the ISO harmonisation project. For all other models, the community of interest needs to perform the required translation/mapping.

It is also important to know that the Process Reference Models in the international standards do not attempt to describe 'how' to implement the processes. (Note: Process Lifecycle models in a later chapter cover this). By avoiding the 'how' aspects, Process Reference Models can be managed to both provide the user with both process implementation and the process assessment aspects.

This chapter will be of interest to anyone designing process implementations, particularly process owners, process experts, and developers of models.

Requirements on Process Reference Models

One of the two dimensions of the ISO/IEC 15504 process assessment standard is the process dimension. This is as equally important as the capability dimension. The process dimension must provide clear process descriptions.

In order to assess an organization's business processes, the processes must be defined in a way that can be assessed. To handle this aspect, the standard refers to the need for a Process Assessment Model, which shall be based upon a Process Reference Model.

A compliant or conformant Process Reference Model defines a set of processes, and consists of statements of process purpose and expected process outcomes. The process purpose describes the high-level objectives of the process, while the process outcomes are the expected results of a successful implementation of the process. Together they describe what to achieve, without prescribing how to achieve the objectives.

Since the standard was initially devised as a software process assessment standard, it has a strong relationship with software lifecycle process standards, particularly ISO/IEC 12207. In the earlier technical report form of the standard, the Process Reference Model and Process Assessment Models were directly based upon ISO/IEC 12207 and incorporated within the standard and its informative parts.

ISO/IEC TR 15504-2:1998 (part 2) described the Process Reference Model. ISO/IEC TR 15504-5 (part 5) described an exemplar (example) Process Assessment Model.

In the latest version of ISO/IEC 15504-2, the standard no longer contains a Process Reference Model but states the requirements for defined Process Reference Models and Process Assessment Models, which are related to the measurement framework defined in the standard.

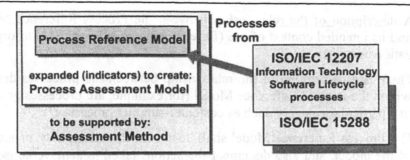

Fig. 16. Process Reference and Assessment model relationships.

The Process Reference Model comprises the processes purpose and outcomes from process life cycle models. ISO/IEC 12207 and ISO/IEC 15288 provide this information and are suitable to use as reference models. However, note that these standards may also provide other information for lifecycle definition purposes (and to clarify their application and use) that is irrelevant for assessment purposes. The Process Reference Model provides the basis for one or more Process Assessment Models.

This conformance requirement on models should enable organizations to compare assessment outputs from different Process Assessment Models that are based on the same Process Reference Model. In other words, an assessor should be able to obtain the same assessment result using different Process Assessment Models.

It should be noted that the expanded detail required for a conformant Process Assessment Model is substantial and not a trivial exercise. Assessment models generally are described in several hundred pages of text, mostly specifying indicator and work product details. This probably means that very few different conformant models are likely to be available.

For a conformant Process Assessment Model, the term 'Translation' is concerned with assuring that assessment results can be converted into an ISO/IEC 15504 process profile in a repeatable and reliable manner. To assure this, the Process Reference Model(s) shall adhere to the following requirements:

a) There is a clear declaration of the domain of the Process Reference Model. For example, it may be for systems, or software or even more specific domains such as space software development.

b) The descriptions of the processes within the scope of the Process Reference Model meet the requirements of clause 6.2.4 of ISO/IEC 15504-2 (with regard to purpose and outcomes).

c) A description of the relationship between the Process Reference Model and its intended context of use (for example, the type and size of organization using it).

d) There is a description of the relationship between the processes defined within the Process Reference Model (for example, are processes grouped in a particular category such as customer-supplier processes?).

e) The Process Reference Model shall document the community of interest of the model, and also document the actions taken to achieve consensus within that community of interest.

   1) The relevant community of interest will be characterized and/or specified (for example, space industry, and automotive industry).

   2) The extent of achievement of consensus shall be documented; or

   3) If no actions are taken to achieve consensus, a statement to this effect shall be documented.

f) The processes defined within a Process Reference Model shall have unique process descriptions and identification.

For ISO/IEC 15504 purposes, the fundamental elements of a Process Reference Model are the set of descriptions of the processes. These process descriptions shall meet the following requirements:

g) A process shall be described in terms of its purpose. The purpose states the high level overall objective of performing the process, and describes the likely outcomes of effective implementation.

h) In any description, the set of process outcomes shall be necessary and sufficient to demonstrate successful achievement of the process's purpose. The outcomes could be:
   1) Production of an artefact (e.g. system, software, document).
   2) A significant change of state.
   3) Meeting of specified constraints, e.g. requirements, goals etc.

i) The process descriptions shall describe the basic processes and not the process capabilities beyond level 1 for ISO/IEC 15504. In other words, they shall describe the process dimension and not the capability dimension.

What does all the above mean?

Basically, ISO/IEC 15504 now allows any type of Process Reference Model to be used, not just a software Process Reference Model.

Therefore, in the future it will be possible to use a model that describes the complete processes of an organization, not just the information technology or software processes (for example, a Process Reference Model covering ISO 9000 can be defined and used). This is an intentional result of the overall harmonization aspect of the standards setting approach for ISO/IEC 15504.

There is a proposal within the standard's user community to create an Enterprise Process Reference Model. Such a model would cover an enterprise architecture as described in the second chapter of this book. One possible candidate is the process model in the FAA iCMM.

Furthermore, organizations and industry associations that perceive a strategic competitive advantage in their business processes, now have the option to create their own Process Reference Model or use an existing process model they already have. They can then create a Process Assessment Model based on this reference model.

However, the effort needed to ensure that the models are compliant or conformant with ISO/IEC 15504 should not be underestimated[26]. It is likely that only large organizations will undertake the step. The European space and automotive industries are taking this step through their industry associations.

Without the steps to ensure conformance, the organization can still assess its own processes using just the capability dimension and its own process descriptions, but this is not considered a conformant assessment.

Several Process Reference Models already generally meet the conformant Process Reference Model requirements. Those that are not yet compatible are being considered for revision or are being revised in line with ISO/IEC 15504.

They include:
- ISO/IEC 12207 Amd.2: 2004 Information technology - Software Lifecycle processes.
- ISO/IEC 15288:2002 Systems Engineering - System Lifecycle processes.
- The ISO 9000 compatible S9K and the European Space Agency S9KS.
- The Software Engineering Institute CMMI® and the FAA-iCMM®.
- Trillium© [27].

---

[26] ISO defines compliance as: "adherence to those requirements contained in standards and technical reports which specify requirements to be fulfilled by other standards, technical reports or ISPs (e.g. reference models and methodologies)." ISO define conformance as "Conformity is fulfilment by a product, process or service of specified requirements."

- Automotive SPICE ®.

The Software Engineering Institute CMMI® and the FAA-iCMM® encapsulate the reference model within their overall model. The process parts of these documents in general meet the requirements for a Process Reference Model, but the overall model descriptions also include the capability dimension, which do not strictly comply with the ISO/IEC 15504 requirements. Rather than describe these models here, they are covered in chapter 6.

Information Technology – Software Lifecycle Processes

First, let us look at the standard that provided much of the process dimension and domain of application for ISO/IEC 15504 part 5. This is ISO/IEC 12207 Information Technology - Software Lifecycle Processes, which established a common framework for software life cycle processes.

The evolution of the software lifecycle process standard and the process assessment standard illustrates many of the characteristics of standards setting including:

- Dependencies between standards.
- The way one standard moves ahead of the other ('leapfrogging').
- How ISO/IEC 15504, while starting as a software process assessment standard, has changed into a more generic process assessment that still integrates with ISO/IEC 12207.

The technical report version of ISO/IEC TR 15504-2 created a software oriented process assessment model that was based upon ISO/IEC 12207:1995. The substantive part of the ISO/IEC 12207 standard sets out for each process the purpose, activities and tasks required to implement the high-level life cycle processes to achieve desirable performance. The combined purpose, activities and tasks thereby specify the requirements for acquirers, suppliers, developers, maintainers and operators of software systems.

The standard groups the purposes and outcomes in a general process architecture within three life cycle process categories: Organizational, Primary and Supporting. The Primary Life Cycle process category defines the core business processes for a software oriented business from acquisition through

---

[27] Trillium© is a proprietary process assessment standard used by Bell Canada to assess the product development and support capability of prospective and existing suppliers to Bell Canada for IT and telecommunications products. It will not be covered further in this book. See Coallier, F. (and others). The Trillium Model. Bell Canada for further details, and http//ricis.cl.uh.edu/trillium.

supply and development to operation. The following figure provides an overview of these categories.

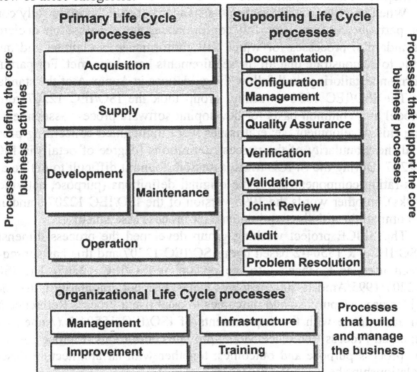

Fig. 16. Overview of the ISO/IEC 12207:1995 Process Life Cycle Model.

Each process category contains a set or processes and sub-processes with purpose statement descriptions. The purpose statement includes additional material identifying the outcomes of successful implementation. These lead to unique functional objectives when instantiated (defined and performed) in a particular environment. In other words, the standard provides a generic purpose statement that should be adapted to the specific situation. This situation will vary according to the two complementary factors in the people-process-product model, which are the people and the products. If a product is used to automate the process, for example testing, then the process definition will be different to when people manually design and perform testing.

The ISO/IEC 12207:1995 standard does not provide a complete description of a process life cycle, for example it does not describe phasing or dependencies between the processes. It does describe some common activities in process groups, and these are described later in this section. It must be elaborated to provide a complete process life cycle description. There is also a chapter on tailoring the standard to suit the organization.

When an organization applies the standard, it can choose to fully conform or partially conform. For full conformance, the organization declares the (standard's) processes for which full conformance is claimed and must be able to demonstrate that all the requirements have been met. For partial conformance, tailoring shall follow the guidelines in Annex A of the standard.

The ISO/IEC 15504 working group took the ISO/IEC 12207 reference model as a common basis for developing software process assessment. During this development, several issues were highlighted concerning processes and the granularity of the process definitions (degree of detail) in ISO/IEC 12207. During the SPICE trials, assessors found it difficult to derive a process-rating component using the original definitions (purpose, activities and tasks), in other words the 1995 version of the ISO/IEC 12207 standard was incompatible with the requirements for process assessment.

The SPICE project working group developed the process dimension in ISO/IEC TR 15504-2 based upon ISO/IEC 12207 and this has subsequently been used as feedback into the update of ISO/IEC 12207. The ISO/IEC 12207:1995/Amd.1: 2002 resolves the assessment granularity issue and provides process purpose and outcomes to establish a Process Reference Model in accordance with the requirements of ISO/IEC 15504-2 (Annex F). The updated Process Reference Model provides definitions of processes in terms of process purpose and outcomes, together with an architecture describing relationships between the processes.

The other changes in the amendment are also significant. There are 6 completely new processes consisting of: User Support, Product Evaluation, Usability, Asset Management, Reuse Programme Management and Domain Engineering.

The management process now consists of 6 sub-processes: Organizational Alignment, Organization Management, Project Management, Quality Management, Risk Management and Measurement, and Training is now greatly expanded to cover Human Resource Management (and also covers knowledge management). In addition to changes promoted by ISO/IEC 15504-2, it also incorporates suggested change aspects from ISO/IEC 14598:1998 Software Engineering – Product Evaluation [9] and ISO/IEC 15939 Software Engineering – Software Process Measurement [10].

The organization must define their processes to conform to the requirements of this standard if they desire compliance to the standard.

The ISO/IEC 12207 process architecture defines the hierarchical relationship among processes, activities and tasks and the invocation rules for the software life cycle processes. The standard does not define how, or in what order, the elements of the purpose statements are to be achieved. These are defined by the organization when it specifies its detailed practices and work products. Once defined, these elements will demonstrate the achievement of process purpose when implemented.

In amendment 1 of the standard, Annex F defines a Process Reference Model. It provides descriptions of process purpose and outcomes. The overall model consists of both process level and activity level detail.

In amendment 2 of the standard[28], the Supply process now has 4 component processes, and Change Request Management has been added as a support process [11].

As is normal with standards development, the published work lags current research. Hence, the model should probably contain additional processes such as innovation processes.

---

[28] ISO/IEC 12207 Amendment 2 was accepted in 2005. Unfortunately, there has been no complete re-issue of the standard. Readers need to obtain the standard and its amendments and combine them to see the complete standard. The diagram of the complete standard was created by the author in the first edition of this book as no such diagram was issued in amendment 2. It should also be noted that the author provided important revision to the acquisition and supply processes to correctly define and locate them in the model.

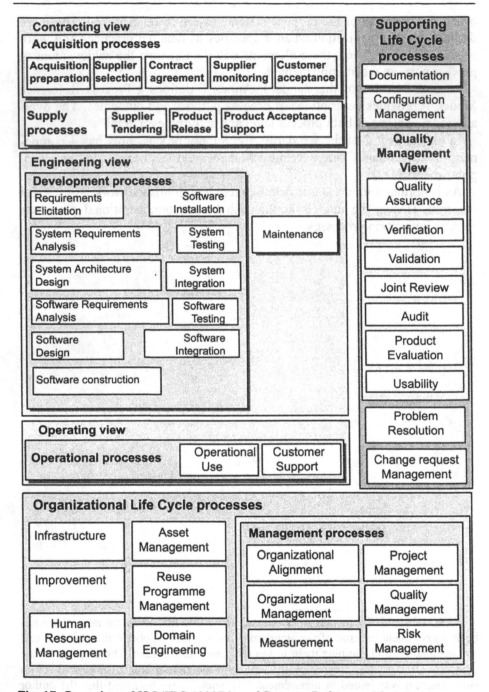

Fig. 17. Overview of ISO/IEC 12207 based Process Reference Model.

The organization must define its own set of applicable processes, taking into account the proposed set of processes described in Annex F of ISO/IEC 12207.

It must firstly consider its business needs, for example, is the focus on software development or use? It then needs to consider its own environmental parameters, for example, is it a small or large organization? It then needs to consider the domain of application, for example, safety critical, automotive, space software, or computer games.

In addition, the organization may define novel or alternative processes that achieve the same goals of those described in this standard, but have different detailed provisions to those prescribed in the body of the standard, including additional outcomes. The tailoring may also eliminate processes that are irrelevant or of little importance to the organization. This tailoring of the standard is explicitly mentioned as part of adoption of the standard.

The resultant organization's set of processes is called their standard process set. This standard process set may be further tailored in use to suit customer requirements; normally this would be done on a project-by-project basis as required.

Annex F allows the organizations own set of processes to be assessed for conformance to the ISO/IEC 12207 standard. The process definitions are evaluated against the statements of Purpose and Outcomes in Annex F for conformance to Process Reference Model requirements. To claim conformance, the organization needs to demonstrate that the implementation of the processes results in the realization of the corresponding Purpose and Outcomes provided in Annex F.

For government and industry associations, the creation of a standard process set to suit their particular domain is attractive; an example would be the V-Model. Single organizations (for example a large system and software developer) may also create conformant process sets for their own business purposes, but are less likely to explicitly validate conformance to the standard. Organizations will find that if they do create a process set based upon the standard, it will ease the process mapping needed before process assessment.

Annex F is also the applicable section for an organization that is assessing its processes in order to determine the capability of these processes. It permits assessment of the effectiveness of the processes in ways other than simple conformity evaluation, even when the organization defines novel or alternate process definitions to those in the main text of the standard.

Annex F can also be used to develop assessment model(s) for assessing processes using ISO/IEC 15504-2. The purpose and outcomes are indicators that demonstrate whether the organization's processes are being achieved. These indicators are useful to process assessors to determine the capability of the organization's implemented process and to provide source material to plan organizational process improvement.

ISO/IEC 12207 Process Reference Model process descriptions

The ISO/IEC 12207 processes are summarized in this section in terms of their process purpose and in some cases their outcomes when successfully implemented. I will describe the Contract and the Engineering processes in a little more detail as these are the focus of the standard (they are grouped in the Primary Life Cycle process category of the standard). I have added some additional comments and explanations.

Both process implementers and process assessors should become familiar with these process descriptions. Please refer to the standard for a full description and guidance. ISO/IEC 12207 uses the following definitions:

Process Purpose: The high level objective of performing the process and the likely outcomes of effective implementation of the process. The implementation of the process should provide tangible benefits to the stakeholders.

Process Outcome: an observable result of the successful achievement of the process purpose. This includes: production of an artefact, a significant change in state and/or meeting of specified constraints, e.g. requirements, goals, etc.

Primary Life Cycle Processes

Primary Life Cycle Processes consist of Acquisition, Supply, Operation, Development and Maintenance processes. They are the main focus of the ISO/IEC 12207 standard and consequently developed in more detail, better documented and therefore easier to understand.

The standard describes a series of views within the process lifecycles. There are two views within the primary lifecycle, the contract view, and the engineering view.

The contract view consists of Acquisition and Supply processes.

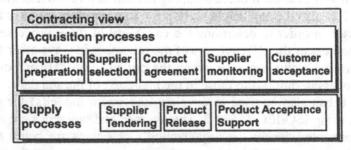

Fig. 18. Acquisition and supply processes

The **Acquisition Process** consists of preparation, supplier selection and monitoring, contract agreement and customer acceptance sub-processes. The purpose of the Acquisition Process is to obtain the product and/or service that satisfy the need expressed by the customer. Note that the standard assumes this is a software oriented product or service – this is apparent in the supply process.

The process begins with the identification of a customer need and ends with the acceptance of the product and/or service needed by the customer. An acquiring organization should specify (and assess) these processes. The outcomes include:

- The acquirer specifies the acquisition needs, goals, product and/or service acceptance criteria and acquisition strategies. These include the concept or the need for the acquisition/development/enhancement; the customer's known requirements; an acquisition strategy; contractual acquisition requirements; supplier selection criteria and validation activities.
- A supplier is chosen.
- The acquirer develops a clear agreement covering the expectation, responsibilities and liabilities of both the customer and the supplier. This is based on the supplier selection criteria, the supplier's proposals, process capabilities, and other contract/customer specific factors. The result is in a negotiated agreement between the customer and the supplier, which covers developing, maintaining, operating, packaging, delivering, and installing the product and/or service.
- The acquisition is monitored to ensure that specified activities are performed. The acquirer monitors constraints are met including cost, schedule and quality. This also includes joint activities between the customer and the supplier; exchange of regular information on technical progress; performance against the agreed requirements; and negotiation of needed/desired agreement changes.
- The acquirer receives products and/or services from the supplier that satisfy the stated needs.
- The customer acceptance is based upon previously agreed acceptance criteria and the requirements of the agreement.
- The acquirer and supplier agree and resolve any identified open items.

The **Supply Process** is the corollary to the Acquisition process. The purpose of the Supply process is to provide a product or service to the customer that meets the agreed requirements. It is therefore of more interest to suppliers. However, acquirers may be interested in how these processes match their acquisition processes, especially when the relationship is a close and/or long term one (for example, in partnering, just in time or Keiretsu relationships). The outcomes include:

- A response to customer's request (Supplier Tendering component process[29]).
- Supply of products and/or services that meet the agreed requirements (Product release component process).
- The products and/or services are delivered to the customer in accordance with the agreed requirements (Product Acceptance Support component process).

The standard in Annex H of Amendment 1 also describes an alternative acquisition process chain, consisting of 17 sub-processes. This process chain would be suitable for organizations that have a significant expenditure in acquisition, where they do not develop products themselves, or where acquired products are a substantial component of the total effort/cost of products (and services) they provide.

The alternate acquisition process chain starts from a policy and strategy level and progresses through proposal request and evaluation, contract agreement, acceptance and contract closure. It encapsulates an acquirer's viewpoint of system/software products, including technical and non-technical aspects such as benefits analysis, legal requirements and financial management. It also depicts the organization within a larger organizational chain by means of sub-processes such as user relationships and supplier relationships.

Annex H is offered as an alternative to the Acquisition process in Annex F. Although not explicitly stated, readers can decide whether to use all or only some of the sub-process descriptions from Annex H together with parts of Annex F.

---

[29] Amendment 1 had only the basic process, but Amendment 2 has the specified three equivalent component processes. Note that initially the component process: Contract Agreement was shown as a supply process until the author's review of the draft amendment 2 convinced the authors that 'as written' it was an acquirer's responsibility and hence an acquisition process.

The Engineering view consists of both development and maintenance processes.

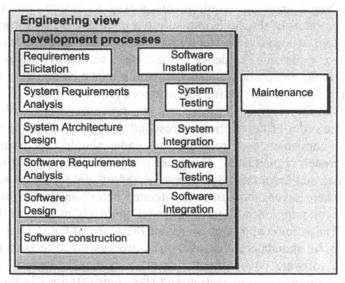

Fig. 19. Development and maintenance processes.

The **Development processes** are described in some detail, as they are a primary focus process area in the standard. The Development Process has 11 sub-processes. These sub-processes are commonly implemented as separate processes in many organizations, but it is possible to combine them. In cases where one process combines several sub-processes, all the relevant purposes and outcomes should still be met.

The development processes are of primary interest to organizations that develop systems containing software (including firmware). They will be of interest to customers (especially technical customers such as systems integrators) that require formal control and monitoring of the supplier development processes. For example, when system integrators specifically order newly developed software-based products or where collaborative development, subcontracting of software development or concurrent engineering is used. Note that no specific life cycle approach, for example, V Model, Waterfall, Iterative, Phased, and Spiral is assumed to be followed.

The purpose of the Development processes is to transform a set of requirements into a software product or software based system that meets the customer's stated needs. The activities of the Development Process are composed for both the Systems Developer role and the Software Developer role. The outcomes include the gathering of development requirements (at software and system levels); development of a software product or software-based system together with intermediate products to demonstrate that the end product is based upon the requirements; a way to ensure consistency between the products of the development process; a means to optimise system quality factors against system requirements, e.g., speed, development cost, usability, etc.; creation of evidence (for example, testing evidence) that demonstrates that the end product meets the requirements; culminating in the end product being installed according to the agreed requirements.

Each of the Development Process area sub-processes are described below. Note that the order of description corresponds to a phased approach but this is only for convenience of reading, the reader should not assume that a phased approach is mandated. There are many possible ways to implement the processes/sub-processes. Some possible approaches include an iterative approach where several processes are iterated before another group are performed, a cyclic approach, a partial parallel approach, as well as the phased approach. The specific approach is outside the scope of the standard.

It is also not mandatory that every sub-process must be performed. For example, a software development organization may be given a complete software requirements specification and start their activities in the Software Design sub-process. Alternately, the organization may deliver software to another organization for system testing.

Finally, there are some common outcomes that occur in every process/sub-process.

- One common outcome is that outputs are defined and 'baselined'. Note that 'baselined' in this context is a recording of the output in a known state, not necessarily being the highly formal meaning of baseline found in military, space or aeronautical specifications. This is communicated to all involved parties.

- Another common outcome is that consistency and traceability between the inputs and outputs of a process are established and maintained (for example, when changes occur). This outcome helps ensure that inter-process relationships are considered and managed, so that the process chain as described in the opening chapter is properly managed.

- Finally, most processes assume that prioritization of outcomes will occur (i.e. some outcome will be implemented first).

The **Requirements Elicitation** sub-process specifies the interface between the customer and the supplier, and how they interact to determine the requirements[30]. The purpose of requirements elicitation is to gather, process,

---

[30] Note: In some process assessment models (including earlier versions of ISO/IEC TR 15504-5), requirements elicitation may appear as a customer-supplier process.

and track evolving customer needs and requirements throughout the life of the product and/or service so as to establish a requirements baseline that serves as the basis for defining the needed work products. Requirements elicitation may be performed by the acquirer or the developer of the system, and therefore is of interest to both organizations.

The outcomes are focused on ongoing and effective communication between the customer and supplier. The supplier agrees requirements with the customer, and defines and baselines them. A change mechanism is established to evaluate changing customer needs/requirements and incorporate agreed changes into the baselined requirements. The customer needs are continuously monitored. The customer can easily determine the status and disposition of their requests. There is identification and management of technological and customer desired enhancements.

The **System Requirements Analysis** sub-process is focused on creation of system level requirements. The purpose of system requirements analysis is to transform the defined stakeholder needs/requirements into a set of system technical requirements that will guide system design. Therefore, this sub-process is of greatest importance to the organization that creates the system level requirements. It may be important to the technical organization of acquirer organizations when complex systems are to be developed.

The outcomes include a defined set of system functional and non-functional requirements describing the problem, and appropriate techniques to optimise the preferred project solution. The system requirements are analysed for correctness, testability and impact on the operating environment. The requirements are prioritised, approved and updated as needed. The system requirements are communicated to all affected parties. There is an evaluation of cost, schedule and technical impact of proposed and implemented changes to the baseline.

The **System Architectural Design** sub-process converts or places requirements into a system architecture. The purpose of system architectural design is to identify which system requirements should be allocated to which elements of the system.

The outcomes include a defined system architecture design comprising the elements of the system that meet the defined functional and non-functional system requirements. The requirements are allocated to the system architecture elements together with their defined internal and external interfaces. The system requirements are verified to be correctly incorporated in the system architecture. The requirements allocated to the system elements and their interfaces are traceable back to the customer's requirements baseline.

Note: where a system architecture uses a product line or product family approach, this process will also consider existing system elements and decide upon reuse or modification of existing elements, or new design.

The **Software Requirements Analysis** sub-process is the first process to focus on specifically on software[31]. The purpose of software requirements analysis is to establish the requirements of the software elements of the system. In some developments, this will be performed by a different organization to the system developer. If this is the case, it becomes an important interface process between the system developer and the software developer. Normally personnel involved in the system requirement process will also have some oversight or review of the performance of the software requirements process to ensure that the system requirements have been properly translated into software requirements.

The outcomes include that the (system and customer) requirements are allocated to the software elements of the system and their interfaces are defined. The software requirements are analysed for correctness, testability and impact on the operating environment. The software requirements' are prioritised for implementation. There is a mechanism to ensure that the software requirements are approved and updated (as needed). There is a mechanism to ensure evaluation of cost, schedule and technical impact of changes to the software requirements.

The **Software Design** sub-process is the first process to focus on the software product rather than requirements for software. The purpose of software design is to provide a design for the software that implements the requirements and can be verified. In some organizations, this may be a dedicated team or designer, in others (e.g. in agile methods) it may be performed by any member of the development team.

The outcomes include a baselined software architectural design describing the software elements that will implement the software requirements, together with internal and external interfaces of each software elements. There is a detailed design describing the software units that can be built and tested.

The **Software Construction** sub-process is where the fundamental software products are created. The purpose of software construction is to produce executable software units that properly reflect the software design. In large development projects, there will probably be several teams each producing one or more sets of software units. In addition, construction may consist of coding and/or selection of existing software units.

---

[31] Even though the standard is titled "Information Technology – Software Lifecycle Processes", as the reader will have noted, there are many processes of a generic nature (management, support) and system development nature that are relevant to software.

The outcomes of Software Construction include the production of software units (defined by the design) and their verification criteria. The software units are verified against the requirements and the design.

The **Software Integration** sub-process brings the diverse outputs of the software construction process together. The purpose of software integration is to combine the software units, producing integrated software items that fulfil the software design. The software integration also ensures that integrated software components satisfy the functional and non-functional software requirements on either an equivalent (e.g. target test bed) or a complete operational platform. The integration may be performed by a dedicated integration team or by co-option or co-operation of the software construction teams.

The outcomes include an integration strategy for software units; consistent with the software design and the prioritised software requirements (for example, iterative software builds would incrementally meet a set of prioritised requirements and would often be iteratively integrated). The verification criteria for software items are developed to ensure compliance with the software requirements allocated to the items, and software items are verified using the defined criteria. The software items (defined by the integration strategy) are produced, tested and results of integration testing are recorded. There is a regression strategy developed and applied for re-verifying software items when a change in software units (including associated requirements, design and code) occur.

The **Software Testing** sub-process is concerned with formal conformance of the software produced. The purpose of Software testing is to confirm that the integrated software product meets its defined requirements.

The outcomes include the development of criteria for the integrated software that demonstrate compliance with the software requirements. The integrated software is verified using the defined criteria and the test results are recorded. There is a regression test strategy developed and applied for re-testing the integrated software when a change in software items is made.

The **System Integration** sub-process is the interface between the developed software (and the organizations producing it) and the other system components (and their involved organizations). The purpose of system integration is to integrate the system elements (including software items, hardware items, manual operations, and other systems, as necessary) to produce a complete system that will satisfy the system design and the customers' expectations expressed in the system requirements. This is very important when using a 'system of systems' approach.

The outcomes of system integration include a strategy to integrate the system according to the system requirements priorities (e.g. there may be several integration repetitions). The system integration criteria are developed to verify compliance against system requirements. The integrated system is verified using the defined criteria and the results recorded. There is a regression strategy developed and applied for re-testing the system when changes are made. The integrated system is constructed. It demonstrates compliance with the system design and validates that a complete set of useable deliverable system elements exists.

In system integration, it is common to use the target environment but an equivalent environment may be an alternative if it closely resembles the target environment. The decision should be based in part upon availability of the target environment and use a risk assessment if the target environment is unavailable.

The **System Testing** sub-process completes the formal aspects of system development and test. The purpose of systems testing is to ensure that the implementation of each system requirement is tested for compliance and that the system is ready for delivery.

The outcomes include the criteria for the integrated system that demonstrate compliance with system requirements. The integrated system is verified using the defined criteria, and test results are recorded. There is a regression strategy developed and applied for re-testing the integrated system when changes are made.

The **Software Installation** sub-process completes the development process life cycle. The purpose of Software installation is to install the software product that meets the agreed requirements in the target environment.

The outcomes include a software installation strategy and criteria for software installation. The software product is installed in the target environment. There is assurance provided that the software product is ready for use in its intended environment.

Some additional notes the reader should consider about the development process. Each of the sub-process in the development process may have one or more outputs that achieve the defined outcomes. This is defined separately by the organization implementing the sub-process.

The sub-processes can be viewed as a process chain (as described in chapter 1). In the process chain, the outputs of one process can become inputs to the next process in the process chain. However, they could also be feedback to the sub-process itself or even be inputs to an earlier sub-process in the process chain (for example in a cyclic or iterative approach). It is partially for this reason that the standard does not specify the actual lifecycle, as it is possible to implement the sub-processes in a wide variety of ways and to use different feedback loops. The way that the processes/process chain is implemented depends upon the organization's business needs, the products it produces and the people involved.

Therefore, for process assessment purposes, we only need to know the purpose and outcomes from ISO/IEC 12207.

The other process in the engineering process view is the **Maintenance Process.** It is normally associated with the development process in the standard as part of the engineering view due to its use or interaction with many of the development sub-processes.

The purpose of the maintenance process is to modify a system/software product after delivery to correct faults, improve performance or other attributes, or to adapt to a changed environment while preserving the integrity of organizational operations. This objective may include retirement of existing system/software products. The outcomes include:

- A maintenance strategy. This is developed to manage modification, migration and retirement of products according to the (system/software) release strategy. (Note: this may require the creation of a release strategy that would normally be a supplier responsibility unless the system and software development is a shared customer/supplier responsibility).
- The impact of changes to the existing system on organization, operations or interfaces are identified and managed.
- The modified products are developed with associated tests or other verification/ validation methods that demonstrate that requirements are not compromised, and the affected system/software documentation is updated as needed.
- The product upgrades are migrated to the customer's environment, and products are retired from use upon request, in a controlled manner that minimizes disturbance to the customers.
- The system/software modification is communicated to all affected parties.

The Operating view consists of the operational process that takes the outputs from the engineering development and maintenance processes and ensures that there is a smooth transition of products and services into customer operation.

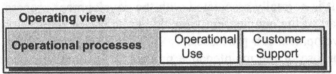

Fig. 20. Operational processes.

The **Operation Process** has 2 sub-processes: Operational Use and Customer Support. The purpose of the overall Operation Process is to operate the software product in its intended environment and to provide support to the customers of the software product. The overall outcomes include identification and evaluation of the conditions for correct operation of the software in its intended environment, operation of the software, and assistance and consultation to the customers of the software product in accordance with the agreement.

The purpose of **Operational Use** is to ensure the correct and efficient operation of the product for the duration of its intended usage and in its installed environment. The outcomes include criteria for operational use, and identification of the operational risks for the product introduction, operation, monitoring and management of the operational risks. The product is operated in its intended environment according to requirements and criteria.

The purpose of **Customer support** is to establish and maintain an acceptable level of service through assistance and consultation to the customer. The outcomes include identification of the service needs for customer support and monitoring. The customer satisfaction is evaluated on an ongoing basis for both the support services being provided and for the product itself. The initiation of operational support to handle customer inquiries and requests, to resolve operational problems, and the customer support needs are met through delivery of appropriate services.

It should be noted that both the operational use and customer support processes have important dependencies and relationships to the contract view (acquisition/supply) and the engineering view (development/maintenance) processes.

Operational use often follows the software installation sub-process (development). However, it should have provided some user environment requirements at the start of development earlier (either through the requirements elicitation process or through the acquisition preparation sub-process). It may also interact with the customer acceptance sub-process when systems/software are acquired rather than developed.

In a similar manner, customer support interacts with the maintenance process (and consequently the development process if software maintenance is performed within the organization). An effective customer support process provides not only support to the customer, but also a means for the software product developer/maintainer to determine what changes and problem solutions are required. For problems, the customer support process may make use of the problem resolution process (in the Supporting life cycle processes group), or use its own process.

Together with operational use, customer support may provide an important source of input for future product development, both for new versions of existing products and for new products.

It is for this reason that the operational use and customer support processes are grouped into the primary lifecycle processes.

Supporting Life Cycle Processes

The second major grouping of processes is the **Supporting Life Cycle Processes.** There are 10 Supporting Life Cycle processes. In general, the supporting life cycle processes can be applied to support the primary and organizational life cycle processes.

Four processes are generic: Documentation, Configuration Management and Problem Resolution. They are generally applicable to the primary and organization processes and outcomes. The other seven (7) processes are focused on supporting quality management[32] of the other processes.

The purpose of **Documentation Process** is to develop and maintain the recorded software information produced by a process.

The purpose of the **Configuration Management Process** is to establish and maintain the integrity of all the work products of a process or project and makes them available to concerned parties.

The purpose of the **Problem Resolution Process** is to ensure that all discovered problems are analysed and resolved and that trends are recognized.

The purpose of the **Change Request Management Process** is to ensure that change requests are managed, tracked and controlled. Previously in Amendment 1 there was no separate process and the problem resolution process was referred to instead. This process now allows non-problem related changes to be recognised and handled.

Fig. 21. Support processes.

---

[32] ISO/IEC 12207 uses the term: Quality Management view, which is focused on application within a project or development programme. There is also the Quality Management process, which is focused on the overall management/organization level.

The following processes are part of the quality management view of processes.

The purpose of the **Quality Assurance process** is to provide assurance that work products and processes comply with predefined provisions and plans.

The purpose of the **Verification process** is to confirm that each software work product and/or service of a process or project properly reflects the specified requirements. It is complementary to many of the testing processes in the primary lifecycle development processes.

The purpose of the **Validation process** is to confirm that the requirements for a specific intended use of the software work product are fulfilled.

The purpose of the **Joint Review process** is to maintain a common understanding with the stakeholders. It should review the progress against the objectives of the agreement and what should be done to help ensure development of a product satisfies the stakeholders. Joint reviews can be held at project management and technical levels throughout the life of the project.

The purpose of the **Audit process** is to independently determine compliance of selected products and processes with the requirements, plans and agreement.

The purpose of the **Product Evaluation process** is to ensure a product meets the stated and implied needs[33] of the users through systematic examination and measurement.

The purpose of the **Usability process** is to consider the interests and needs stakeholders to optimise support and training, increase productivity and quality of work, improve human working conditions and reduce the chance of user rejection of the system.

The supporting life cycle processes were initially devised as a group to support the primary life cycle processes, especially the development process. Some of the process descriptions still reflect this relationship (for example verification focuses on the software product). However, processes such as joint review, product evaluation and usability are also highly applicable to the acquisition process and the operational processes.

The audit process is not only applicable to the primary life cycle processes, but to any process in the model, and provides an important input to the Quality Management process in the organizational life cycle.

---

[33] See ISO/IEC 14598, Software product evaluation for requirements for performing product evaluations.

Organizational Life Cycle Processes

The Organizational life cycle consists of a set of management processes and a set of organizational processes. These processes are important to establish (build and manage) and maintain the organization's primary life cycle processes as suited to their own business needs. Organizations that have effective organizational and management processes are likely to be more efficient and effective in their other processes and in establishing projects.

Organizations that do not have effective organizational and management processes tend to be inconsistent in managing work and do not sustain long term improvement programmes.

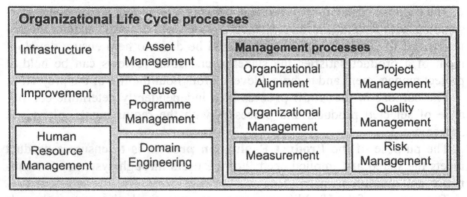

Fig. 22. Organizational processes.

The purpose of the **Management processes** is to organize, monitor, and control the initiation performance and consistency of any process to achieve their goals in accord with the business goals. While these practices are inherent to the management of an organization, they are intended to be instantiated for use by each of the organization's projects. The overall outcomes of the six management processes include:

- The definition of the scope of the process to be managed, and the identification of the activities and tasks to achieve the purpose of the process.
- The evaluation of the feasibility of achieving process goals with available resources and within existing constraints.
- The establishment of the resources and infrastructure required to perform the identified activities and tasks, the implementation of the activities and monitoring of performance.
- The review of the work products resulting from the process activities and analysis and evaluation of the results.
- Modification of performance of a process when it deviates from the identified activities and tasks or fails to achieve the goals.

There are 6 management sub-processes, which describe management in greater detail: Organizational Alignment, Organizational Management, Project Management, Quality Management, Risk Management and Measurement.

The purpose of the **Organizational Alignment** sub-process is to enable the software processes to provide software products and services, and be consistent with its business goals.

The purpose of the **Organization Management** sub-process is to establish and perform software management practices that are consistent with the business goals of the organization.

The purpose of the **Project Management** sub-process is to identify, establish, co-ordinate, and monitor the project activities, tasks, and resources in order to produce a product and/or service, within project constraints.

The purpose of **Quality Management** sub-process is to achieve customer satisfaction by monitoring the quality of the products and services to ensure they meet customer requirements.

The purpose of **Risk Management** sub-process is to identify, manage and mitigate risks at both the organizational and project level.

The purpose of **Measurement** sub-process is to collect and analyse data relating to the products developed and processes implemented within the organization and its projects. Measurement should support effective process management and objectively demonstrate the quality of the products.

There are 6 additional organizational processes. These processes should apply across the entire organization, although it is possible for the organization to apply them on a Business unit or departmental basis (especially when the organization is large and complex).

The purpose of the **Infrastructure** process is to maintain a stable and reliable infrastructure to support the performance of any other process. The infrastructure may include hardware, software, methods, tools, techniques, standards, and facilities for development, operation, or maintenance.

The purpose of the **Improvement** process is to establish, assess, measure, control, and improve a software life cycle process. It contains three subprocesses. The **Process Establishment** process purpose is to establish a suite of organizational processes for all life cycle processes as they apply to business activities (i.e. a establish standard process library). The **Process Assessment** process determines the extent to which the organization's standard processes contribute to the achievement of its business goals and to help the organization focus on the need for continuous process improvement[34]. The **Process Improvement** process is used to continually improve the organiza-

---

[34] In the author's view, it should focus on the need for 'continual' process improvement (continuous improvement is a non-sequiter).

tion's effectiveness and efficiency through the processes used and aligned with the business need.

The purpose of the **Asset Management** process is to manage the life of reusable assets from conception to retirement.

The purpose of the **Reuse Program Management** process is to plan, establish, manage, control, and monitor an organization's reuse program and to systematically exploit reuse opportunities.

The purpose of the **Domain Engineering** process is to develop and maintain domain models, domain architectures and assets for the domain[35].

The purpose of the **Human Resource** process is to provide the organization with adequate human resources.

- The purpose of the **Human Resource Management** sub-process is to provide the organization and projects with individuals who can perform their roles effectively and work together as a cohesive group (preferably as a team).
- The purpose of **Training** sub-process is to provide the organization and project with individuals who possess the needed skills and knowledge to perform their roles effectively
- The purpose of **Knowledge Management** sub-process is to ensure that individual knowledge; information and skills are collected, shared, reused and improved throughout the organization.

ISO/IEC 12207 Amd.1:2002 has labelled some processes as sub-processes (for example, the 6 management sub-processes) while others are labelled as processes (the 6 organizational processes). In addition, it labels processes as basic, component, extended or new processes, depending upon their relationship to the process descriptions in the 1995 version of the standard. Amendment 2 uses similar descriptions.

In general, related sub-processes are grouped under a process description (for example, management, and development). When a process has sub-processes, there is a description of process purpose and outcomes at the two levels (process level and sub-process level). One advantage of this is that an organization could use the top-level process description when this is sufficiently detailed for their business purposes (for example in a small organization or where the process is relatively less critical), or could use the sub-process descriptions when needed (for example in a larger and more complex organization).

The grouping of processes must be seen as a convenience for the process implementer, rather than a strict rule. The process implementer needs to con-

---

[35] There is considerable debate about which process category should contain Domain Engineering.

sider all the relationships between the processes (well, at least those important to the business of their organization).

Other standards have created different process groupings, for example IEEE Std 1517 [12] has a process group called Cross-Project processes that span more than one software project. In this group is Domain Engineering, which provides an ability to produce products useable in multiple projects as well as take input from multiple projects. This standard is based upon ISO/IEC 12207, and was an input to the amendment of ISO/IEC 12207. For example, Asset Management and Reuse Programme Management are based in part upon IEEE Std 1517. For more information on this standard, see Carma McClure's book: Software Reuse – A Standards-Based Guide [13].

The process assessor needs only consider that the actual processes implemented in an organization have been mapped to the process dimension as described. For process assessment purposes, Annex F provides a process purpose and outcomes for each process/sub-process so either level of description can be chosen as appropriate.

Systems Engineering – Systems Life Cycle Processes

The Systems Engineering – Systems Life Cycle Processes standard is identified as ISO/IEC 51288 [14].

This standard covers the life cycle of man-made systems. This starts from the conception of ideas and progresses through to the retirement of a system. It covers acquiring and supplying systems. In addition, it also provides for the assessment and improvement of its own processes.

The standard specifies a set of processes that provide the basis to allow an organization to create their own system life cycle model. The organization can create a total environment (with a product infrastructure of methods, procedures, techniques and tools) and include the trained personnel who use this to perform and manage projects through the entire system life cycle.

The organization may also use the standard as a basis for a customer (acquirer) - supplier agreement of an appropriate system life cycle. In these cases the standard can help to define the interfaces between the organizations. Alternately, the organization may decide to adopt a few of the component processes, rather than the entire life cycle.

It should also be noted that although the standard is focused on man-made systems, it is not restricted to man-made artefacts. It can include naturally occurring entities (for example water in an ecologically suitable environmental management system, or actual air movement/turbulence inputs into an aircraft flight control system) as well as the actions of the operators or personnel involved in the life cycle. This view of what comprises a system is a more holistic approach than that described in ISO/IEC 12207 as it allows for naturally occurring entities as part of an overall system. Such natural (including human) entities may have a major impact in analysis and design of the man-made system.

The consideration of the total environment is becoming increasingly necessary as humans realise how their activities impact the environment. For an even more holistic approach to managing systems and the environment, readers are recommended to read the author's book: Reach for the STARS [15].

The life cycle staging or phasing is not prescribed (for example it may be waterfall, concurrent, iterative or recursive), nor whether the system is unique, mass-produced or customized. The standard is meant to be applied to systems of widely varying scope, complexity, innovation, domain, life span and evolution. This is one reason why it addresses investment management.

When an organization applies the standard, it can choose to fully conform or partially conform. For full conformance, the organization declares the (standard's) processes for which full conformance is claimed. It must be able to demonstrate that all the requirements of these processes have been met. For partial conformance, tailoring shall follow the guidelines in its Annex A.

The standard recognizes and interfaces with ISO/IEC 12207[36]. It has some process overlap. For example, the Implementation process (in the Technical processes group) could explicitly use ISO/IEC 12207 for the software related processes (as well as the requirements analysis, integration and operation processes). There are a number of similar processes, for example the acquisition and supply processes, which have the same purpose but are not completely identical.

An organization should consider these commonalities when creating and tailoring their process framework. However, as will be described in the following text, the types of processes and the process viewpoint in ISO/IEC 15288 is quite different to ISO/IEC 12207.

The processes in ISO/IEC 15288 have been used to create an exemplar System Life Cycle Process Assessment Model, identified as ISO/IEC 15504 Part 6. Therefore I will focus on the processes that form the reference model for this assessment model.

---

[36] It should be noted that the ISO/IEC 15288 and ISO/IEC 12207 standards are not fully harmonized with each other. The current planning is to harmonize the standards in 5 years. Current draft standard proposals are attempting this harmonization.

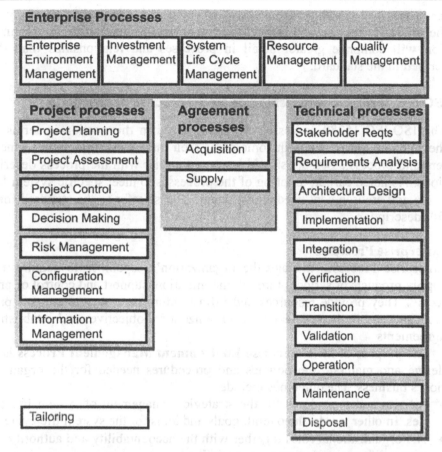

Fig. 23 ISO/IEC 15288 System Life Cycle processes used for ISO/IEC 15504-6.

The standard's processes are grouped into 4 main categories: Agreement processes, Enterprise processes, Project processes and Technical processes. There is also a tailoring process. This is a component of the system life cycle management process, but the standard does explicitly describe tailoring in an annex. It applies to every process in the standard.

It is immediately apparent that the processes are grouped differently to ISO/IEC 12207, and some are unique processes. There is a corresponding change in focus or overall purpose for each group. In ISO/IEC 12207, there is just one project management process, while this standard describes four processes (Project planning, assessment, control and decision making) together with three supporting processes.

The processes may be performed in any order (or concurrently) as needed and there is no explicit hierarchy of processes, or phasing. However, the inter-process relationships should be performed and managed as carefully as the processes themselves. Hence, the actual implementation in an organization will comprise greater detail in processes and relationships than described in the standard.

ISO/IEC 15288 Process Reference Model process descriptions

The ISO/IEC 15288 processes are summarized in this section in terms of their process purpose and in some cases their outcomes. Process implementers and process assessors should become familiar with the process descriptions. As noted earlier, tailoring of the processes to meet specific system life cycle and environment needs must occur. Please refer to the standard for a full description.

Enterprise Processes
Enterprise Processes manage the organization's capability to acquire and supply products or services through the initiation, support and control of projects[37]. They provide resources and infrastructure necessary to support projects and ensure the satisfaction of organizational objectives and established agreements.

The purpose of the **Enterprise Environment Management Process** is to define and maintain the policies and procedures needed for the organization's business. The outcomes include:
- Policies and procedures for the strategic management of system life cycles. In other words, the overall goals and aims for the system life cycle.
- The organizational roles together with the accountability and authority for system life cycle management are defined.
- A policy for the improvement of system life cycle processes is provided. This provides goals and aims for the management of the system life cycle.

The purpose of the **Investment Management Process** is to initiate and sustain projects to meet the objectives of the organization. This process invests organization funding and resources, and sanctions the authorities needed to establish the selected projects. It performs qualification of projects to confirm they justify the investment made. If it is found that they are not meeting the investment guidelines, it refocuses (or cancels) the projects. The outcomes include:
- Investment opportunities are assessed and selected. This may include investigating return on investment, opportunity costs, etc.

---

[37] In the current redrafting of the standard, it is proposed to rename Enterprise Processes to Project Enabling Processes. They are not a complete set of processes that enable strategic management of the organization's business.

- The initial resources, for example the core project team or project manager are allocated. In addition, the type and quantity of resources for the entire project are identified and budgeted.
- Project management accountability and authorities are defined. This is often called a project directive. It describes the project authority and accountability at a level that ensures agreement between project and organizational management.
- Projects meeting the agreement, stakeholder and organization requirements are established and sustained. Most organizations do not commit an entire investment at project start; hence investment management sustains the project as it meets its goals.
- Projects not meeting the agreement, stakeholder or organization requirements are refocused (for example new or altered project goals are set) or the project is terminated.

The criteria that projects need to meet may be temporal (i.e. change over time) as well as functional and financial. Hence, it may be valid to invest in a particular opportunity and start a project, but at some later time or circumstance to redirect or terminate the project. It is therefore appropriate to use mechanisms that stage or guide investment. One such method is the Stage-Gate approach [15].

The purpose of the **System Life Cycle Processes Management Process** is to assure that effective system life cycle processes are available for use by the organization. This process provides system life cycle processes that are consistent with the organization's goals and policies. This involves defining processes, adapting and maintaining them in a consistent way in order to meet the nature of individual projects. It also involves ensuring they are capable of being applied using effective, proven methods and tools. The outcomes include:

- Defined system life cycle processes and process chains.
- A policy on how to apply system life cycle processes.
- A policy or procedure on how to adapt system life cycle processes to meet the needs of individual projects (this is performed in the tailoring process).
- Measures are defined to evaluate the application of the system life cycle processes. Note that these measures may be simple and qualitative. They may also meet the requirements of ISO/IEC 15504 Capability Level 4 for quantitative process measurement.
- A way to improve the definition and application of system life cycle processes is established and used. This may meet the requirements of ISO/IEC 15504 Capability Level 3 or Level 4 if using quantitative measurements from the previous point.

The purpose of the **Resource Management Process** is to provide resources to projects. It provides resources, materials and services to support both the organization and project objectives throughout the life cycle. This includes educated, skilled and experienced personnel qualified to perform the life cycle processes. This process assures that there is effective coordination and sharing of resources, information and technologies.

The purpose of the **Quality Management Process** is to assure that products, services and implementations of life cycle processes meet enterprise quality goals and achieve customer satisfaction.

Agreement Processes

Agreement Processes specify the requirements for the establishment of agreements with organizational entities external and internal to the organization. The Agreement Processes consist of an Acquisition Process – used by organizations for acquiring products or services; and a Supply Process – used by organizations for supplying products or services. These are similar in scope to ISO/IEC 12207 and are not described further here

Project Processes

The **Project Processes**[38] are used to establish and evolve project plans, to assess actual achievement and progress, and to control project performance through to fulfilment. Individual project processes may be used any time in the project. They may also need to be used due to unforeseen or unplanned events. The level of rigour and formality depends on the risk and complexity of the project. For large and complex projects requiring substantial investment (and higher risk), the level of rigour is normally much higher than for small and short-term projects with low investment and risk.

The purpose of the **Project Planning Process** is to produce and communicate effective project plans. This process determines the scope of the project management and technical activities. It identifies outputs, tasks and deliverables, establishes schedules, achievement criteria, and the required resources to accomplish project tasks. The focus here should be on good planning, not on producing a 'glossy' document.

The purpose of the **Project Assessment Process** is to determine the status of the project. This process evaluates the progress and achievements against requirements, plans and overall business objectives. The evaluation may be done periodically and/or at defined events (for example at a design mile-

---

[38] The standard assumes everything is done in projects, but this could be interpreted as organizational unit activities. Hence some of the project processes could occur as 'business as usual' activities in an organizational unit.

stone). It may use process assessment, audit, project reviews and even ongoing measurement and review for this purpose.

The purpose of the **Project Control Process** is to direct and guide project performance according to plans, schedules and budgets. If project planning is correctly performed, the plans, schedule and budgets should reflect the technical objectives. Project control personnel redirect or refocus the project activities to correct deviations and variations from plans, as well as technical goals.

The purpose of the **Decision-making Process** is to select the most suitable course of action (where alternatives exist). The people performing this process respond to a request for a decision encountered during the system life cycle. They analyse alternative actions and select the most suitable action(s). Actions may need to reach specified, desirable or optimised outcomes. The decisions and their rationale are recorded to support future decision-making.

The purpose of the **Risk Management Process** is to reduce the effects of uncertain events that may result in changes to quality, cost, schedule or technical characteristics. People using this process identify, assess, mitigate and monitor risks during the entire life cycle, responding to each risk in terms of appropriate action or acceptance.

The purpose of the **Configuration Management Process** is to establish and maintain the integrity of all identified outputs of a project or process and make them available to concerned parties. This includes the tailored processes.

The purpose of the **Information Management Process** is to provide relevant, timely, complete, valid information to designated parties. People using this process generate, collect, transform, protect, retain, retrieve, disseminate and dispose of information. They manage designated information, including technical, project, enterprise, and agreement and user information.

Technical Processes

The **Technical Processes** are used to define the requirements for a system, and manage activities through production and use. In addition, the processes cover disposal of the product when it is retired from service.

The enterprise (and projects) use the technical processes to optimise the benefits and reduce the risks that arise from technical decisions and actions. People using these activities, are able to ensure that products and services possess the timeliness and availability, the cost effectiveness, and the functionality, reliability, maintainability, producibility, usability and other qualities[39] required by both the acquirer and supplier. They also enable products

---

[39] Commonly referred to in short form as the 'alities' and 'ilities'.

and services to conform to the expectations or legislated requirements of society, including health, safety, security and environmental factors. This latter aspect covers how the standard considers both project products and the environment in which they operate.

Common outcomes for most of the technical processes include traceability and consistency between inputs and outputs, and between processes that form a process chain.

The purpose of the **Stakeholder Requirements Definition Process** is to define the requirements for a system that can provide the services needed by users and other stakeholders in a defined environment. It identifies stakeholders, or stakeholder classes, involved with the system throughout its life cycle. Stakeholders identify their needs and desires. People using the process analyse and transform these needs and desires into a common set of stakeholder requirements. These express the intended interaction the system with its operational environment. They become the reference against which each resulting operational service is validated in order to confirm that the system fulfils the stakeholder needs. The outcomes include:

- The required characteristics and context of use of services.
- The constraints on a system solution.
- The basis for defining the system requirements.
- The basis for validating the conformance of the services.
- A basis for negotiating and agreeing to supply a service or product.

Stakeholders should include both immediate and remote organizations, persons and entities. Immediate stakeholders include the enterprise, the customers and the system developers. Remote stakeholders can include legislative authorities, such as environmental authorities who have an interest in how the system affects the environment during operation and later disposal.

The purpose of the **Requirements Analysis Process** is to transform the stakeholder, requirement-driven view of desired services into a technical view of a required product that could deliver those services. People using this process build a representation of a possible future system that will meet stakeholder requirements. Within known constraints, this should not imply any specific implementation, but rather a generalized set of measurable system requirements.

The purpose of the **Architectural Design Process** is to synthesize a solution that satisfies the measurable system requirements. People using this process encapsulate and define areas of solution as a set of separate problems of manageable, conceptual and realizable proportions. They identify and explore implementation strategies consistent with the system's technical and commercial requirements and risks. From this, they define an architectural design solution in terms of the requirements for the set of system elements. Normally, they perform the process one or more times as requirements and risks become better defined. The specified architectural requirements are the basis for verifying the realized system and for creating an assembly and verification strategy. The outcomes include:

- An architectural design baseline.
- The set of system element descriptions.
- The interface requirements.
- A basis for verifying the system elements.
- A basis for the integration of system elements.

The purpose of the **Implementation Process** is to produce a specified system and system element(s). People using this process transform specified behaviour, interfaces and implementation constraints into one or more system elements. They do this within the capabilities and constraints of the selected implementation technology. They employ appropriate technical specialities or disciplines to construct or adapt system elements by processing the materials and/or information in the selected technology. This process results in system elements that satisfy architectural design requirements.

The purpose of the **Integration Process** is to assemble a system from the system elements that are consistent with the architectural design. People using this process combine system elements to form complete or partial system configurations to create the product specified in the system architectural requirements. Hence, it is feasible that different systems can be created using one common library of system elements.

The purpose of the **Verification Process** is to confirm that the specified design requirements are fulfilled by the system. People using this process provide information required to take any needed remedial actions to correct non-conformances in the system or the processes that act on it.

The purpose of the **Transition Process** is to first establish a capability and then provide required services in the operational environment. People using this process install the system, together with relevant enabling systems, e.g. operating system, support system, operator training system, user training system, as defined in agreements. The outcomes include:

- A system transition strategy.
- A system installed in its operational location.
- A system capable of delivering the required services.
- A recorded system configuration.
- Corrective actions and reports as needed.
- An operational service sustained by the enabling systems.

The purpose of the **Validation Process** is to provide objective evidence that the services provided by a system comply with stakeholders' requirements. People using this process perform a comparative assessment and confirm that the stakeholders' requirements are correctly defined and implemented. Any variances are identified, recorded, and guide corrective actions. Stakeholders ratify system validation.

The purpose of the **Operation Process** is to operate the system to deliver its services. People using this process assign personnel to operate the system, and to monitor the services and operator-system performance. They identify and analyse any operational problems with respect to agreements, stakeholder requirements and constraints in order to remedy them. They ensure that the required service is provided. The outcomes include:

- An operation strategy.
- Services that meet stakeholder requirements.
- Approved corrective action requests, which are satisfactorily completed.
- Stakeholder satisfaction is managed and maintained.

The purpose of the **Maintenance Process** is to sustain the capability of the system to provide a service. People using this process monitor the system's capability to deliver services, record problems for analysis, take corrective, adaptive, perfective and preventive actions and confirm restored capability and service.

The purpose of the **Disposal Process** is to end the existence of a system entity. People using this process deactivate, disassemble and remove the system and any waste products. They return the environment to its original or an acceptable condition. People using this process reuse, recycle, reclaim, store or destroy system entities and waste products in an environmentally sound manner. They need to consider the relevant legislation, agreements, organizational constraints and stakeholder requirements. Where appropriate or required, they maintain records of the health of operators and users, and the safety of the environment, so that it is properly monitored. The outcomes include:

- A system disposal strategy. This strategy should be formulated during the investment management process as part of the requirements and constraints for project selection.
- Disposal constraints as inputs to requirements (feed forward loop).
- The system elements to be disposed are destroyed, stored, reused, reclaimed or recycled.
- The environment is returned to its original or an agreed state.
- Records of disposal actions and the analysis of long-term hazards are kept and made available.

As stated in the introduction to this standard, ISO/IEC 15288 takes a different systems viewpoint to ISO/IEC 12207 (which only partially addresses systems). The ISO/IEC 15288 standard is oriented towards a total lifecycle from idea formulation to retirement and disposal. When an organization defines and implements specific processes, the process implementers are recommended to consider this standard as a potential input.

Parts of the standard can be replaced by ISO/IEC 12207 (for example, some of the technical processes), but there are many processes that are unique. The enterprise process group comprises processes such as Enterprise Environment Management and Investment Management, which are beyond the scope of software lifecycle standards. They not only address engineering issues, but also market issues.

Processes such as Decision Making and Resource Management explicitly address inter-personnel issues. Where these processes are considered important to an organization, it is recommended that they be investigated more closely in the standard as they provide a useful basis for an organization to implement its own processes.

In addition, when an organization needs to consider the development of systems that heavily interact with natural entities such as the external environment, the standard can provide a useful basis for definition of processes that handle this interaction. In particular, the disposal process provides a useful forward looking viewpoint for handling systems that reach end of life.

For organizations performing internal assessments for the purpose of improvement, it is recommended that the process assessors become more familiar with this standard. Since it provides a systems view of processes and additional process descriptions, it provides potential inputs for process assessment and improvement.

For persons and organisations that wish to embrace holistic management and systems approaches, the author's book: Reach for the STARS provides a method to integrate the various disciplines and techniques [15].

Other Candidates for Process Reference Models

There are several other candidates for Process Reference Models. It is expected over time that some of these industry specific models will be developed further to better serve the particular needs of that industry. These include:

- ITIL® (Information Technology Infrastructure Library – currently considered for further development as ISO 20000)
- COBIT® (Control Objectives for Information and related Technology) – when used with ITIL, HERMES or similar model.
- OOSPICE (Component Based Development – already developed)
- S9K (SPICE for ISO 9000 – draft developed)
- Automotive SPICE

- V Model [16]

A brief overview of ITIL®, OOSPICE® and S9K are provided here.

Information Technology Infrastructure Library

The Information Technology Infrastructure Library [17] recognizes that organizations are increasingly dependent upon Information Technology (IT) to satisfy their corporate aims and meet their business needs. Information Technology Service Management is concerned with delivering and supporting Information Technology services that are appropriate to the business requirements of the organization.

ITIL® provides a comprehensive, consistent and coherent set of best practices for IT Service Management processes, promoting a quality approach to achieving business effectiveness and efficiency in the use of information systems. The best-practice processes described in the ITIL book both support and are supported by the British Standards BS 15000:2000, Specification for IT Service Management [18], and in turn underpin the ISO quality standard ISO 9000 for IT related quality management. They are currently being drafted in several parts as ISO 20000.

ITIL® processes[40]:

- Configuration Management
- Change Management
- Release Management
- Incident Management
- Problem Management
- Service Desk
- Service Level Management
- Capacity Management
- Financial Management for IT Services
- Availability Management
- IT Service Continuity Management
- Customer Relationship Management
- ICT Infrastructure Management
- Application Management
- Security Management
- Environmental infrastructure processes
- Project Management

---

[40] Taken from the Institution's Code of Practice for IT Service Management (PD0005)

OOSPICE

The OOSPICE project consortium gathered academic and industry partners to produce a development model and a process assessment model. The consortium includes Kepler University Linz, Computer Associates Belgium, WAVE Solutions Information Technology, Huber Computer Datenverarbeitung GmbH, University of Boras, Volvo Information Technology, Griffith University and COTAR, UTS [19].

OOSPICE started looking at Object Oriented technologies and has expanded to cover Component Based Development. The purpose of component-based development is to increase the quality of products by better specifying application design, component provisioning and assembly of applications (integration centric development) [20].

OOSPICE provides extensions to the ISO/IEC 15504 Process Reference Model to cover component based software engineering. The OOSPICE project provides a comprehensive set of documents covering:

* Component based process model
* Component based process methodology
* Process Reference Model
* Process Assessment Model and methodology
* Process Assessment tool.

In this section, I will briefly describe the Process Reference Model aspects, and in chapter 6, I will describe the Process Assessment Model.

OOSPICE groups processes into 8 groups, of which 3 groups are focused on engineering (where the most important impacts of component based development occur). The 3 groups are Modelling, Application Assembly and Component Provisioning (see the OOSPICE Process Model diagram for an overview of these processes and their component processes). In addition, there are Customer-Supplier, Support, Management, Organization and Human Resources process groups.

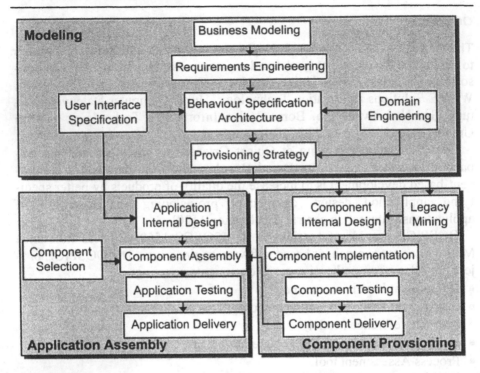

Fig. 24. OOSPICE Engineering Processes.

The underlying architecture is based on the four-layer (metamodeling) framework of the Object Management Group (OMG) [21]. Using the Unified Modelling Language (UML) Architecture to model the OOSPICE process model in the OPEN Framework can be represented as follows.

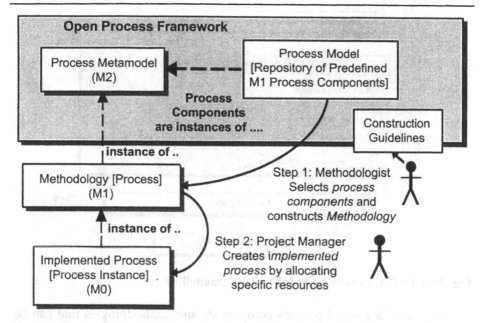

Fig. 25. Mapping OOSPICE Process Model using OMG/UML framework.

The OOSPICE process model is similar to the process component repository in OPEN. It specifies purpose, outcomes, tasks and associated work products. The OOSPICE process model also uses the UML modelling terminology. Two main actors are defined, the Methodologist who constructs the methodology based upon use of existing process components, and the project manager who implements the methodology as a specific process instance by allocating resources to the various process components.

If we expand the above to illustrate the mapping to the UML architecture, we have the process model that comprises the set of process components specifying what needs to happen (but not *how*), and specific process component descriptions specifying how to implement the process components (tasks and techniques). These are combined with tailoring guidelines to provide the methodology. The tailoring guidelines are also used by the project manager when implementing the processes (process components).

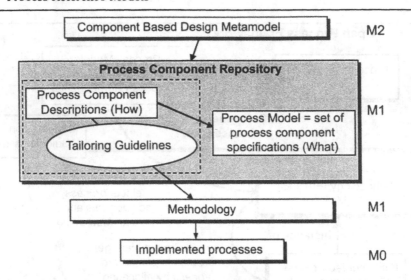

Fig. 26. OOSPICE mapping to OMG/UML modelling.

The results is a set of process components and methodologies that can be used directly by industry for component based development and assessment.

The Process Model covers the tasks (as required to meet the Object Management Group modelling), and the purpose and outcomes needed for a Process Reference Model conformant to ISO/IEC 15504.

The OOSPICE Process Reference Model follows the ISO/IEC 15504 recommendations and specifies only the purpose and outcomes (similar to ISO/IEC 12207 Amd.1 Annex F).

For a more detailed description of the component based development models and methodologies, reader should obtain the book Business Component-Based Software Engineering [22] or refer to the OOSPICE website at www.oospice.com.

SPICE for ISO 9000

The SPICE for ISO 9000 (S9K) project has developed an ISO/IEC 15504 conformant assessment and reference model for ISO 9000 [23].

It has been derived from a European Space Agency funded project called SPICE for Quality Management in the Space Industry (S9KS) [24]. By definition, space quality assurance within European Space Agency overlaps strongly with the scope and goals of quality management addressed by the ISO 9000 family of standards and the project derived a process assessment approach covering both ISO 9000 and the space specific quality standards created by the European Cooperation for Space Standardisation.

The S9K reference model documents the set of quality management system processes that are fundamental to good quality management systems and cover practices that are required to perform these practices. The processes are described in terms of process purpose and a list of outcomes that support achievement of the process purpose.

The S9K Process Reference Model groups the Purposes and Outcomes into the six process categories of quality management system, i.e., Organizational, Customer Focus, Resource and Facilities Management, Purchasing Assurance, Core Processes (for Quality Management) and Measurement, Analysis and Improvement.

Customer Focus	Organisation
Requirements Determination	Management Direction
Customer Communication	Quality establishment
Customer Property	Management Review
Product Acceptance and Delivery	Document Control
	Record Control

Core Processes	Resource and Facilities Management
Design & Development Management	
Design & Development Control	Infrastructure Management
Technical Review	Work Environment Management
Production & Service Provision	Human Resource Management
Control	Control and Monitoring of
Product Preservation	Measuring Devices
Design & Development	
Change management	
Product Identification	

Purchasing Assurance	Measurement, Analysis and Improvement
Supplier Selection	Internal Audit
Purchasing Requirements	Process Monitoring & Measurement
Supplier Monitoring	Product Monitoring & Measurement
Incoming Inspection	Non conforming Product Control
	Corrective Action
	Preventive Action
	Continual Improvement

Fig. 27. S9K Process Reference Model.

The organization must define the various detailed activities, tasks, and practices being carried out to produce work products. These performed tasks, activities, and practices, and the characteristics of the work products produced, are indicators that demonstrate whether the specific purpose is being achieved.

Automotive SPICE

A group of automotive manufacturers through the automotive special interest group in the procurement forum and the SPICE User Group have created an automotive industry specific Process Reference Model. The manufacturers comprise AUDI, BMW, Daimler Chrysler, Fiat, Ford, Jaguar/Land Rover, Porsche, Volkswagen and Volvo.

The Process Reference Model [25] is based upon the ISO/IEC 12207 standard, although it does not use all the processes from this standard. It has a number of processes from Annex H of ISO/IEC 12207 (Amendment 1), which specifically contains an alternate acquisition process life cycle. In addition it uses automotive sector terminology and reflects the sector application preferences.

The most obvious and important difference to the ISO/IEC 15504 Part 5 Process Reference Model is the acquisition process life cycle. This uses a more detailed and elaborate acquisition life cycle which reflects the automotive industry use of many parts and component suppliers. The specification and elaboration of requirements between the automotive manufacturers and their suppliers is a well developed process life cycle that covers technical, legal and project requirements. Hence these aspects are handled in separate processes within the acquisition process life cycle.

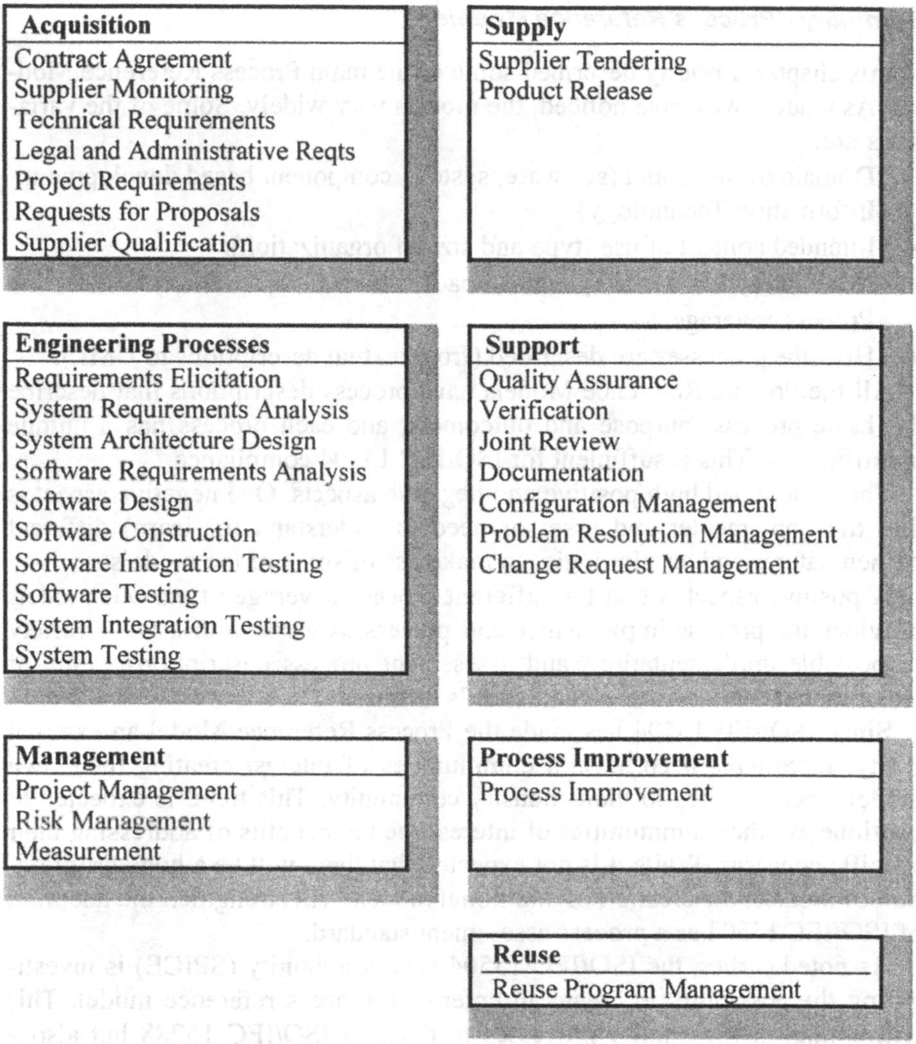

Acquisition	Supply
Contract Agreement	Supplier Tendering
Supplier Monitoring	Product Release
Technical Requirements	
Legal and Administrative Reqts	
Project Requirements	
Requests for Proposals	
Supplier Qualification	

Engineering Processes	Support
Requirements Elicitation	Quality Assurance
System Requirements Analysis	Verification
System Architecture Design	Joint Review
Software Requirements Analysis	Documentation
Software Design	Configuration Management
Software Construction	Problem Resolution Management
Software Integration Testing	Change Request Management
Software Testing	
System Integration Testing	
System Testing	

Management	Process Improvement
Project Management	Process Improvement
Risk Management	
Measurement	

Reuse
Reuse Program Management

Fig. 28. Automotive SPICE Process Reference Model.

The Process Reference Model specifies the process identifier, name, purpose and outcomes for each of the above processes. In addition it defines the automotive oriented terminology in Annex A and a key concept of automotive systems in Annex B. This illustrates the key relationships between systems, hardware, software, requirements, and implementation and testing, which provides the context for the terminology used.

Summary - Process Reference Models

In this chapter, I briefly described some of the main Process Reference Models. As readers will have noticed, the models vary widely. Some of the variations are:

- Domain of the model (software, system, component based development, Information Technology).
- Intended context of use (type and size of organization).
- Community of interest (general, space, automotive, aviation).
- Process coverage.
- How the processes are described (from textual descriptions to UML).

All the Process Reference Models have process descriptions that describe the basic process (purpose and outcomes), and each process has a unique identification. This is sufficient for ISO/IEC 15504 compliance.

The variety had both positive and negative aspects. One negative aspect is that the implementer and assessor need to understand (or learn) different nomenclatures and terminologies to make use of some of the models.

A positive aspect is that the different process coverage of various models provides the process implementer and process assessor with a wide variety of possible implementations and assessment process descriptions, some of which may better suit the organization's business.

Since ISO/IEC 15504 has made the Process Reference Model an external entity, there have been several communities of interest creating their own models, better suited to their industry/community. This trend is expected to continue as other communities of interest see the benefits of addressing their specific concerns. While it is not expected that there will be a huge proliferation of models, the creation of additional models will strengthen the adoption of ISO/IEC 15504 as a process assessment standard.

As noted earlier, the ISO/IEC 15504 user community (SPICE) is investigating the possibility to create an enterprise process reference model. This will contain many similar processes to those in ISO/IEC 15288 but also a significant number of processes that have not been previously defined.

Process Assessment Models

Process Assessment Models

This chapter describes conformant Process Assessment Models that are needed to perform process assessments. This includes ISO/IEC 15504 requirements and the exemplar model in ISO/IEC 15504-5. Other conformant models include ISO/IEC 15504-6, SPiCE for SPACE, OOSPICE, and Automotive SPICE. This is followed by an overview of the SEI CMMI® and the FAA-iCMM®. Finally, I look at how to use the assessment indicators in these Process Assessment Models in rating the capability of processes. This chapter will be of interest to anyone designing or assessing processes, including assessors, process owners, process experts, and developers of assessment models.

ISO/IEC 15504-2 Requirements

ISO/IEC 15504-2 requires that a conformant or compliant Process Assessment Model provides a level of detail that ensures consistent assessment results. The Process Reference Model alone cannot be used as the basis for conducting reliable and consistent assessments of process capability since the level of detail is not sufficient.

Therefore, a Process Assessment Model is needed to form the basis for the collection of evidence and rating of process capability. The Process Assessment Model shall be based on process management principles, using the approach that the capability of a process can be assessed by demonstrating the achievement of each of its process attributes. Stated another way, this means that an overall assessment of capability can be built up from assessment of each of its components.

Any conformant Process Assessment Model must provide at least a **two-dimensional view** of process capability. In one dimension, it describes a set of process entities (process areas) that relate to the processes defined in the specific Process Reference Model (s); this is termed the **Process Dimension**. In the other dimension, the model describes capabilities that relate to the process Capability Levels and process attributes defined in ISO/IEC 15504-2; this is termed the **Capability Dimension**.

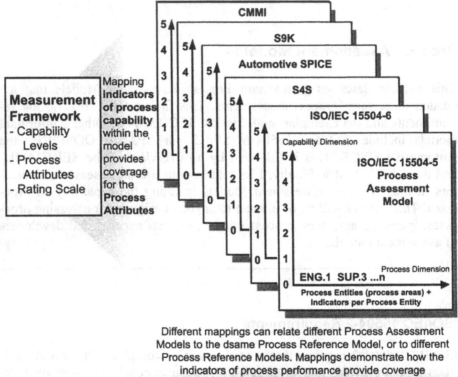

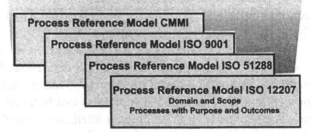

Fig. 29. Process Assessment Model Relationships.

The diagram depicts several important aspects in the standard:

- It is possible to have many conformant Process Reference Models (horizontal axis at bottom).
- It is possible to have many conformant Process Assessment Models.
- It is possible to map one or more Process Assessment Models to one or more Process Reference Models.
- All the Process Assessment Models must map to the Measurement Framework of ISO/IEC 15504 (Capability dimension on vertical axis). Hence ISO/IEC 15504 specifies the common measurement framework that can either be adopted 'as is' into the assessment model or mapped. The mapping must provide a clear, unambiguous translation from the assessment model indicators to the measurement framework.

For conformance, a Process Assessment Model shall be related to (at least) one conformant Process Reference Model. For example, ISO/IEC 12207 provides the basis for ISO/IEC 15504-5, for SPICE for SPACE (S4S) and for Automotive SPICE. The latter two build upon the basic Process Reference Model with additional/altered process entities and indicators. Similarly ISO/IEC 15288 provides the basis for ISO/IEC 15504-6, and ISO9001 provides the basis for S9K. CMMI provides a unified model (as does the FAA iCMM).

In order to ensure consistency and repeatability of assessments, a Process Assessment Model shall contain a definition of its purpose, scope, elements and indicators, mapping to the Measurement Framework and specified Process Reference Model(s), and a mechanism for consistent expression of results.

Nature and Use of indicators

A process assessment model must document a set of indicators of process performance and process capability that enable judgments of process capability to be soundly based on objective evidence [see clause 6.3.4 ISO/IEC 15504-2]. The assessment indicators represent various types of objective evidence that might be found when a process is used, and therefore provide a basis to judge achievement of capability. There is a clear expectation that the indicators will fall into two categories, related to the two dimensions of the model:

- Factors that indicate the performance of the process.
- Factors that indicate its capability.

In selecting a model, clear attention should be given to the use of indicators in the model, the comprehensiveness of the indicator set, and the applicability of the indicator set.

- **Indicators of process performance** provide coverage for the purposes and outcomes of the process.
- **Indicators of process capability** within the model provide coverage for the process attributes at the various capability levels.

At **Capability Level 1,** the Process Attribute is of process performance and is written in ISO/IEC 15504-2 in such a way as to be common to all processes. However, the evidence that demonstrates the process is performed is specific to each process.

The relevant **process performance indicators** will be different from process to process but will generally consist of:

- identified work products that are input to the process (input work products) and their characteristics;
- identified work products that are produced by the process (output work products) and their characteristics; and
- activities that transform the input work products into output products (Base Practice indicator) and indicate a change of state.

A base practice is an indicator that is equivalent to an activity or task that addresses the purpose of a particular process. When the organization consistently performs activities equivalent to the base practices associated with a process, it will consistently achieve its process purpose. A coherent set of base practice indicators is associated with each process in the process dimension. The base practice indicators are described at an abstract level, identifying "what" should be done without specifying "how" (they represent the unique, functional activities of the process). Note that the term 'indicator' is normally not used consistently in the standard's text and hence it describes base practices as if they are the actual activities. Hence the standard assumes that base practices are performed. It should really state that activities achieve the purpose and outcomes of base practice indicator. Hence, it is assumed here and in the standard that the term 'base practice' is interchangeable with 'base practice indicator'.

A base practice indicator of process performance for software testing is normally different to one for project management. An example of the former is performing a software test, while the latter could be monitoring project progress. In some cases there will be similar base practices, for example writing a plan, however the plan contents will be different (different work product or work product characteristics). In a few cases, the assessment model may refer to the same work product for different processes. For example, many processes list a report as a work product. There are several of these work products, but the assessor should expect the contents to vary by the process creating or using it.

Like all indicators in assessment models, the base practices represent an assessment view of the activity, rather than the activity itself. Hence the assessor needs to use his or her judgement to compare the base practices in the model with the actual activities performed. In many cases they will be almost the same, but the assessor should not assume they are exactly the same. An experienced person may perform activities differently to an inexperienced person; in other words, meet the required base practices differently.

In an assessment, the output work products and actions taken (refer Base Practices) are the main indicators of process performance for Capability Level 1. Hence, the assessment model focuses on two of the three elements of the **people-process-product** model, namely the process and the product.

An assessor needs to also consider the people performing the process, but the standard does not explicitly address this. For example, a highly skilled person or team can generally achieve the required outcomes with a 'lighter' process definition than a less skilled person or team. Similarly, teams that are closely coupled through co-location and shared roles, normally require less formal process definition because they use greater levels of communication. The effect of people aggregates even more across an organization, what is commonly referred to as organizational culture. This is described in more detail in the Practical Guide book [5] as well as in Reach for the STARS [15]. In brief, the assessor needs to consider the people in the assessment and should adjust his or her assessment accordingly.

In the higher levels of the capability dimension, the **indicators of process capability** are related to the definitions of the attributes of process capability for each Capability Level. In ISO/IEC 15504-2, there are two process attributes per Capability Level for levels 2 to 5 and these work together to enhance the capability of process performance (in other words, how well the process is performed). Each Process Attribute describes some facet of the overall capability of managing the effectiveness of a process in order to achieve its process purpose.

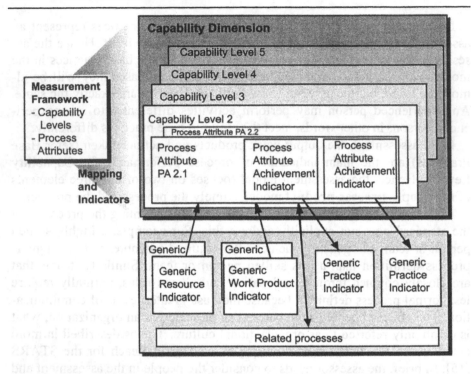

Fig. 30. Capability Levels, Process Attributes and Practice Indicators.

The Process Attribute(s) consists of a summary, generic description of the attribute for the particular Capability Level and a list of process achievement attribute indicators. The achievement attributes describe the type of evidence that would substantiate an assessor's judgment of the extent that the attributes of process capability outcomes are achieved. These attributes are called Process Capability Indicators, and are the principal indicators of process capability.

The Process Attribute is supported by four types of Process Capability Indicators that provide evidence of process capability. In the draft version of ISO/IEC 15504-5 are called:

- Generic Practice Indicators (GPI)
- Generic Resource Indicators (GRI)
- Generic Work Product Indicators (GWI)
- Related Process Indicators (RPI)

The **generic practice indicators (GPI)** are generic activities that provide guidance on implementation to ensure the achievement of the process attribute. There are generally several indicators for each process attribute. Each indicator focuses on one aspect of the achievement of the process attribute.

The practices support and build on the process performance as it is characterized at level 1. Many are management practices. There are at least as many generic practice indicators as attribute achievement items.

The **generic resource indicators (GRI)** are the associated resources. They are resources that can be used when performing the process in order to achieve the attribute outcomes. These resources may include human resources, tools, methods and infrastructure.

The **generic work-product indicators (GWI)** are the typical work products of the process. They are often the generic component of work products defined as process performance indicators in Capability Level 1, for example, a report or plan. Related processes often produce these work products. They contribute to the achievement of the process attribute. They are related to the Process Attribute in the standard and the Capability Levels of the Process Assessment Model.

The **related-processes indicators (RPI)** identify processes from the process dimension of the Process Assessment Model that support achievement of the attribute. The performance of a related process supports the organizational unit to achieve the outcomes of the process attribute. An example is the measurement process, which support the measurement Process Attribute (PA4.1).

Note: In a specific Process Assessment Model, the terminology used for the indicators may be different and may even be combined. In ISO/IEC TR 15504-5, the terminology used was different to that now contained in the standard.

CAUTION: A Process Assessment Model contains descriptions of processes, often grouped in process categories for convenience in *assessing* process performance. No Process Assessment Model is a complete description of all implemented business processes nor is it a specific description of any actual process implementation. Rather the model attempts to describe generically *what* a business process should achieve and provides typical *example* types of evidence. While it provides a useful supplemental source of practices and work products for a process, process implementers should take care to first ensure their processes meet organizational needs. This may validly lead to a different composition of processes to those described in a Process Assessment Model. Consequently, assessors should take care to convert/translate the Process Assessment Model indicators against what the organization actually does.

The ISO/IEC 15504-5 Exemplar

Part 5 of ISO/IEC 15504 describes one particular example of a conformant Process Assessment Model (called an exemplar model). As I will describe later, there are other conformant Process Assessment Models that use such a different approach, but ISO/IEC 15004-5 provides a simple example.

The published version is ISO/IEC 15504-5:2005 [26]. Part 5 is useable as a complete Process Assessment Model and in fact is the basis for many assessment models currently in use. It provides an additional level of detail required to perform reliable and consistent assessments, consisting of sets of attribute indicators for process performance and capability.

In addition, part 5 also provides an example of how to define and document a conformant assessment model that can be followed when a model developer wishes to create their own Process Assessment Model. Part 5 uses terminology specified in the previous section, except that it does not include the term indicator.

- **Process Attribute indicator**: an assessment indicator that supports the judgment of the extent of achievement of a specific process attribute. Indicators may be related to performance of a particular process (specific base practice) or the capability of a process (generic practice).
- **Base Practice**: an assessment indicator for an activity that contributes to achieve the purpose of a particular process. In other words, a basic practice or activity, this may be a managerial, engineering or service activity.
- **Generic Practice**: an assessment indicator of an activity that addresses the implementation of a specific Process Attribute at Capability Levels from level 2 to level 5.
- **Generic Resource**: an assessment indicator of the associated resources.
- **Generic Work Product**: an assessment indicator of the typical work products associated with a process attribute.

Structure of the Process Assessment Model

The Process Assessment Model structure in ISO/IEC 15504-5 is based upon the Process Reference Model in ISO/IEC 12207 and its amendments 1 and 2. This is combined with the capability dimension of ISO/IEC 15504 Part 2.

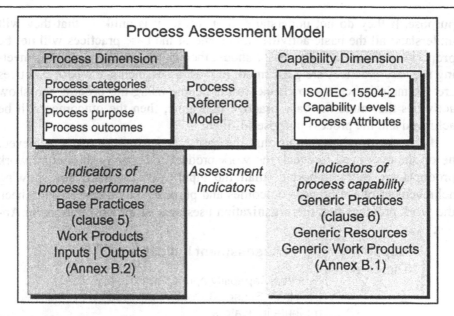

Fig. 31. Process Assessment Model structure and relationships.

In the diagram, the process dimension is based on the Process Reference Model (from ISO/IEC 12207 and amendments) with the expansion of indicators as base practices and work products. The capability dimension expands the capability levels and process attributes in part 2 by use of generic practices, resources and work products.

In clause 5 of the standard, each process is described in seven tabular fields, as follows:

- Process ID: An acronym identifying the process within a process group.
- Process name: The descriptive title of the process.
- Process Purpose: The statement of purpose taken from the process reference model.
- Process Outcomes: The outcomes from successful process implementation, from the process reference model.
- Base Practices: The assessment indicators of an activity that addresses the implementation of a specific process
- Work Products: Two columns with input work products on left and output work products in the right column.

Clause 5 is the main section of interest to assessors. It provides the basic information about each process. When performing an assessment, the assessor refers first to this clause to determine the basic activities to assess. The assessor checks that the people using the process understand the process purpose. If they do not understand the purpose, it is unlikely that they will understand all the basic activities and some of the base practices will not be properly performed. The assessor should then check whether activities meeting the base practices are performed. In most assessments, the base practices are the main indicators to check. In the people using the process can show activities that meet the base practice indicators, then the outcomes will be achieved and the process purpose fulfilled.

If the assessor is uncertain that the base practices are properly achieved, he or she may need to check the work products. Normally the output work products are more important than the input work products for showing achievement of the process outcomes and purpose. The assessor will check the work products that the organization uses against the descriptions in Annex B.2.

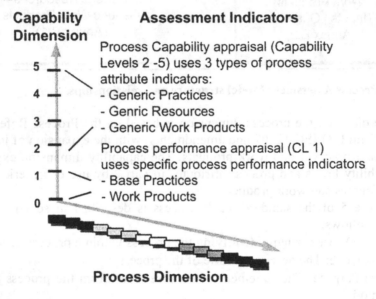

Fig. 32. Assessment Indicators by Capability levels.

If the assessor is also assessing the process to higher levels of capability, he or she then refers to clause 6. Clause 6 describes each capability level and the associated Process Attribute(s). The standard describes each capability level as follows:

- Capability level description.
- Process Attribute description and list of outcomes
- Generic Practice description and list of outcomes or results
- Generic Resource list

- Generic Work Products with a list of expected characteristics.

The assessor focuses first on the generic practices and check to see if the actual practices achieve the Process Attribute purpose and outcomes. The assessor uses the generic resources and work products as supporting evidence.

Process Dimension

The ISO/IEC 15504-5 Process Assessment Model groups the related processes in the process dimension into 3 categories and 9 groups. The categories and groups are:

- Primary Life Cycle Process
  - Acquisition
  - Supply
  - Engineering
  - Operation
- Organizational Life Cycle
  - Management
  - Process Improvement
  - Resources and Infrastructure
  - Reuse
- Supporting Life Cycle

The grouping of processes follows the guidance of ISO/IEC 12207, but there are some differences. First, the Usability support process is not included in the Process Assessment Model. Secondly, the Improvement subprocesses are separated, hence process establishment, assessment and improvement are included as separate processes. Thirdly, the training process is included, rather than as a sub-process of human resource management.

In addition the process identifiers have been changed from those in the technical report version of the standard. For example, the Customer-Supplier processes were formerly identified as CUS. They are now separated into an Acquisition group identified as ACQ, and a Supply group identified as SPL. Operation processes now use OPE, Process Improvement uses PIM, Resource and Infrastructure uses RIN, and Reuse uses REU.

In general the processes are defined for assessment of more complex software based products and systems. The assessment indicators, consisting of the base practices and work products, are intended to cover nearly all possible software based products and related services. When the scope of work or the products and services are limited, the assessor needs to tailor the process assessment indicators. This will normally consist of using only those indicators that are relevant (i.e. simplifying the assessment using a reduced set of indicators). There are no simple rules defined in the standard, this is where assessor judgment is required.

Another general point to note; an assessor can use the assessment indicators at process or even indicator level for non software oriented work assessment. This applies to nearly all the processes and process groups, except the Engineering process group, which is specifically oriented towards software based products and services. The assessor may need to make some expert judgment about the relevance of the assessment indicators. He or she may even choose to add or 'borrow' specific indicators from other processes or models. So while part 5 is oriented towards software based products, it is not exclusive.

Primary Life Cycle Processes

The primary life cycle processes cover acquisition, supply, engineering and operation of software based systems.

The **Acquisition** process group are processes that a customer uses to acquire products and services. It includes preparation, selection, contract agreement, supplier monitoring and customer acceptance. The preparation, supplier selection and contract agreement processes are designed to allow acquisition of more complex software based products. If a customer acquires existing products, for example, Commercial Off The Shelf (COTS) software, then the process will need tailoring. The supplier monitoring process assumes that the acquisition takes time, for example the product or service may need to be developed, and hence the supplier needs to be monitored. Similarly, the customer acceptance process assumes that several acceptance activities are needed, including planning of acceptance. Therefore, the assessor needs to understand the actual scope of the work performed and select the process assessment indicators that are relevant.

For example, the Acquisition Preparation process [ACQ.1] consists of six base practices [BP] and thirteen work products [WP]. If the assessment is for work associated with acquiring Off The Shelf (OTS) software, the following may be a valid tailoring of the assessment.

Table 5. Example of use of Acquisition Preparation Base Practice indicators.

Base Practice	Short description	Tailoring
ACQ.1.BP1	Establish the need	Person identifies software to perform work (short note).
ACQ.1.BP2	Define the requirements	Person verbally or in writing describes what is needed to person who makes purchase (if different persons).

ACQ.1.BP3	Review require-ments	Occurs during BP2 if verbal or may require some checking of COTS capa-bilities.
ACQ.1.BP4	Develop acquisi-tion strategy	For simple COTS, no strategy is needed, just a decision to buy.
ACQ.1.BP5	Define selection criteria	Not separately needed.
ACQ.1.BP6	Communicate the need	Occurs as part of BP2.

The above example assumes a simple software product of negligible cost is purchased and there is minimal bureaucracy required. What is negligible cost can vary, but is an amount that is readily spent without the need for extensive technical and cost review ('just do it').

In the example BP4 and BP5 are not needed and the level of formality and work products used in BP1, BP2, BP3 and BP6 are low. The only work products may be a purchase order and receipt (whether electronic or paper based). A similar situation would exist for the other acquisition processes, with few base practices being needed.

At the other extreme, acquiring large, costly, complex software based product or service that could make or break an enterprise, may require a process with virtually all the base practices and many work products implemented. Therefore, the assessor would expect to see evidence that meets nearly all the assessment indicators of the five acquisition processes.

The other issue to consider is whether an activity will meet several assessment indicators, or whether multiple activities are required to meet one assessment indicator.

In summary, it is important that the assessor using the process assessment model employs his or her judgment, based on the scope of the work.

The **Supply** process group consists of three processes. They are Supplier Tendering, Product Release and Product Acceptance Support. Supplier tendering is about offering products and services, and may reduce to a simple, fixed offer for COTS. For example, the first base practice is to establish a communication interface, which could be a web site. Many of the associated base practices may be automated using e-business processes. Product release is about defining, configuring and delivering the product. Product acceptance support is about support the customer so they can properly use the product.

The **Engineering** process category [acronym: **ENG**] consists of twelve processes. The twelve engineering processes provide a complete life cycle for specifying, developing, testing, installing and maintaining a software based system.

The life cycle comprises Requirement elicitation, System requirements analysis, System architectural design, Software requirements analysis, Software design, Software construction, Software integration, Software testing, System integration, System testing, Software installation, and software and system maintenance.

The life cycle uses the processes as amended in the ISO/IEC 12207 standard with little or no variation. Note that the processes cover both system and software levels, although the emphasis remains on software enabled systems.

The life cycle starts with the capture of the requirements (Requirements Elicitation). People using this process elicit (ask, discuss, collect and capture) requirements from the 'customer' for the system. Who the customer is and whether or not they are the user of the system is not specified. In some earlier versions of the assessment model, this process was part of the customer-supplier process lifecycle.

This leads to another important observation for assessors. The assessor should not assume that a process is restricted to a particular lifecycle or process category. Requirement Elicitation is as much a customer-supply related process as an engineering process. Even when an organization does not perform the actual design, construction and testing of software, it may still perform the requirement elicitation. Hence, an assessor should consider whether to assess a process based upon its importance to the assessment of the organization, regardless of its process category and the stated focus of the organization.

Organizational Life Cycle Processes

The **Management** process category [acronym: **MAN**] consists of processes that establish overall goals of the organization (including vision, mission and culture) and may be used on any type of project or process associated with software. The category includes Organizational alignment, Organizational management, Project management, Quality management, Risk management, and Measurement. This process category was formerly partly organizational processes [ORG] and management processes [MAN] in the technical report version of the standard.

Several processes are focused on organizational level, specifically Organizational alignment, and Organizational management. Project management is focussed on project level. The other processes can operate at organizational or project level. The assessor therefore needs to consider which level is required for effectively achieving the process purpose and outcomes. For example, risk management may be effectively performed at project level, unless it is found that risks are common across projects and affect the achievement of the process, especially at higher capability levels. At capability level 4, risks may impact on statistical process control. In such a case, the organization should ensure that risk is also handled at organizational level.

The **Process Improvement** process category [acronym: **PIM**] consists of organization-wide processes that develop process assets. It consists of Process establishment, Process assessment, and process improvement. With changes to the definition of capability level 3 to define both standard and deployed processes, process establishment is now more focussed on organizational level. Process assessment, which did not exist in early versions of the standard, is now separately defined. Process improvement is focussed on processes, but could be part of an organization's overall improvement process.

The **Resource and Infrastructure** process category [acronym: **RIN**] consists of processes, which establish human and infrastructure resources. It consists of Human resource management, Training, Knowledge management, and Infrastructure. The first three processes are people focussed. Training is a sub-process of human resource management in the reference model, but is separately defined here for clarity. Knowledge management is not just an elaborated form of information management. It is concerned with both knowledge capture and use from a person and organizational perspective. Infrastructure covers all physical and information infrastructure aspects.

The **Reuse** process category [acronym: **REU**] consists of processes, which cover creation and reuse of artefacts associated with software based systems. It consists of Asset management, Reuse program management, and Domain engineering. While the process group is located within the organizational life cycle, it is also strongly associated with the engineering life cycle. In other standards (e.g. IEEE-1517), the reuse processes were contained in a separate category called 'cross-project' processes.

Domain engineering is used to devise common domains in which software can be reused. These domains may be user-centric, architectural (design) or component oriented. Reuse program management is focussed on establishing and running an organization wide reuse program. This is important as reuse requires investment which is best recovered over multiple projects. Asset management is focussed on establishing and running a library of reusable assets. While software assets are naturally expected to be managed, assets can be of any type. Existing templates, planning documentation, design, requirements, operation and test assets may all be managed as assets. Asset management should establish selection rules for assets, based upon business needs. One such rule may be related to the effort to create an asset and to re-use/adapt that asset for other projects. If any extra effort to create a standard item is later recouped by multiple reuse, then the item should be selected as an asset.

Supporting Life Cycle Processes

The **Support** process category [acronym: **SUP**] consists of processes, which may be employed, by other processes (from any process category) at various points in the software product/service life cycle. It consists of Quality assurance, Verification, Validation, Joint review, Audit, Product evaluation, Documentation, Configuration management, Problem resolution management, and Change request management.

The introduction of amendments in ISO/IEC 12207 affected the number of processes in this category, in particular the addition of change request management and product evaluation. The usability process was not included. Unlike ISO/IEC 12207, the processes are not differentiated into sub-groups.

Assessors may need to discuss the difference between verification, and the various testing process in the engineering life cycle which verify the system and software. In general, the verification process can be considered as supplementary, it covers aspects that the engineering processes do not cover. However, an organization may wish to group all its verification activities in this process.

Process Performance

Each process in the assessment model is described in terms of a process purpose statement. These statements contain the unique 'functional' objectives of the process when instantiated (implemented) in a particular environment. The purpose statement leads to a set of process outcomes. If the outcomes are achieved, then the process purpose is achieved.

There is a set of base practices associated with each process. Each base practice is an indicator of an activity that addresses part of the purpose of the process. Consistent performance of the base practices will help to consistently achieve the outcomes and process purpose.

The base practices are described at an abstract level, identifying "*what*" should be done (the functional activities) without specifying "*how*" it should be done.

Implementing the activities indicated by the base practices of a process is the first step in achieving process Capability Level 1. They produce work products that are at least marginally usable in achieving the purpose of the process. In this Process Assessment Model, each work product has a defined set of characteristics that may be used to assess the effective implementation of a process. If the activities are performed and the work products demonstrate achievement of the process purpose, then the process will be assessed as achieving process Capability Level 1.

However, the performance of the base practices at this level does not ensure that the process is performed consistently. It also does not ensure it is properly planned, predictable or result in products that necessarily meet all their requirements. The performance of the process to meet these requirements needs to meet higher Capability Level process attributes (see next section).

ISO/IEC 15504-5 clause 5 contains a complete description of the base practices. Annex B.2 lists the key characteristics of the work products.

Capability Dimension

The Process Assessment Model uses the process attributes from the Process Reference Model to determine process capability. The current part 5 model uses the attributes from ISO/IEC 15504-2:2003.

Capability Level 5 Optimising PA 5.1 Process Innovation PA 5.2 Process Optimisation	The process is continually improved to meet relevant current and projected business goals
Capability Level 4 Predictable PA 4.1 Process Measurement PA 4.2 Process Control	The process is enacted consistently within defined limits
Capability Level 3 Established PA 3.1 Process Definition PA 3.2 Process Deployment	A defined process is used, based on a standard process
Capability Level 2 Managed PA 2.1 Performance Management PA 2.2 Work Proeduct Management	The process is managed and work products are established, controlled and maintained
Capability Level 1 Performed PA 1.1 Process Performance	The process is implemented and achieves its purpose
Capability Level 0 Incomplete	The process is not implemented or fails to achieve its purpose

Fig. 33. ISO/IEC 15504 Capability dimension.

Each of the above process attributes [PA] describes one aspect of the organizational unit's capability to manage and improve the effectiveness of a process. The aim is to achieve the process purpose and contribute to the business goals of the organization in a more effective and efficient manner.

The Capability Levels are described in detail in chapter 4 of this book [Measurement Framework]. The process assessment model provides the following information in clause 6:

• Capability level description.
• Process Attribute description and list of outcomes
• Generic Practice description and list of outcomes or results
• Generic Resource list
• Generic Work Products with a list of expected characteristics.
• Related processes

Each Capability Level provides a major enhancement in the capability to perform a process to achieve its purpose. Each represents a set of process attributes at its own level that support this capability. The process attributes build capability on top of those at the lower capability level. Hence the effect of the process attributes and capability levels are cumulative, rather than separate and discrete. For process improvement purposes, the levels constitute one way of progressively improving the capability of any process.

Assessing the achievement of a Capability Level requires assessment of achievement of all lower level process attributes. For example, to achieve Capability Level 3, the process attributes for level 2 and level 1 must be fulfilled. In addition, the process assessment model specifies additional resource and work product characteristics that the assessor should look for that support the generic practices at Capability Level 3. Although not all the resources are mandatory, the existent of these will make the achievement of the generic practice easier to achieve. Similarly, if the organization has implemented the related processes, then the assessor is likely to find more consistent evidence that the management practice has been consistently implemented across multiple instances.

The assessor focuses first on the generic practices and check to see if the actual practices/activities achieve the generic practice indicators. If these are achieved, the Process Attribute outcomes will be achieved. If both process attributes are achieved, then the Capability Level will be achieved.

If it is not clear whether a generic practice indicator is achieved, the assessor may refer back to the Process Attribute outcomes or also assess the generic resource list and/or the generic work products. In general, the assessor uses the generic resources and work products as supporting evidence. It is not uncommon for the meaning of the generic practice indicator to be unclear for the people using a process. Sometimes this is because of the language used to describe them in the assessment model, and sometimes it is because the organization uses different interpretations. The assessor needs to be able to explain both the intent and meaning of the indicators, especially the generic practice indicators. In these cases, the generic resource and work products can help the understanding of the practices.

In addition, the assessor can use the information in clause 6.6, which provides a table of related processes for each process attribute. People using a process may use a related process to achieve specific generic practices. For example, most of the support processes (quality assurance, verification, joint review, etc.,) support achievement of Process Attribute PA 2.2, work product management. While it is not mandatory for these processes to exist in order to achieve a particular Process Attribute, it is likely that some of them will exist.

The level of detail for the practice performance characteristics is much greater than the generic practice description (and there is additional detail in the resource and infrastructure characteristics), in order to support the assessor's ability to reliably and consistently judge the achievement of the assessment indicator.

In conclusion, Part 5 of ISO/IEC 15504 sets out a Process Assessment Model that is compatible with the Process Reference Model in ISO/IEC 15504-2 by means of simple elaboration of the Process Reference Model.

The Process Assessment Model scope covers all the processes and all the Capability Levels in a one-to-one mapping of the Process Reference Model.

Additional conformant Process Assessment Models

There are several other conformant Process Assessment Models that have been or are being developed. I look in the following sections at some of these in brief.

The SPiCE for SPACE and OOSPICE Process Assessment Models were initially conformant to the earlier ISO/IEC TR 15504-2:1998 version of the standard. SPiCE for SPACE and Automotive SPICE have been updated with the revisions to ISO/IEC 15504.

Model developers (and to a lesser extent users) need to consider changes introduced by the normative part 2 of the ISO/IEC 15504 standard. In particular, they need to consider the measurement framework capability dimension aspects and the removal of a Process Reference Model in this part of the standard. They also need to consider changes introduced into the associated Process Reference Model (for example, ISO/IEC 12207 and ISO/IEC 15288). There is an ISO working group initiative to harmonise these two standards that is in early committee draft form. This will alter the contents of both standards, early drafts have already indicated the scope of change, but they are not yet ready for release as standards.

In addition, the ISO/IEC TR 15504-5:1998 exemplar was used as a basis for some of the conformant Process Assessment Models, therefore changes introduced in the exemplar need to be considered, including terminology, layout and descriptions.

SPiCE for SPACE

SPiCE for SPACE (S4S) is a method for the assessment of software processes for the space industry. SPiCE for SPACE comprises a Process Assessment Model, a Process Reference Model, an assessment method, a rating process and a tool for evaluating space software processes. The method was developed by a consortium of space software suppliers and software quality experts under a study contract from the European Space Agency (ESA) [27] for the European space industry.

ESA's goals were to encourage production of the best possible software products and services; develop customer-supplier relationships based on trust, not control; promote and disseminate best practice concepts proven across the software industry; and widen their supplier base to companies traditionally outside of aerospace. The method has been in use since 2000 for assessments of space software suppliers.

SPiCE for SPACE provides both capability determination for space relevant processes and process improvement opportunity outputs. An additional advantage is that the process dimension of SPiCE for SPACE can be tailored to different classes of safety-critical software and includes an optional risk oriented dimension (Risk for Space) and target profiles.

The Process Assessment Model adopted the same overall approach as ISO/IEC TR 15504-5. It has been updated in part with the release of ISO/IEC 15504-5. It has added specific inputs from the European Cooperation for Space Standardisation (ECSS) standards [28]. The ECSS Management, Engineering and Quality standards are compatible with ISO/IEC 12207 and its amendments, which simplified their incorporation into the SPiCE for SPACE assessment model, while allowing the dual assessment purpose to be included.

The capability dimension from the Assessment Model in ISO/IEC 15504-2 was adopted as-is.

Requirements from ECSS documents or activities from space software process models were matched with Assessment Model processes and base practices. In addition, the process dimension was augmented with space specific processes and base practices. New work products and work product characteristics were created to represent the space standard outputs not covered by the ISO/IEC 15504-5 exemplar model. These new processes and process indicators properly incorporate space software needs into the SPiCE for SPACE Process Assessment Model.

SPiCE for SPACE has been prepared as a potential ECSS Handbook and was undergoing industry review at the time of writing this edition of the book.

Acquisition
ACQ.1 Acquisition Preparation
ACQ.2 Supplier Selection
ACQ.3 Contract Agreement
ACQ.4 Supplier Monitoring
ACQ.5 Customer Acceptance
ACQ.6 Contract Maintenance

Supply
SPL.1 Supplier Tendering
SPL.2 Product Release
SPL.3 Product Acceptance Support

Engineering
ENG.1 Requirements Elicitation
ENG.2 Systems Requirements Analysis
ENG.3 System Architecture Design
ENG.4 Software Requirements Analysis
ENG.5 Software Design
ENG.6 Software Construction
ENG.7 Software Integration
ENG.8 Software Testing
ENG.9 System Integration
ENG.10 System Testing
ENG.11 Software Installation
ENG.12 Software and System Maintenance

Support
SUP.1 Quality Assurance
SUP.2 Verification
SUP.3 Validation
SUP.4 Joint Review
SUP.5 Audit
SUP.6 Product Evaluation
SUP.7 Documentation
SUP.8 Configuration Management
SUP.9 Problem Resolution Management
SUP.10 Change Request Management
SUP.11 Safety and dependability assurance
SUP.12 Independent software verification and validation

Reuse
REU.1 Asset Management
REU.2 Reuse Program Management
REU.3 Domain Engineering

Operation
OPE.1 Operational use
OPE.2 Customer support

Management
MAN.1 Organisational alignment
MAN.2 Organisation Management
MAN.3 Project Management
MAN.4 Quality Management
MAN.5 Risk Management
MAN.6 Measurement
MAN.7 Information Management

Resource and Infrastructure
RIN.1 Human Resource Management
RIN.2 Training
RIN.3 Knowledge Management
RIN.4 Infrastructure

Process Improvement
PIM.1 Process Establishment
PIM.2 Process Assessment
PIM.3 Process Improvement

Fig. 34. SPICE for SPACE.

The process dimension expands upon the process dimension in ISO/IEC 15504 to include Space industry related processes, base practices, work products and explanatory notes. In comparison with ISO/IEC 15504-5, SPiCE for SPACE has:

- 4 New Processes:
  - ACQ.6   Contract Maintenance
  - MAN.7   Information Management
  - SUP.11   Safety and Dependability
  - SUP.12   Independent Software Verification and Validation
- 41 New Base Practices
- 73 New Notes
- 22 New Work Products

Additional differences between ISO/IEC 15504-5 and SPiCE for SPACE include 2 new categories of work products. The first is an ECSS Instance. This is a specific instance of an existing ISO/IEC 15504 work product, which inherits the generic characteristics of the work products but has additional characteristics added from ECSS (space standards) requirements; an example is a Maintenance Plan, which is an ECSS instance of a Plan. The second is a specific extension. This is an extension of an existing ISO/IEC 15504 work product, which has added characteristic(s) to existing ISO/IEC 15504 work products; an example is a Compliance Matrix, which is an extension of Software Product Assurance Plan.

Example Process Assessment Indicator

The following example is for a specific SPiCE for SPACE process, Contract Maintenance. It illustrates the standard layout used for describing a process assessment indicator.

Table 6. Example SPiCE for SPACE process assessment indicator.

Process ID	ACQ.6
Process name	Contract Maintenance
Process Purpose	The purpose of the contract maintenance process is to maintain and change the business agreements during the development process. Either the customer or the supplier may propose contract modifications, while the complementary actor responds to the proposal.
Process Outcomes	As a result of the implementation of the Contract Maintenance process: 1) each business agreement is clearly identified and accomplished;

	2) the need for a contract change is identified, with the reason and scope defined; 3) a contract change is proposed; 4) the impact of the change on all aspects of the product is assessed; and 5) the customer and supplier negotiate the contract modification reflecting the agree requirements
Base Practices	**Base Practices ACQ.6.BP1: Propose contract modifications.** Identify the need, scope and impact of modification of the original contract. [Outcomes: 1, 2, 3] NOTE A: ECSS-M-40 requires that for an evolution requested by the customer, the corresponding change proposal include the description of the change to the requirement documents, when they are affected, derived from the customer's request and as a result from the changes of requirements ECSS-M-40 requires that for an evolution proposed by a supplier, the corresponding change proposal contain: • The change descriptions related to the desired change • Description of any modification to business agreement provisions (e.g. cost, schedule, special clauses, data requirements, etc.) *ECSS Ref. M-40B 5.3.2.1a, 5.3.2.1c, 5.3.2.2a, 5.3.2.2b, 5.3.2.2c, 5.3.2.3, 5.3.2.5,* *5.3.2.6a, 5.3.2.6b* **ACQ.6.BP2: Respond to contract modification request.** Review the reason and scope and conduct an impact assessment on all products, including contractual, technical, quality, dependability and safety aspects. [Outcomes: 4] *ECSS Ref. M-40B 5.3.2.4* **ACQ.6.BP3: Agree on contract modification.** Review reply to change request. Negotiate and incorporate changes into new contractual agreement. [Outcomes: 5] *ECSS Ref. M-20B 5.3.1a, 5.3.1i, 5.3.3e*

Work Products

Input Work Products	Output Work Products
WP02-01 Commitment / agreement [Outcomes: 1, 5] WP13-16 Change request [Outcomes: 3] WP17-00 Requirement specification [Outcomes: all] WP60-01 Request for waiver [Outcomes: 2, 3]	WP02-01 Commitment / agreement [Outcomes: 5] WP13-16 Change request [Outcomes: 3] WP15-01 Analysis report [Outcomes: 4]

The layout follows the exemplar assessment model layout

Enhancements to SPiCE for SPACE

The following enhancements were made in order to incorporate European space software development practices.

ISVV Process

ISVV (Independent Software Verification and Validation) is one of the organizational ways to achieve the independence of Verification and Validation. A well-defined set of standard life cycle processes is repeated by an actor completely independent from the supplier. ECSS documents require this two-fold process instantiation for highly critical software. For space projects this is applicable for software criticality class B or higher.

ISO/IEC 15504-5 does not describe explicitly such an ISVV instantiation of processes although it has similar practices throughout verification, validation, audit, joint review, as well as all of the engineering processes.

Only the establishment and management of an ISVV program are not addressed by ISO/IEC 15504-5. Thus, the new ISVV process includes Base Practices such as 'Define scope of ISVV' (SUP.12.BP1) and concludes with 'Report ISVV activities and results' (SUP.12.BP4). Particular work products created include ISVV plan and ISVV report. This process can be assessed even if only one of the two (independent verification or validation) is performed.

Safety and Dependability Assurance Process

In ECSS terminology, safety is a state in which the risk of harm (to persons) or damage is limited to an acceptable level [ECSS-P-001A].

ISO/IEC 15504-5 does not specifically address the safety of the software system. To underline the importance of the SPA requirements related to safety, a new process was incorporated into the Process Assessment Model within the SUP process category. This process covers all activities required to ensure the safety of the system. In addition, the author ran a project that looked at systems of various safety criticality to define target process capability profiles. This is described further in the Practical Guide.

Dependability is the degree to which the software product is available, reliable and maintainable. In the ISO/IEC 12207 Reference Model, no process specifically ensures software dependability. Again, in order to underline the importance of this issue for space software, a new process was added to the assessment model. The base practices are worded such that they are applicable to both the dependability and the safety process. Therefore, both processes were merged into one process, which is called "Safety and Dependability Assurance Process" (SUP.11).

Numerical Accuracy (Requirements, Design, Verification)

As an important issue to be addressed in requirements specification, design specification and testing, numerical accuracy is explicitly mentioned in notes added to the corresponding work product characteristics.

Memory Occupation and Timing (Budgeting, Design, Verification)

Memory occupation and timing are usually constraints, which are imposed through system requirements. These requirements need to be propagated and addressed through the software life cycle. Work products like Requirements Specification, Software Components Design Documents and Test Reports should document that such issues are treated carefully. Extra characteristics were added to the corresponding work products if not mentioned in the original ISO/IEC 15504-5 work product description.

Lessons Learned

In ISO/IEC 15504-5, the lessons learned process is a continuous process improvement process (PIM.3), which is not restricted to the end of a project.

Alert System

Alerts may be raised as a reaction to non-conformance reports. The duty of the contractors is to ensure the provision of all information related to any non-conformance reported to the final customer. ISO/IEC TR 15504-5 did have a Problem Resolution process. In ISO 15504-5 SUP.9 provides the basis to support an alert system. A new base practice, "Prepare preliminary alert information", was added to SUP.9.BP11 to support this practice. If an alert is broadcasted by ESA, the contractor, or its alert coordinator, must disseminate the alert within his organisation and take corrective actions as necessary. Another new base practice "Support processing of alerts" (SUP.9 BP12) describes the activities performed to respond to incoming alerts.

Information Management

During a space software project life cycle, every actor must be able to readily access all the information he needs in order to perform his task. Although not space-specific, the flow of information inside a project organisation is of paramount importance to success of space projects and is described by a new process, Information Management (MAN.7) in the Process Assessment Model.

Contract Maintenance

During the evolution of a software project, many circumstances may demand a revision of the business contract. As the duration of the contract increases, this possibility also increases. Major space systems and platform contracts ran for many years. In ISO/IEC 15504-5 no process specifically addresses contract maintenance and modification. A new process (ACQ.6) was proposed within the acquisition process category that admits a customer-supplier exchange and may result in a contract change.

Risk Management

Risk management is an integral part of space projects, where risks cannot be reduced to zero. Several base practices were added to MAN.5 to stress the importance of communicating and accepting risk. "Recommend acceptance", "Communicate risks" and "Accept residual risks" ensure that after risk reduction, risks are known and understood by the responsible management.

Interfaces to System Processes

In space projects, software is mostly embedded in a complex hardware system. To assure coherence between the software and other components of the system, software processes must be linked to the corresponding system processes. ISO/IEC 15504-5 defines such interfaces at the beginning (ENG.2 System Requirements Analysis and Design) and at the end of the development phase (ENG.9 System Integration and Testing, ENG.12 System and Software Maintenance). Space standards require further interfaces between software and system processes. For example, system PA requirements have to be considered when establishing the software PA plan, and software safety and dependability plans should be in line with the corresponding policy on the system level. In addition, milestone reviews have to be coordinated with the corresponding system reviews. SPiCE for SPACE covers these aspects in defining appropriate input work products for the relevant processes.

Software Re-use

The re-use of software impacts both the organisation and engineering process categories. The ISO/IEC 15504-5 Reuse process (REU.2) describes the production and management of software for re-use, including the definition of a re-use strategy and the establishment of a re-use infrastructure.

Regarding software engineering processes, alternative re-use solutions are analysed during the software design phase and implemented during the software construction. To reflect these activities, two new base practices, "Identify and analyse reusable components" and "Reuse software units" were added to the Software Design (ENG.5) and Software Construction (ENG.6) processes, respectively.

OOSPICE

OOSPICE provides a Process Assessment Model and methodology. The Process Assessment Model covers 8 groups of processes. I described Process Reference Model in the previous chapter [29].

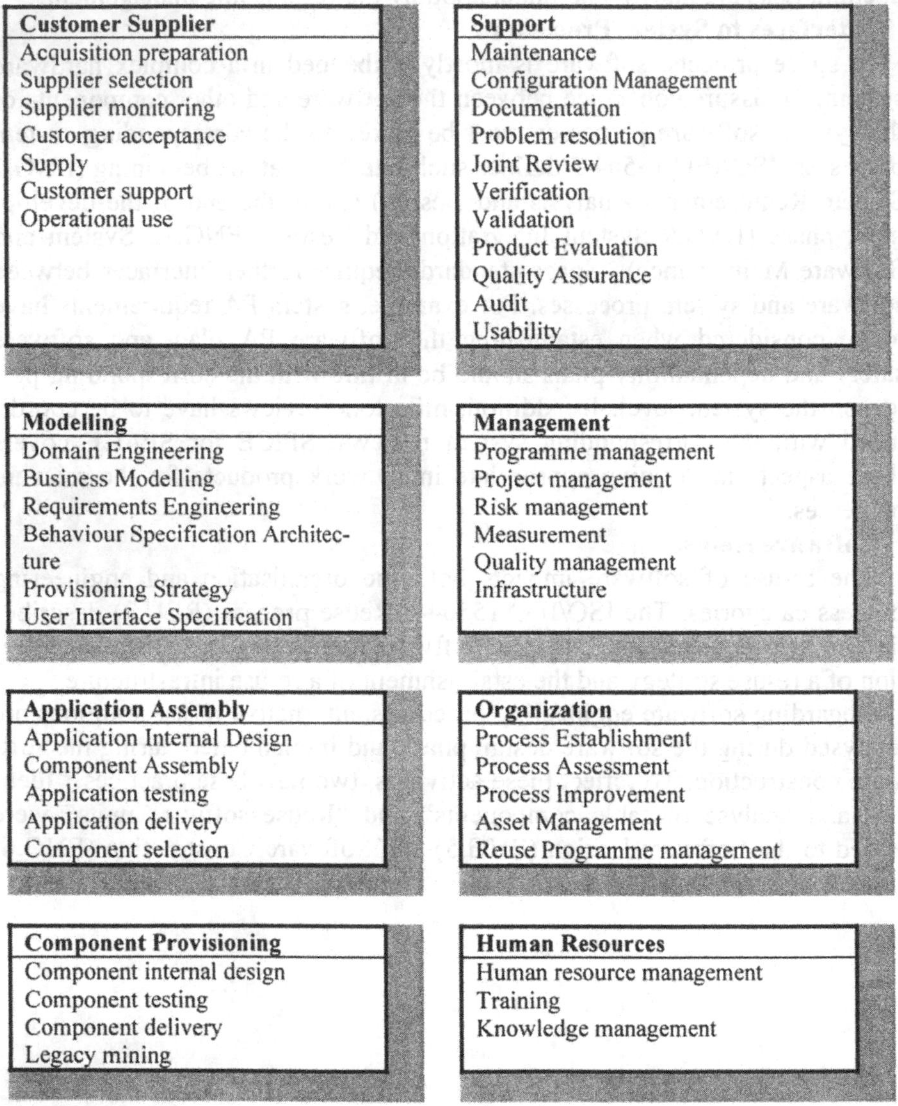

Customer Supplier	Support
Acquisition preparation	Maintenance
Supplier selection	Configuration Management
Supplier monitoring	Documentation
Customer acceptance	Problem resolution
Supply	Joint Review
Customer support	Verification
Operational use	Validation
	Product Evaluation
	Quality Assurance
	Audit
	Usability

Modelling	Management
Domain Engineering	Programme management
Business Modelling	Project management
Requirements Engineering	Risk management
Behaviour Specification Architecture	Measurement
Provisioning Strategy	Quality management
User Interface Specification	Infrastructure

Application Assembly	Organization
Application Internal Design	Process Establishment
Component Assembly	Process Assessment
Application testing	Process Improvement
Application delivery	Asset Management
Component selection	Reuse Programme management

Component Provisioning	Human Resources
Component internal design	Human resource management
Component testing	Training
Component delivery	Knowledge management
Legacy mining	

Fig. 35. OOSPICE Process Assessment Model.

The main extensions to ISO/IEC 15504 are for the 3 engineering process areas: Modelling, Application Assembly and Component Provisioning.

The OOSPICE Process Assessment Model is integrated within the OOSPICE process model that describes the component based development methodology and the implemented processes, as well as providing the framework for the process component repository.

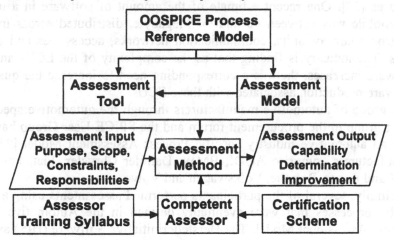

Fig. 36. OOSPICE Assessment Methodology..

The Process Assessment Model describes for each process:
- Process Identifier and Name
- Purpose
- Outcomes
- Tasks
- Work Products

The capability dimension of ISO/IEC TR 15504:1998 has been adopted.

An assessment tool has been designed, based upon the SPICE-1-2-1 tool. For more details, see www.oospice.com.

Automotive SPICE

The leading automotive manufacturers around the world have increased the use of electronics both as control aids and as consumer features in the current and future development of the automobile. The use of electronic control units (ECUs) is increasingly dependent upon software for functionality and features [30]. One recent estimate of the amount of software in a modern automobile was between 40 and 90 Megabyte, distributed across multiple electronic control units, communication networks, accessories and display units. The industry is finding that as the complexity of the ECUs and their software increases, there is a corresponding need to increase the quality of software production associated with these ECUs.

A group of automotive manufacturers through the automotive special interest group in the procurement forum and the SPICE User Group have created an automotive industry specific Process Assessment Model [31]. The manufacturers comprise AUDI, BMW, Daimler Chrysler, Fiat, Ford, Jaguar/Land Rover, Porsche, Volkswagen and Volvo.

Initially, several of the participants performed assessments using a subset of the processes that were eventually defined in the Automotive SPICE Process Assessment Model. The Herstellerinitiative Software (HIS) assessed a subset of ten processes in what is now the Automotive SPICE model. These were:

- Supplier Monitoring
- System Requirements Analysis
- Software Requirements Analysis
- Software Design
- Software Construction
- Software Integration Testing
- Software Testing
- System Integration Testing
- Configuration Management
- Project Management

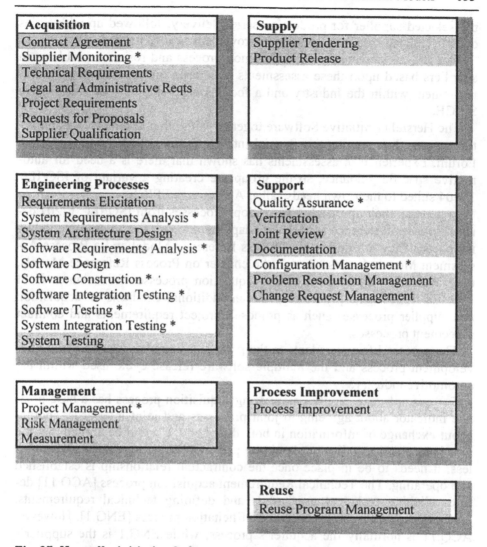

Acquisition	Supply
Contract Agreement	Supplier Tendering
Supplier Monitoring *	Product Release
Technical Requirements	
Legal and Administrative Reqts	
Project Requirements	
Requests for Proposals	
Supplier Qualification	

Engineering Processes	Support
Requirements Elicitation	Quality Assurance *
System Requirements Analysis *	Verification
System Architecture Design	Joint Review
Software Requirements Analysis *	Documentation
Software Design *	Configuration Management *
Software Construction *	Problem Resolution Management
Software Integration Testing *	Change Request Management
Software Testing *	
System Integration Testing *	
System Testing	

Management	Process Improvement
Project Management *	Process Improvement
Risk Management	
Measurement	

	Reuse
	Reuse Program Management

Fig. 37. Herstellerinitiative Software process assessment subset.

Using this basic subset (the 10 processes marked with an *), they assessed the relevant processes of suppliers with an aim that suppliers achieve Capability Level 2. They have set three ratings for suppliers based upon the assessments; the first is equivalent to fully achieved Capability Level 2 (> 85%), the second is above 75% achievement, and the third is anything less than this. The assessment strategy was to assess multiple potential suppliers in short assessments on a few key processes and then do a full assessment of the selected supplier for production series delivery, followed up with series delivery related measures and any improvement actions needed.

The HIS also created a list of common process and resource problems in suppliers based upon these assessments as a basis for opportunities for improvement within the industry and a focus for development of Automotive SPICE.

The Herstellerinitiative Software together with other automotive manufacturers formed an Automotive Special Interest Group within the Procurement Forum. Experience in assessments has shown that there is a need for automotive specific guidance, so the group are creating a variant of ISO/IEC 15504 suited to their own needs called Automotive SPICE.

In general, their approach was to adopt processes from ISO/IEC 12207 derived Process Reference Model and adapt them to suit the automotive industry needs. They are defining a Process Reference Model and a Process Assessment Model. As described in the chapter on Process Reference Models, they decided to adopt most of the acquisition processes from Annex H of ISO/IEC 12207. The processes place an additional emphasis on acquisition and supplier processes such as proposal, project requirements and contract agreement processes.

The process lifecycle adapts to the parallel system/hardware/software development process and the multiple software release cycle used within the automotive industry.

For example, the supplier monitoring acquisition process has a base practice indicator about agreeing to joint processes and joint interfaces, another about exchange of information in both directions. It could be argued that the first base practice indicator should be part of contract agreement; nevertheless, it needs to be in place once the contractual relationship is established and operating. The Technical Requirement acquisition process [ACQ.11] defines eliciting technical user needs and defining technical requirements, partly in parallel to the Requirements Elicitation process [ENG.1]. However, ACQ.11 is normally the acquirer's process, while ENG.1 is the supplier's process. In addition to technical product requirements, the process also includes environment evaluation, safety, security, supportability and tracking changing technology. The scope of this acquisition process is defined in more detail than in part 5 of ISO/IEC 15504. In a similar manner, the Legal and administrative requirement process [ACQ.12] defines a more detailed approach to handle these aspects, as does the project requirements acquisition process. It is important to note that these are processes performed by the acquirer and not the supplier.

The software release cycle can be summarized as: "Release-Change Request (or Problem Resolution)-Update Release" in a semi-continual cycle (multiple repetitions for one product, until replaced by a new product). While this type of multiple release cycle is also used for software in other industries, it is more complicated in the automotive industry due to the parallel hardware ECU development cycles. In addition, it is possible that during the prototype development stage, there are competing suppliers providing both hardware and software. This requires extra emphasis on processes covering software release and configuration management.

Due to the multiple release strategy adopted when developing software for automotive Electronic Control Units, Change Request Management is an important process to manage these changes, and configuration management becomes important in tracking the many versions of software released both during development and in the units that are included in the delivered automobiles.

Annex D of the Process Assessment Model provides a key concept schematic that shows the relationship between systems, software, specifications and processes.

Annex E provides a depiction of bilateral traceability. This is traceability between the specification and construction work products, and laterally to the test specifications/test cases.

Capability Maturity Model Integration

The Software Engineering Institute's latest versions of CMM® are the Capability Maturity Model Integration (CMMI® $^{v1.2}$). There are two types of CMMI[41] models, the continuous model and the staged model. The staged model is based upon the staged representation first formulated for the SW CMM®; in brief, it requires processes to be implemented in a specific order to attain a maturity level. This approach is not fully compatible with the requirements of ISO/IEC 15504 and will not be described further here (refer to the separate SW CMM and CMMI chapter later in this book for further details). For more detail on this model, see the Software Engineering Institute CMMI Handbook [32] or the CMMI website [33].

The CMMI provides both a Process Reference Model and Process Assessment Model. Because the Process Assessment Model encapsulates the reference model, it is described here, rather than in chapter 5.

The CMMI continuous model has been designed to be conformant to ISO/IEC 15504[42]. There are several variants of this model available, each presenting a different scope of activity. The most comprehensive model is briefly summarized here. This is the CMMI for Development v 1.2 [34]. The model consists of the following process areas.

- Process Management
  - Organizational Process Focus (B)
  - Organizational Process Definition (B)
  - Organizational Training (B)
  - Organizational Process Performance (A)
  - Organizational Innovation and Deployment (A)
- Project Management
  - Project Planning (B)
  - Project Monitoring and Control (B)
  - Supplier Agreement Management (B)
  - Integrated Project Management for IPPD (Integrated Product and Process Development) (A)
  - Risk Management (A)
  - Integrated Training (A)
  - Integrated Supplier Management (A)
  - Quantitative Project Management (A)

---

[41] CMMI and CMMI® are used interchangeably and are acknowledged as registered trademarks of the SEI^{SM}.

[42] It should be noted that work is still ongoing to ensure a fully conformant model is achieved.

- Engineering
  - Requirements Management (B)
  - Requirements Development (B)
  - Technical Solution (B)
  - Product Integration (B)
  - Verification (B)
  - Validation (B)
- Support
  - Configuration Management (B)
  - Process and Product Quality Assurance (B)
  - Measurement and Analysis (B)
  - Decision Analysis and Resolution (A)
  - Organizational Environment for Integration (A)
  - Causal Analysis and Resolution (A)

The CMMI continuous model groups processes into process areas to highlight the specific interactions, but the process areas also often interact and have an effect on one another regardless of their defined group.

The engineering process areas are written in a general engineering terminology so any technical discipline involved in the product development process (e.g., software engineering, mechanical engineering) can use them for process improvement. At the same time, the CMMI is oriented towards organizations that develop systems and software, and not to organizations that do not do this.

The CMMI also differentiates between basic process areas (shown as (B) in the process areas list) and advanced process areas (for example, Organizational Process Performance and Organizational Innovation and Deployment are advanced process areas – shown as (A) in the process areas list). It therefore guides users to consider implementing the basic process areas before the advanced process areas to have a good foundation to build upon – especially when attempting to achieve higher Capability Levels.

The layout of CMMI® provides for each process area:

- Purpose
- Introductory notes
- Related Process Areas
- Specific Goals
- Generic Goals
- Practice to Goals relationship
- Specific Practices by Goal
- Generic Practices by Goal

For the purpose of a conformant Process Reference Model, the purpose, specific and generic goals descriptions are sufficient. The goals provide the equivalent description to process outcomes. For example, the Process and Product Quality Assurance process area consists of the following description [35]:

Purpose
The purpose of Process and Product Quality Assurance is to provide staff and management with objective insight into processes and associated work products.
Specific Goals
SG 1   Objectively Evaluate Processes and Work Products [PA145.IG101]
Adherence of the performed process and associated work products and services to applicable process descriptions, standards, and procedures is objectively evaluated.
SG 2   Provide Objective Insight [PA145.IG102]
Noncompliance issues are objectively tracked and communicated, and resolution is ensured.
Generic Goals
GG 1   Achieve Specific Goals [CL102.GL101]
The process supports and enables achievement of the specific goals of the process area by transforming identifiable input work products to produce identifiable output work products.
GG 2   Institutionalize a Managed Process [CL103.GL101]
The process is institutionalized as a managed process.
GG 3   Institutionalize a Defined Process [CL104.GL101]
The process is institutionalized as a defined process.
GG 4   Institutionalize a Quantitatively Managed Process [CL105.GL101]
The process is institutionalized as a quantitatively managed process.
GG 5   Institutionalize an Optimising Process [CL106.GL101]
The process is institutionalized as an optimising process.
CMMI-SE/SW/IPPD, V1.2

Fig. 38. Example CMMI process area description.

The model presented must be adapted and tailored by the organization to their business needs. The CMMI® provides guidance for users to transition from the older CMM® standards and EIA/IS 731 [36] to CMMI® with the aim to allow assessments to achieve ISO/IEC 15504 conformance.

US FAA iCMM

This section is based upon information kindly provided by Linda Ibrahim, the US FAA Chief Engineer for Process Improvement. I have edited the input to place it within the context of the book and added some comments comparing the FAA iCMM® to other process assessment standards, especially ISO/IEC 15504.

The United States Federal Aviation Administration (US FAA) has created its own model called the FAA iCMM® [37]. The US Federal Aviation Administration commenced process improvement using various forms of the SEI Capability Maturity Model. In 1997, they integrated three of the capability maturity models (CMMs): the software, systems engineering, and software acquisition CMMs. This became the integrated CMM (or FAA iCMM® v1.0 for short) and was published and deployed in 1997.

The US FAA soon recognized that integrating CMMs alone did not provide sufficient process improvement guidance for broad and complex enterprises like the FAA and others who have adopted the FAA iCMM. Thus, the US FAA created version 2.0 in 2001. This integrated several important improvement approaches including ISO/IEC TR 15504 (SPICE), ISO 9001:2000, ISO/IEC CD 15288, ISO/IEC 12207, Electronics Industries Alliance (EIA) 731, Malcolm Baldrige National Quality Award, and Capability Maturity Model Integration. By integrating beyond CMMs, and incorporating international standards and perspectives, the iCMM now contains cohesive guidance for improving business and technical processes ranging from enterprise management to operation and disposal.

The FAA iCMM continues to evolve, with work currently underway to include international safety and security standards as part of the framework. There are detailed mapping tables indicate how the practices and principles from source standards and documents are integrated into the FAA iCMM.

Any organization pursuing process improvement examines its business objectives and the processes it performs to accomplish those objectives. The organization selectively compares its practices to those in the relevant parts of the FAA iCMM to identify areas where improvements might be pursued.

The model provides process improvement coverage for internal and external organizations to the FAA. Its primary focus was initially internal and governmental organizations, but it is gaining wider acceptance. It covers high-level (for example strategic direction) and low-level (for example task management) issues. It can be used for process assessment of external organizations in combination with an FAA Assessment method [38].

General Structure of the FAA iCMM.

The practices in the iCMM are structured into 2 parts: the process dimension, with practices specific to performing a selection of processes, and the capability dimension. The FAA deliberately followed the recommended guidance for process assessment models in ISO/IEC 15504. The Base Practices are specific to each process, while the Generic Practices are used to improve the way any process is performed. Within the process dimension, practices are grouped into Process Areas, and within the capability dimension, practices are grouped into Capability Levels. Both Process Areas and Capability Levels contain goals expressing what should be achieved if their associated practices are performed. Some practices in the process dimension provide additional detail regarding practices in the capability dimension. This structure is illustrated below.

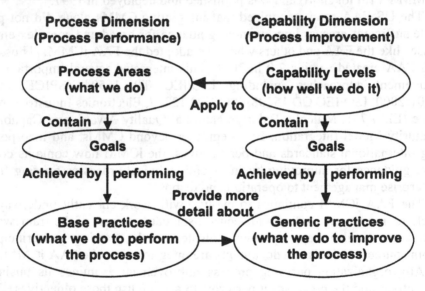

Fig. 39. FAA iCMM Dimensions, Goals and Practices.

The Capability Dimension.

There are 6 capability levels in the capability dimension of the iCMM. Any of the processes in the process dimension may be being performed at any of these capability levels.

Table 7. FAA-iCMM Capability Dimension.

FAA-iCMM Capability Dimension: Capability Levels, Goals, and Generic Practices
CAPABILITY LEVEL 0: INCOMPLETE
One or more of the goals of the process area are not achieved. (No goal or generic practices at this level)
CAPABILITY LEVEL 1: PERFORMED
Goal: The process achieves the goals of the process area.
Generic Practices 1.1 Identify Work Scope 1.2 Perform the Process
CAPABILITY LEVEL 2: MANAGED: PLANNED AND TRACKED
Goal: The process is institutionalized as a managed (planned and tracked) process.
Generic Practices 2.1 Establish Organizational Policy 2.2 Document the Process 2.3 Plan the Process 2.4 Provide Adequate Resources 2.5 Assign Responsibility 2.6 Ensure Skill and Knowledge 2.7 Establish Work Product Requirements 2.8 Consistently Use and Manage the Process 2.9 Manage Work Products 2.10 Objectively Assess Process Compliance. 2.11 Objectively Verify Work Products 2.12 Measure Performance 2.13 Review Performance with Higher-level Management 2.14 Take Corrective Action 2.15 Coordinate with Stakeholders
CAPABILITY LEVEL 3: DEFINED
Goal: The process is institutionalized as a defined process.
Generic Practices 3.1 Standardize the Process 3.2 Establish and Use a Defined Process 3.3 Improve Processes
CAPABILITY LEVEL 4: QUANTITATIVELY MANAGED
Goal: The process is institutionalized as a quantitatively managed process.
Generic Practice: 4.1 Stabilize Process Performance
CAPABILITY LEVEL 5: OPTIMIZING
Goal: The process is institutionalized as an optimizing process
Generic Practice: 5.1 Pursue Process Optimization

The capability dimension of the FAA iCMM uses a similar concept of continuous capability levels, but a different definition of each capability level when compared to ISO/IEC 15504.

The major differences include:

- At Capability Level 2, the following generic practices are specifically addressed:
  - Establish Organizational Policy
  - Document the Process
  - Ensure Skill and Knowledge
  - Review Performance with Higher-level Management
  - Coordinate with Stakeholders
  - Measure Performance
- At Capability Level 2, the following generic practices are further evolved than in ISO/IEC 15504:
  - Consistently Use and Manage the Process
  - Objectively Assess Process Compliance
  - Take Corrective Action
- At Capability Level 3, the following generic practice is addressed:
  - Improve Processes

Note: These differences in the practices for the capability levels makes it difficult to translate or compare the results of the FAA iCMM capability levels directly to ISO/IEC 15504 capability levels (and process attributes).

The Process Dimension.

- There are 23 process areas in the process dimension of the iCMM. Some of these process areas pertain to **Management** activities, some to **Life Cycle** activities, and some to **Support** activities.

  Management
  - PA 00   Integrated Enterprise Management (ML3)
  - PA 11   Project Management (ML2)
  - PA 12   Supplier Agreement Management (ML2)
  - PA 13   Risk Management (ML3)
  - PA 14   Integrated Teaming (ML3)

  Life Cycle
  - PA 01   Needs (ML3)
  - PA 02   Requirements (ML2)
  - PA 03   Design (ML3)
  - PA 06   Design Implementation (ML3)
  - PA 07   Integration (ML3)
  - PA 08   Evaluation (ML2)
  - PA 09   Deployment, Transition, and Disposal (ML2)
  - PA 10   Operation and Support (Not staged)

Support

PA 04   Alternatives Analysis (ML3)

PA 05   Outsourcing (ML2)

PA 15   Quality Assurance & Management (ML2)

PA 16   Configuration Management (ML2)

PA 17   Information Management (Not staged)

PA 18   Measurement and Analysis (ML2)

PA 20   Process Definition (ML3)

PA 21   Process Improvement (ML3)

PA 22   Training (ML3)

PA 23   Innovation (ML5)

Most of these process areas are assigned a maturity level designation (ML) providing guidance on which process areas might be improved together, or next. These designations also offer iCMM maturity levels for the purpose of benchmarking with organizations that measure their accomplishments using the maturity levels of a variety of CMMs that are sources to the iCMM.   Since the iCMM integrates many standards and models besides CMMs however, some process areas that are not in other CMMs are designated as "not staged" for benchmarking purposes.

Maturity Level Definitions:

- Maturity Level 2: To achieve maturity level 2, nine process areas staged at maturity level 2 must have satisfied capability levels 1 and 2 (or be not applicable) according to an iCMM appraisal. See the process table below for the ML2 processes.

- Maturity Level 3: To achieve maturity level 3, 20 process areas staged at maturity level 2 and maturity level 3 must have satisfied capability levels 1, 2, and 3 (or be not applicable) according to an iCMM appraisal. See the process table below for the additional ML3 processes.

- Maturity Level 4: To achieve maturity level 4, 20 process areas staged at maturity level 2 and maturity level 3 must have satisfied capability levels 1, 2, and 3 (or be not applicable) and selected process areas additionally must have satisfied capability level 4 according to an iCMM appraisal.

- Maturity Level 5: To achieve maturity level 5, 21 process areas staged at maturity levels 2, 3, and 5 must have satisfied capability levels 1, 2, and 3 (or be not applicable) and selected process areas additionally must have satisfied capability levels 4 and 5 according to an iCMM appraisal.

Table 8. Sample Process Description.

PA 00 INTEGRATED ENTERPRISE MANAGEMENT
Goals
1. Vision, mission, values, performance goals and objectives are established, maintained, and communicated to all employees. 2. Strategies are developed and projects are launched that visibly support goal achievement. 3. Projects are continued, changed, or terminated based on performance, within the capability of the organization, and with acceptable risk and potential benefit to the organization.
Practices
BP 00.01   Establish and Maintain Strategic Vision BP 00.02   Align to Achieve the Vision BP 00.03. Establish and Maintain Strategy BP 00.04. Develop and Deploy Action Plans BP 00.05. Review Performance BP 00.06. Act on Results of Review BP 00.07. Fulfil Public Responsibility

Note: One of the positive features of the FAA iCMM is that it contains processes at organization executive levels (for example, Integrated Enterprise Management as shown above), as well as processes like Outsourcing and Deployment, Transition, and Disposal. It does not assume that the enterprise is involved in software development.

Generic Attributes

The iCMM contains a feature used to measure the results of process performance, independently of capability level. There are 2 generic attributes defined:

- Usefulness: the extent to which work products or services provide the needed benefits in actual use
- Cost effectiveness: the extent to which the benefits received are worth the resources invested.

Note: The generic attributes are business related, rather than process assessment related and are a worthwhile feature of the model. This approach aligns well with the improvement focus.

For more information on how a business related improvement focus, provides tangible business benefits, readers are advised to read the related Practical Guide book, especially the improvement business case and the Team Based Business Design Improvement sections.

Some Advantages/Disadvantages.

Advantages:

- The FAA iCMM provides an integration of various International and National standards into one model.
- The model is being extended to cover specific areas of application. For example, it provides an 'application area' for safety and security related applications.
- The model follows the ISO/IEC principle of allowing an organization to select only the processes relevant to its business needs. Thus an organization can decide to implement one process (or at least one process for a specific business area).
- The model covers executive level management.
- The model is the basis for an enterprise assessment model.
- The model adopts the 6 capability level continuous measurement framework approach of ISO/IEC 15504.

Disadvantages and areas requiring care in application:

- The FAA iCMM uses a different capability dimension to ISO/IEC 15504, making assessments incompatible with the measurement framework of the International standard. This is probably the most serious disadvantage, if compatibility with the ISO/IEC 15504 measurement framework is critical.
- The FAA iCMM and the SEI CMMI capability levels and maturity levels are also not completely compatible.
- The FAA iCMM has integrated the Malcolm Baldrige National Quality Award criteria, which makes it useful for US institutions. However this also makes it somewhat incompatible with the European Quality Award criteria and the Japanese Quality Award criteria. This creates differences on a cultural basis, which should be recognised and handled.
- There is currently no guidance on the desired capability levels for specific applications (for example, safety critical application).

Use of assessment indicators in rating processes

An assessment indicator is defined in ISO/IEC 15504 as an "objective attribute or characteristic of a practice or work product that supports the judgment of the performance or capability of an implemented process". The assessment indicators must provide a greater level of detail for each Process Attribute in order for the assessor to be able to rate that process attribute.

The Process Assessment Model provides sets of the process attributes and sets of their characteristics for each process in the model (Process Dimension). These are, in brief, the specific process purpose, outcomes and process attributes for each process (base practices) and the work products with descriptions of their content.

CAUTION: The process categories in a Process Assessment Model represent convenient groupings of processes for assessment purposes, but may not represent the actual process implementation of a business.

The name, format and allocation of the characteristics of the work products for each process are not mandatory. It is up to the assessor and the organizational unit coordinator to relate the actual work products produced in their organization to the associated work products for each process. Assessors need to convert/translate the process dimension to the actual business processes during assessment preparation.

The model also provides a set of indicators of each management practice consisting of extended descriptions containing the indicator description, the practice performance characteristics, the resource and infrastructure characteristics and the associated processes (Capability Dimension).

The assessment indicators in the model give examples of types of evidence that an assessor might obtain, or observe, in the course of an assessment. The assessors must map the actual objective evidence onto the set of assessment indicators to enable them to correlate the implemented process with the processes that are defined in the Process Assessment Model. The assessment indicators are guidance to the assessors to collect the objective evidence needed to support their judgment of capability; they are not a mandatory set of check-lists/products.

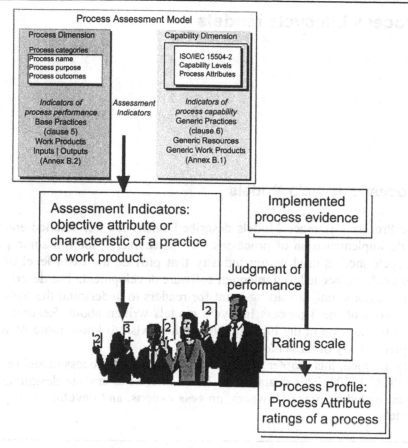

Fig. 40. Use of assessment indicators and process profiles.

The output from a process assessment is a set of process profiles, one for each instance of each process within the scope of the assessment (it is possible to assess several instances of a particular process in one assessment, for example the assessors may assess the project management process in several projects).

Each process profile consists of a set of the Process Attribute ratings for an assessed process. Each Process Attribute rating represents a judgment by the assessor of the extent to which the attribute is achieved, and comprises the set of assessment indicators fulfilled by the accumulated evidence. This evidence may come either from the examination of work products of the processes assessed, or from statements made by the performers and managers of the processes.

Process Lifecycle Models

Process Lifecycle Models

The Process Reference Models described earlier are not detailed enough to guide implementation of processes. In this chapter, I look at some process lifecycle models used within industry that provide the extra level of detail and guidance needed to implement software development. The description in this chapter is only a starting point for readers to understand the basic characteristics of the 3 process lifecycle models written about. Readers should refer to the texts in the bibliography if they wish to know more or wish to implement any of these models.

In addition, this chapter briefly looks at how each process model relates to ISO/IEC 15504. This chapter will be of interest to anyone designing processes, including process owners, process experts, and developers of process models.

German V-Model

Overview of V-Model

The V-Model is an internationally recognized standard [39] for development of IT systems for the German Federal government[43]. It comprises:
- the Lifecycle Process Model,
- the Allocation of Methods, and
- the Functional Tool Requirements.

---

[43] The standard is non-proprietary and not copy-protected, which means that the V-model can be copied as often as is wished for one's own use without infringing license regulations.

The V-Model (1997) [40] specifies what steps are to be taken and which methods are to be applied for the development tasks and which functional characteristics the tools to be used must have. The V-Model realizes some of the processes in ISO/IEC 12207 in a specific and detailed manner [41]. The model is structured into three parts:

- Part 1: Regulations. This part contains binding regulations concerning work steps to be performed (activities) and results (products). This is the document set of interest for process assessment.
- Part 2: Supplements with regard to Authorities. This part covers civilian and military fields with instructions to apply the Lifecycle Process Model in the respective field.
- Part 3: Collection of Manuals. This part contains a set of manuals dealing with special topics, such as IT security or use of object-oriented languages.

The V-Model was developed with several applications in mind, including as the basis for contracts, for instruction and for communication. The provisions of the V-model are independent of the form of organization. They are restricted to the technical development process. The V-model was developed as a standard in public administration and is used in the private sector in German banks, insurance companies, car manufacturers, manufacturing industry and energy producers.

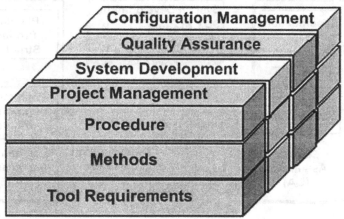

Fig. 41. V-Model levels and areas of activity.

The standard has the following three levels of detail, which specify the 'what', 'how' and 'what with'. Hence the model defines processes in a greater level of detail than a process assessment or reference model. The 3 levels are:

1. Procedure. "*What* has to be done?" This level establishes what activities are to be performed in the course of system development, which results are to be produced in this process and what contents these results must have.
2. Methods. "*How* is something to be done?" Here it is determined what methods are to be used to perform the activities established in the first level and what means of presentation are to be used in the results.
3. Tool Requirements. "*What* is to be used to do something? " At this level, what is established is what functional characteristics must the tools have which are to be used during system development.

At all levels, the regulations are structured according to the areas of activity into sub-models that consist of Project Management, System Development, Quality Management and Configuration Management.

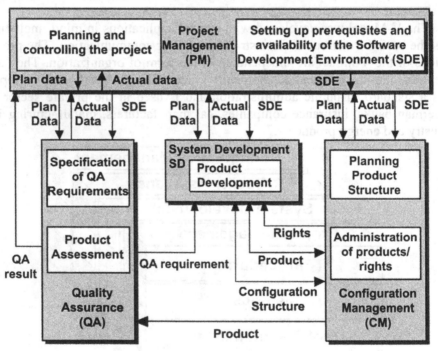

Fig. 42. Coordination of V-Model activity areas (sub-models).

For each activity area, the V-Model provides a sub-model, activities and sub-activities, products and roles of personnel. When we look at the System Development sub-model, it comprises the following activities:

• System Requirements Analysis (SD 1): Description of the requirements for the system under development and its technical and organizational environment; realization of a threat and risk analysis; drafting a user-level model for functions, data and objects.

- System Design (SD 2): Segmentation of the system into segments and software and hardware units.
- Software/Hardware Requirements Analysis (SD 3): The technical requirements made for the software and, possibly, for the hardware units are detailed. From here onwards, the further progress is split into software development and hardware development.
- The software development of a software unit is performed in four steps/major activities (SD 4-SW to SD 7-SW).
- Similarly, the hardware development of a hardware unit is performed in four steps (SD 4-HW to SD 7-HW).
- System-Integration (SD 8): Integration of the various software and hardware units into a segment and integration of the segments (if they exist) into the system.
- Transition to Utilization (SD 9): Description of all activities that are necessary to install a finished system at the appointed point of operation and to put this into operation.

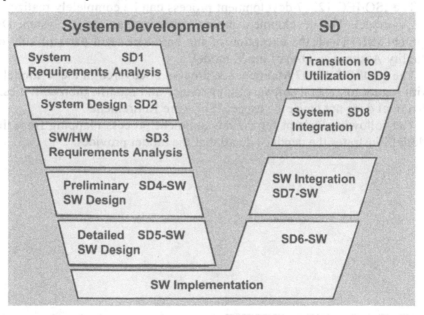

Fig. 43. V-Model System Development Activities overview.

V-Model mapping to ISO/IEC 12207 and ISO/IEC 15504

The V-Model contains a comprehensive mapping shows conformance of the V-Model to parts of ISO/IEC 12207[44] (which is a conformant Process Reference Model for ISO/IEC 15504)[45]. The V-Model mapping can be directly used with a process mapping of ISO/IEC 12207 to ISO/IEC 15504 for process assessments.

When performing an assessment, the assessors should work with the participating process personnel from the organizational unit to ensure that the process mapping is checked during the planning. When the V-Model is implemented consistently in an organization, the process mapping can be performed once for the entire organization and then used as needed in each process assessment.

Primary Lifecycle Processes

In the V-Model, the ISO/IEC 12207 Acquisition and Supply processes are partially covered by the V-model. The ISO/IEC 12207 Operation process has not been covered (although there is a limited coverage described).

The ISO/IEC 12207 development process can be completely realized with the V-model. The development process includes sub-model System Development (SD) (with the exception of the hardware) and parts of sub-model Quality Assurance (QA) of the V-model.

The ISO/IEC 12207 Maintenance process is covered in the V-model only with regard to general software maintenance and modification activities. The V-model does not cover the aspect "Software Retirement".

The following excerpt for the development process mapping from the V-Model illustrates the depth of detail that the model provides.

---

[44] Please note that the mapping is against ISO/IEC 12207 and not against Amendment 1 of ISO/IEC 12207

[45] The mapping tables are taken directly from the section: The V-Model in the ISO and AQAP environment, of General Directive No. 250 "Lifecycle Process Model".

Table 9. Allocation of Primary Lifecycle Engineering Processes - V-Model.

Development Process		
Activities acc. to ISO/IEC 12207	Activities according to V-Model	
Process Implementation	PM1.3 PM1.4 PM 4	"Generation of Project-Specific V-Model" "Toolset Management" "Detailed Planning"
System Requirements Analysis	SD 1.2 SD 1.5 QA 4	"Description of Application System" "User-Level System Structure" "Product Assessment"
System Architectural Design	SD 2.1 SE 2.4 SD 2.5 QA 4	"Technical System Design" "Allocation of User Requirements" "Interface Description" "Product Assessment"
Software Requirements Analysis	SD 3 QA 4 PM 6	"SW/HW Requirements Analysis" "Product Assessment" "Phase Review"
Software Architectural Design	SD 4.1-SW SD 4.2-SW PM 6	"SW Architecture Design" "Design of Internal and External SW Interfaces" "Phase Review"
Software Detailed Design	SD 5.1–SW QA 1.2 PM 6	"Description of SW Component/Module/Database" "Generation of Assessment Plan" "Phase Review"
Software Coding and Testing	SD 6.1-SW SD 6.2-SW QA 2.3 QA 4	"Coding of SW Modules" "Realization of Database" "Definition of Test Cases" "Product Assessment"
Software Integration	SD 4.3-SW SD 7-SW PM 6	"Specification of SW Integration" "SW Integration" "Phase Review"
Software Qualification Testing	QA 4 CM 2 PM 6	"Product Assessment" "Product and Configuration Management" "Phase Review"
System Integration	SD 8 QA 2.3 QA 4	"System Integration" "Definition of Test Cases" "Product Assessment"
System Qualification Testing	QA 4 PM 6	"Product Assessment" "Phase Review"
Software Installation	SD 9 PM 6	"Transition to Utilization" "Phase Review"

Each of the activities in the table is linked to an extensive description.

Supporting Processes

The V-model does not include any separate documentation activity. *Documentation* is not contained in the realization of activities. Therefore, the allocation of V-model activities is not possible, even though the documentation process in the entire V-model is naturally completely realized.

Apart from the configuration management and the change management of the V-model, the *Configuration Management* process of the ISO/IEC 12207 standard also handles "Configuration Evaluation". There is no similar description in the V-model.

According to ISO/IEC 12207, the *Joint Review, Audit, Verification* and *Validation* are handled as techniques of the process *Quality Assurance*. However, since the quality assurance process has only been roughly described, an explicit placement of these techniques is missing. Though the V-model covers all of the listed QA aspects, a 1:1 allocation between V-model and ISO/IEC 12207 is not always possible, based on the general information given in the ISO/IEC 12207 and the mixture between activities (tasks) and methods (techniques).

The V-model always distinguishes between the activities process assessment, product assessment and phase review, and, on pages with method allocations, between audit, review (technical review and phase review), and testing, whereby the reason for applying a certain method depends on the objects tested (software, product, activity, project development).

Organizational Processes

The two processes *Management* and *Infrastructure* are covered by the V-model, sub-model PM. The V-model does not contain an actual *Improvement* process; however, this can be achieved by means of process assessments and the resource project history, where results can be derived for the improvement process.

The V-model includes training and introduction information for staff members and personnel for the *Training* process.

In summary, the V-Model mapping is a good example of detailed process mapping against the ISO/IEC 12207 Process Reference Model and provides a reliable basis for process assessment.

Rational Unified Process

The Rational Unified Process ® (RUP) [42] is a software engineering process architecture that is iterative, use case driven and system architecture centric. It is founded on a process architecture that provides commonality across a family of processes. It is a configurable process, and should be tailored to various size project teams.

It provides an approach that assigns tasks and responsibilities in a (project) team, comprising requirements management, design, test, project management and configuration management. It provides project teams with access to a knowledge base with guidelines, templates and tools for all critical development activities. When the team accesses the same knowledge base, which uses common language and processes, it helps to create a team view. This tool support for the knowledge base is an important productivity and management component of the Rational Unified Process.

It focuses on addressing high-risk areas early in system/software development including defining a system architecture. The overall approach uses iterative requirements analysis/definition and development. To manage the changes implied in an iterative approach without losing control, it encompasses change control processes (supported by tools) to manage change.

The activities in the Rational Unified Process develop and maintain models (using Unified Modelling Language nomenclature), which are semantically rich representations of the software system under development.

The Rational Unified Process is supported by several products, which automate parts of the process. They are used to create and maintain the various artefacts—models in particular—of the software engineering process including the visual models, programming, testing, etc.

The Rational Unified Process encompasses the overall process attributes required for a Capability Level 3 process – it specifies both a standard and a defined process. I will briefly describe later what is required in implementation to achieve this Capability Level.

The main practices and process lifecycles are briefly described here, but readers should consult the numerous texts and books from IBM® and Rational®.

Practices:

- Develop software iteratively, thereby increasing understanding of the problem through successive refinements. Incrementally grow an effective solution over multiple iterations. The aim of this iterative refinement and incremental development is to reduce risk through frequent, executable releases that enable continuous end user involvement and feedback. Implementations may have release cycles as short as 2 weeks, although larger projects often use a 2, 3 or 6 month release cycles. The number of iterations may be between 3 and 9. These iterations and release cycle times are not fixed by the process itself, but rather by the customer requirements and the project team implementation.
- Manage requirements through a requirements elicitation process with the customer. Manage and document the required functionality and constraints. Track and document tradeoffs and decisions made during the elicitation process. The customer's business requirements are captured in use cases and scenarios (Business Modelling).
- Use component-based architectures with early development and base lining of a robust executable architecture (this is often incomplete and also iteratively developed). Use iterative and incremental component-based software development.
- Visually model the software to capture the structure and behaviour of architectures and components. If visual abstraction is correctly performed, it helps show how the elements of the system fit together. When the building blocks are consistent with the code, it helps to maintain consistency between a design and its implementation. Visual modelling can also help promote unambiguous communication when described using the industry standard Unified Modelling Language (UML).
- Verify software quality with respect to the requirements based on reliability, functionality, application performance and system performance.
- The process assists in the planning, design, implementation, execution, and evaluation of test types, using objective measurements and criteria.
- Control changes to software including the ability to make certain that each change is acceptable, and being able to track changes (including backtracking).
- The Rational Unified Process provides individual and team workspace by describing how to automate integration and build management.

The Rational Unified Process can be described in two dimensions, or along two axes:

- The horizontal axis represents time and shows the dynamic aspect of the process as it is enacted, and it is expressed in terms of cycles, phases, iterations, and milestones.
- The vertical axis represents the static aspect of the process: how it is described in terms of activities, artefacts, workers and workflows. This dimension is the corollary of the process areas/processes in the process dimension of ISO/IEC 15504, but not directly equivalent.

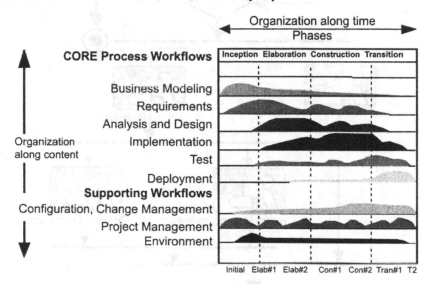

Fig. 44. The Rational Unified Process dimensions.

The static aspects of the process in terms of activities and workflows are further elaborated with the Rational Unified Process. For example, the Analysis and Design Process consists of 6 sets of activities as shown in the diagram.

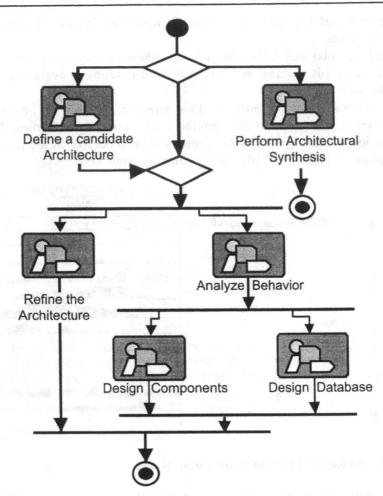

Fig. 45. Rational Unified Process Analysis and Design process.

The Rational Unified Process uses a process composition that can be mapped to a Process Reference Model such as ISO/IEC 12207 and subsequently to a Process Assessment Model such as ISO/IEC TR 15504-5.

The following information shows the Rational Unified Process mapping to the Process Assessment Model in ISO/IEC TR 15504. The processes were mapped to the equivalent CUS, ENG, SUP, MAN and ORG processes, and then compared with the capability dimension. The results come from a comprehensive report prepared by Rational Software [43]. The report provides an analysis of the processes to ISO/IEC 15504 process assessment processes and work products, and an analysis of the capability dimension process attributes to management practice (MP) detail level.

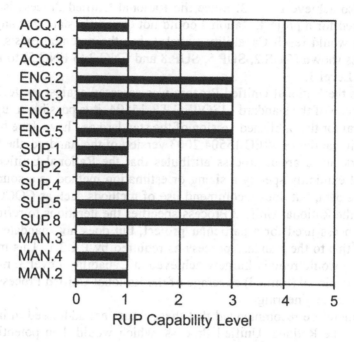

Fig. 46. RUP to ISO/IEC 15504 processes and Capability Levels.

For example, the Analysis and Design process shown earlier is mapped to ENG.2, ENG.3, ENG.4 and ENG.5.

The process mapping and capability determination can generally be considered conservative when assessing the potential of a process to achieve a particular Capability Level. In the above figure, the Capability Level rating is shown when the level is fully or largely achieved. The report notes that these results are the *potential* Capability Levels if all the processes are implemented as specified, so tailored implementations may have a different process capability.

At Capability Level 1, the Rational Unified Process is prescriptive enough to be able to find clear process mappings to most process assessment base practices and work products.

The second aspect is how some processes (when properly implemented) would lead to a rating at Capability Level 3.

The Rational Unified Process provides a lot of process implementation guidance. If this guidance were followed, then the process would reach Capability Level 3. For example, if the guidance is followed for the Analysis and Design process, then an instance of *any* process component (ENG.2, ENG.3, etc), which was individually assessed as fully achieving Level 1, could also achieve Level 3. Since the Rational Unified Process is meant to be tailored for a project, Rational could not explicitly state that any process instance would reach Capability Level 3, but the potential exists for those processes shown (CUS.2, SUP.5, SUP.8 and ENG.2 to ENG.5) to reach Capability Level 3.

While the Rational Unified Process was assessed against the technical report version of the standard - ISO/IEC TR 15504, it is possible to update this in general for the published version of the standard as I have done here.

Looking at the ISO/IEC 15504:2003 version of the standard, the following can be deduced about process attributes that the Rational Unified Process does not explicitly specify a sizing or estimation method as a source of appropriate data, but does recommend use of methods such as COCOMO 2.0. Finally the Rational Unified Process specifies the iterations to refine the defined process used for a particular project, but does not mandate the feedback of this to the standard process as required by PA 3.1. This means that the rating would remain Largely achieved at Capability Level 3, mainly due to the intentional (limited) coverage of the Rational Unified Process, focused on software engineering.

It is therefore recommended that these issues are addressed in implementation of the Rational Unified Process, which would then potentially fully achieve Capability Level 3, and as a minimum partially achieve Capability Level 4 when COCOMO 2.0 is used. The main process attributes lacking at Capability Level 4 are for PA 4.2 Process Control.

In the next section, I describe eXtreme Programming. For readers interested in a comparison between RUP and XP from Rational's viewpoint, see the paper: A comparison of the IBM Rational Unified Process and eXtreme Programming [44].

Assessors and Assessment Teams

Assessor Competence and building assessment teams

The chapter describes at the personal requirements for persons to become competent assessors. In addition, it looks at the registration and certification requirements for assessors. Finally, it briefly describes the requirements when assembling an assessment team.

This chapter will be of interest to assessors and assessment sponsors, and bodies wishing to become certification authorities.

ISO/IEC 15504-3 requires assessors to gain, demonstrate and maintain a level of competence to be recognized as Competent Assessors. The judgment of competence is dependent upon education, training and experience, as well as performing regular assessments. The assessor must demonstrate his/her competence to carry out process assessments.

- The assessor's competence is based upon:
  - their knowledge of the processes;
  - their skills in the principle technologies of ISO/IEC 15504 including the reference model(s), the Process Assessment Models, methods and tools and in the ability to rate processes; and
  - personal attributes which contribute to effective performance, including:
    o Professionalism and the ability to develop and maintain the confidence of the assessment participants including creating an open and honest spirit of communication between people so that interviewed personnel will freely discuss issues.
    o The persistent in carrying out the duties that are expected of them and the ability to resolve any conflicts and handle any resistance that they may experience from assessment participants.
    o No conflict of interest in performing the assessment. (one potential conflict may be the inclusion of managers who evaluate the performance of individuals involved in a project being assessed);

o The ability to assure that the assessed organization has confidence in their judgment and respect for their leadership; and

o The ability to communicate the findings of the assessments in a clear, non-judgmental style by both verbal and written means.

- The assessor's knowledge, skills and personal attributes are gained by a combination of education, training and experience.

When the assessor has yet to demonstrate their competence in performing assessments, an alternative is to validate an intending assessor's education, training and experience. This is a precursor to becoming a provisional assessor.

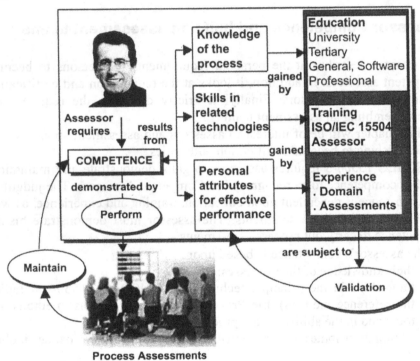

Fig. 47. Assessor Competence.

ISO/IEC 15504 provides mechanisms for demonstrating competence and mechanisms for validating education, training and experience respectively. These annexes were created in order to set up an assessor registration and certification scheme, but can be used by any organization as the basis for selection of persons to be competent assessors.

Gaining and maintaining competence

Step 1 – Becoming a provisional assessor

A person wishing to perform assessments must first become a provisional assessor. The provisional assessor must have the required levels of education, training and experience, but may not necessarily have participated in assessments conducted according to the provisions of ISO/IEC 15504.

A provisional assessor should be trained and experienced in the process as well as in process assessment or quality assessment. As ISO/IEC 15504 has several Process Reference Model s describing the process (for example, ISO/IEC 12207, ISO/IEC 15288), it is necessary for the provisional assessor to have competence in at least one of the key process areas in one process model (for example software engineering in accordance with ISO/IEC 12207) that he/she will assess. An assessor should be familiar with software development and maintenance including various life cycle models such as Iterative, Waterfall or Rapid Prototyping. In addition, an assessor should show an understanding of the activities required to support the software process, methods and tools, including when and how they should be applied according to the development model chosen within the application domain in which the assessor is experienced. Lastly, an assessor should be familiar with a range of relevant software engineering standards.

Assessors should demonstrate competence in aspects of the assessment pertaining to ISO/IEC 15504, particularly the core aspects included in parts 2 to 5.

- Overview of the framework for process assessment.
- The process assessment architecture.
- Performing process assessment.
- Conformant assessment models.
- Relevant software standards.

A provisional assessor should also have evidence of an acceptable level of education, both general education (for example covering management) and system/software related education (for example, systems engineering, software engineering, and computer science). When validating the provisional assessor's competence it is important to consider the general and specific education together with a combination of training and experience in both system/software development activities and process assessments.

In order to be familiar with software development and maintenance processes, the assessor should have been trained, or have documented experience, in all the processes in the Engineering process category. Project management or technical leadership training provides a background in the Acquisition, Supply and the Organizational process categories. Assessors need not have been trained in each process in the two process categories, but should be familiar and conversant with the topics. Assessors should have extensive training in at least one of the processes in these two process categories.

Acceptable levels of education may comprise one or more of the following:

- Tertiary courses offered by a college or university (Bachelor Degree or higher);
- Professional courses organized by recognized local or international bodies;
- Vendor sponsored courses; and
- Employer sponsored courses.

When validating the assessor's education, training and experience, consider the balance of general and specific education in terms of:

- Duration: The amount of time the assessor has spent in a particular process category.
- Range: The assessor's breadth of exposure to the process categories.
- Depth: The level of specialization.
- Responsibility: The extent to which an assessor has held responsibility in terms of both range and depth.
- Currency: How recent is the assessor's education, training and experience, and the extent to which the assessor's knowledge and skill have been updated.

Assessors should maintain documented evidence of their education in terms of certificates and course outlines for validation. The following levels of educational achievement may be considered as appropriate in the categories of general education and software education.

For provisional assessors sufficient education and training may be used as an alternative to demonstration of competence.

The provisional assessor must undergo assessor training on ISO/IEC 15504 (and/or any accepted conformant assessment standard such as CMMI® or Automotive SPICE). The training may be:

- Training provided by recognized local or international bodies (for example, the standards organizations); or
- Training provided by vendors and trainers based on the guidance in this part of the International Standard.

There is an interaction between experience and training: training is normally of limited duration and alone is insufficient to achieve full competence in a given process area or to provide the broad experience level needed for assessments. Practical experience is needed to understand detailed application of a process. In addition, experience covering several processes is needed to understand interactions and process interfaces.

Experiences in different roles will aid the overall ability to assess processes as many processes (and their interfaces) are seen from various perspectives. For example, team leaders or project managers may have had contact with software configuration management and software quality assurance functions. The experience gained may help understanding of a number of process categories in any particular assessment.

Due to the nature of ISO/IEC 15504 process assessment where both base practices of a process (process dimension) and management/generic practices (capability dimension) have to be assessed together, recent graduates, or individuals who have spent their entire working lives in a single process category, are unlikely to have accumulated sufficiently broad experience.

Acceptable levels of experience may comprise one or more of the following:

- Direct practical experience in specialist areas such as software engineering, software development/maintenance, software quality, or quality assurance (requires more than just documentation development).
- Management experience overseeing software specialist areas such as software engineering, software development/maintenance, software quality or quality assurance (especially project management experience).
- Participation in customer and supplier interaction activities within an organizational unit with a recognized quality management system (for example, ISO 9000 where the processes will have been documented). The provision of customer references aids verification of the person's experience.
- Development of plans and the measurement of performance against these plans covering the support process category. Relevant experience includes developing project or user documentation. Assessors should be able to demonstrate familiarity with software quality assurance and quality management systems.
- Experience as managers, consultants or assessors involved in the processes in the organization process category.

In lieu of personal experience, the teaching of the particular subject at a suitable level may suffice, but would require critical examination of the content of course taught.

Step 2 - Becoming a competent assessor

To become a competent assessor, the provisional assessor should have participated in assessments conducted according to the provisions of the International Standard. It is recommended that:

- The provisional assessor participate in at least two assessments led by a competent assessor; or
- The provisional assessor participate in at least one assessment and as an observer in three assessments led by a competent assessor; and
- The provisional assessor leads at least one process assessment under the supervision of a competent assessor.

Competent assessors should maintain a record of ongoing professional activities to demonstrate continuing competencies of skills, knowledge and training.

Step 3 - Maintenance of competence

Competent assessors should maintain their competence by updating their knowledge and skills as well as performing further process assessments, including:

- on the job experience as a competent assessor;
- attending professional seminars;
- giving presentations;
- teaching or developing courses;
- engaging in professional association activities;
- publishing articles or books;
- self training or education using this International Standard;
- working on the standard working group for the standard; and
- active involvement or leadership in the organizational unit's improvement teams.

ISO/IEC 15504 Specific Training

Provisional assessors need to have received training in ISO/IEC 15504. Several such courses are available, and cover the following subjects.

- Background
- Architecture and principles
- The component parts of ISO/IEC 15504
- Vocabulary and definitions
- Comparison of ISO/IEC 15504 with other standards and/or methodologies
- Assessment vs. auditing

- How to use the parts of ISO/IEC 15504

The process assessment architecture

Based on ISO/IEC 15504-2: *Performing an assessment*
- The Process Dimension:
  - Life cycle process groupings
  - Process categories
  - Basic and component processes
  - Process purposes
- The Capability Dimension:
  - Capability levels
  - Process attributes
- Rating processes and the process Capability Level model
- Requirements for conformant models
- How to use ISO/IEC 15504-2.

Process Assessment

Based on ISO/IEC 15504-3: Guidance to performing assessments
- Defining the assessment input
- Responsibilities
- The assessment process:
  - Planning
  - Data validation
  - Process rating
  - Reporting
- Recording the assessment output
- Selection and use of a documented assessment process:
  - Using indicators
- Selection and use of assessment instruments and tools
- How to use ISO/IEC 15504-3

Conformant models for assessment

Based on ISO/IEC 15504-2: *Performing an Assessment*; ISO/IEC 15504-3: *Guide to performing assessments*; and ISO/IEC 15504-5: *An exemplar Process Assessment Model,* or any other conformant model.
- The purpose of an assessment model
- Compatibility with the reference model:
  - Purpose and scope of the assessment model

- Model elements and indicators
- Mapping the assessment model to the reference model
- Translating assessment results to process profiles
• Selection and use of a conformant model in assessments

The training should include a case study process assessment that the course participants use to perform a practice assessment.

Maintenance of records

ISO/IEC 15504 specifies a set of records that should be maintained by all assessors and intending assessors:

• educational certificates and course outlines;
• training records describing training courses attended, hours involved, date place and details of the training provider, and specifically verified records of attending training course(s) in the standard (a certificate from the training provider is sufficient);
• verified records of experience in the process domain(s) relevant to process assessment, using the process categories from the Process Reference Model (for example, Engineering); an overview of involvement in different processes within each category and the level of involvement (for example as a trainee, practitioner, manager, assessor); period or dates of involvement; and verification (by manager, referee);
• verified records of participation in assessments conducted according to the provisions of the standard (by team leader/competent assessor/sponsor);
• verified assessment logs listing date and overview of each assessment (purpose, scope, team size, personal role), duration, process categories assessed; and
• logs of professional activities listing dates, professional activity description, location and duration.

It should be noted that all training, experience and assessments records should be verified by a competent authority. It is suggested by the author that when a person is not performing assessments on a regular basis, the simplest solution to maintaining records is to keep the details as a specific extension of a personal Curriculum Vitae.

The following template is suggested and may be used to record an assessor's participation as a provisional assessor or as an observer in assessments conducted according to the provisions of ISO/IEC 15504.

Table 10. Record of Participation.

Name of the person:	
Date:	
No. of days for the assessment:	
Scope of the assessment:	
Process categories/areas assessed by the person:	
Organization/Organizational unit:	

Effective Communications:
Were the discussions with the customer reasonable?
Was a satisfactory understanding of ISO/IEC TR 15504 shown?
Was the inter team relationship satisfactory?
Judgment and Leadership:
Were the assessment activities completed in a timely manner?
Were the interviews conducted satisfactorily?
Integrity:
Reasonable sample taken?
Range of activity satisfactory?
Depth of questioning satisfactory?
Review of results consistent?
Rapport :
Communication - telling the good and bad news:
Review of the programme:
Conduct:
Team Management:
Comments: (on Diplomacy, Discretion, Persistence and Resistance handling ability)

Performance: Acceptable/More Experience Required/Not acceptable
Name and signature of assessment sponsor/competent assessor/ team leader:

The involvement in assessments should be verified by the sponsor of the assessment, a competent assessor or the assessment team leader. Each assessment is recorded in a format similar to the one below.

Note: ISO/IEC 15504 Guide to qualification of Assessors provides a detailed description of the requirements and example records and logs and should be consulted if further information is required.

Assessor registration and certification

ISO/IEC 15504 proposed an assessor registration system together with validation that assessors met the requirements to be competent assessors.

ISO/IEC 15504 suggests a mechanism for assessing the education training and experience of a (potential) assessor. Annex G provides checklists that can be used to validate the education, training, experience of (potential) assessors for software process knowledge, assessment technologies (of

ISO/IEC 15504) and personal qualities. These are then summed in an Assessor Certification Criteria scoring table.

Table 11. Validation of the software process competence.

Items to validate	Adequacy				Items to Examine	Notes and Commentary
	F	P	N	U		
Software process						
a. Education					• Education accreditation • Degree earned • Number of credit hours • Subject studied	Base or higher degree in a software related discipline preferred.
b. Training					• Training supplier • Type (e.g. instructor led) • Classroom hours • Subject matter • Other assessment models	Training and education alone are not sufficient to become a competent assessor.
c. Experience					• Covers assessment scope • Expertise in at least one process. • Business domain • Application domain • Process variants, if applicable • Other assessment accreditation • Level of responsibility attained	Experience in specific process categories or processes, which are applicable to the assessment scope, should be indicated.

Table 12. Validation of assessment technology competence.

Items to validate	Adequate				Items to Examine	Notes and Commentary
	F	P	N	U		
Assessment Technology						
a. Education					• Educational Institution • Degrees or certificate earned • Classroom hours	Formal education may be used to gain understanding of ISO/IEC TR 15504. Education alone is insufficient to become a competent assessor.

b. Training					• Trainer credentials
					• Type (video, instructor led etc.)
					• Coverage (clause 6.3):
					  – Components of the standard
					  – The reference model
					  – Compatible models
					  – Performing assessments
						Training may be used to obtain knowledge of the components of ISO/IEC TR 15504; assessment methodologies; managing and conducting an assessment.

c. Experience					• Previous assessments conducted • Previous assessment and assessor evaluations • Assessment methodologies used • Satisfied the basis to be a provisional assessor • Creating an assessment methodology, if applicable • Assessment tools and methodologies	This validates the set of experience for consideration of an assessor as a competent assessor.

Table 13. Validation of personal attributes.

| Items to vali-date | Adequate | | | | Items to Examine | Notes and Commentary |
	F	P	N	U		
Personal At-tributes						
a. Education					• Education accreditation • Degree earned • Number of credit hours	Formal education may include courses in ethics or business philosophy.

b. Training					• Training supplier
					• Type (e.g. instructor led)
					• Classroom hours
					• Subject matter:
					  – Total Quality Management
					  – effective meetings
					  – team building
					  – communication skills
					  – change management
						Look for training completion, understanding and application of principles.

c. Experience					Assessment evaluations Presentations Writing skills Leading change (self-assessments)	Experience is the most reliable indication that an individual possesses the personal attributes desired of an assessor.

Adequacy key:

F: Fully adequate: The information submitted clearly demonstrates that the assessor has the competence in the specific area to successfully perform assessments conducted according to the provisions of ISO/IEC 15504.

P: Partially adequate: The information submitted indicates that the assessor has at least some of knowledge and skills necessary to successfully perform assessments conducted according to the provisions of ISO/IEC 15504. Additional information may be requested. Alternately, the composition of the assessment team may be altered to include individuals whose knowledge and skills can augment those of the assessor.

N: Not adequate: The information submitted clearly indicates that the assessor does not possess the knowledge and skills in the specific areas to successfully perform assessments conducted according to the provisions of ISO/IEC 15504.

U: Unknown: The information submitted does not address the specific knowledge, skills and experience outlined in this part of ISO/IEC 15504. Additional information may be needed before a determination can be made.

Table 14. Assessor Certification Criteria Scoring.

Assessor Certification Criteria	Points
Education (Maximum = 4, Minimum = 2)	
Degree or equivalent level of education in any discipline.	1
Any formal course in the Software Process, Computer Science, Software Development, Software Engineering, or Software Quality	1
Degree or equivalent level of education in the Software Process, Computer Science, Software Development, Software Engineering, or Software Quality	2
Assessor education in terms of a national or an international scheme.	2
Training (Maximum = 5, Minimum =3)	
Customer/Supplier process category [CUS]	1
Engineering process category [ENG]	1
Management process category [MAN]	1
Support process category [SUP]	1
Organization process category [ORG]	1
Training based on ISO/IEC 15504	3
Experience (Maximum = 5, Minimum = 3)	
Customer/Supplier process category [CUS]	1
Engineering process category [ENG]	1
Management process category [MAN]	1
Support process category [SUP]	1
Organization process category [ORG]	1
Scoring: 9 or above: suitable to be certified; 5 to 8: more education, training & experience needed; below 5: not suitable at present.	

The Software Quality Institute [45] in Australia maintains a register of assessors trained to the standard called the SQI Assessor Programme. This scheme is open to assessors trained through the Software Quality Institute.

The International Assessor Certification Scheme [46] has commenced a registration and certification scheme for assessors. This has replaced the former Certified SPICE Assessor programme.

The International Assessor Certification Scheme operates under the ISO criteria for certification of personnel and is administered by the ASQF (Arbeitskreis Software Qualität Franken, based in Germany). The ASQF ensures that the scheme meets the needs of current method providers, and ensures a harmonisation route for the certification of assessors worldwide. An international Governing Board and Advisory Board will manage the scheme under the general regulations for Certification Schemes, and will include international representation from Certification Bodies, training bodies, assessors, professional bodies, industry representatives and The SPICE User Group.

The scheme provides for three levels of assessor competence: provisional assessor, assessor, and principal assessor. In addition, it will certify training courses and providers. The scheme will address the specific needs of assessors operating in domains such as space, automotive and medical software.

The information required for an assessor to be certified is as explained in the preceding sections of this chapter; including the requirements for education, training, work and assessment experience, and continuing professional development. The logs and forms required are available on the website and are derived from ISO/IEC 15504.

The scheme details are available at www.int-acs.org.

Assembling assessment teams

When a sponsor wishes to perform an assessment, he/she should choose an assessment team leader who:

- is a good team builder and leader;
- understands the process domain to be assessed in order to both be able to assess the processes and be able to select team members who complement his/her process and assessment skills.

The appointed assessment team leader needs to define the assessment scope in response to the sponsor's assessment purpose. Refer to the Generic Assessment Procedure in the earlier chapter for detailed activities. For alternative assessment methods, readers should refer to the Practical Guide book which defines participative and self assessment methods.

When the assessment scope and organizational units to be assessed are known, the appointed assessment team leader should form a team that will:

- cover the processes to be assessed;
- have at least one competent assessor;
- preferably have at least one additional assessor;
- have a balanced set of skills, experience and organizational/process knowledge; and
- preferably include observers.

Therefore, the team leader may need to interview potential team members and/or refer to their assessor records to determine the most suitable team members. In early adoption of process assessments, it is important to build a team that can communicate well with assessment participants. This aims to build a reputation for helpfulness and avoid a negative 'examination' connotation. This is very important as assessments should not be audits and should not create barriers between the assessed organization and the assessors.

The other assessors should preferably be at least Provisional Assessors but for internal process improvement assessment it is also useful to include persons from the assessed organizational unit to improve commitment, understanding and manage any cultural issues (observers) and/or those who will implement the assessment results.

If absolutely necessary, the team composition may change when covering many organizational unit processes, in this situation the team leader should consider each grouping as a separate team and note which persons were involved in assessing specific processes.

Process Assessment to Capability Level 5

Assessing a process to Capability Level 5

In this chapter, I interpret how to rate a process for all Capability Levels up to level 5. These interpretations are provided as examples to aid as assessor in learning how to apply their expert judgment. They are not a substitute for the assessor's experience, qualifications, training and judgement.

The reader needs to refer to the Process Assessment Model in ISO/IEC 15504 Part 5 for the complete description of the processes, the Process Attributes and the various practices. In the example, I refer to the more important aspects of the attributes and practices and provide interpretations that may help an assessor to better understand the text in the standard. Note that Part 5 specifies each Process Attribute and practice in some detail, although it no longer specifically describes associated processes, but instead describes Generic Resources. While this is more precise, it is also less useful for an assessor. Hence, I provide some associated processes that are likely to achieve the described Generic Resources and support the Generic Practices. This chapter will be of interest to assessors.

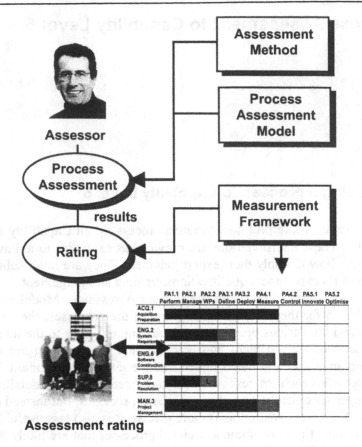

Fig. 48. Rating process capability.

The greatest challenge to assessors is understanding and applying the process assessment model assessment indicators to determining the rating of processes at the various Capability Levels[46].

Generally, the Base Practices are easier to assess. The generic (management) practices seem to cause more problems in interpretation, and deciding upon the rating between partially and largely for each Capability Level.

To help assessors interpret the evidence and findings of an assessment, I have provided both general interpretations, interpretations based upon the projects size and criticality, and a few sample scenarios.

---

[46] The biggest challenge to most organizations is to achieve and sustain Capability Level 5.

- Small projects are defined as : <10 KDLOC (Developed Lines Of Code), or < 10 person-years effort (two teams of 5 people working for one year), and are not mission or safety critical software systems.
- Medium projects are defined as: between 10 KDLOC and 150 KDLOC, or between 5 and 150 person-years effort.
- Large Projects are defined as : >150 KDLOC, or >150 person-years effort, are generally of greater complexity, and may be mission or safety critical.
- Safety or mission critical projects will have requirements on work products and documentation of processes that will be more demanding than for an equivalent sized non-critical project. Safety critical projects in general have a greater level of additional requirements.

Where project size or criticality is less important, then only the general interpretation is provided.

Assessing the Project Management process to Level 5

The following example illustrates a possible interpretation of the various assessment indicators using ISO/IEC 15504-5 for the Project Management process (MAN.3). Readers should read this chapter alongside the relevant sections in part 5.

The Project Management process identifies, establishes co-ordinates and monitors the activities, tasks and resources needed for a project to produce a product or service to requirements. It does this within defined constraints. The process defines 7 major outcomes. These include:

- A scope of work meeting the project goals.
- The feasibility to achieve the project goals is evaluated (and a decision made whether and how to proceed).
- The tasks to achieve the scope of work are defined, sized and the required resources are estimated.
- Internal project teams/groups/interfaces and external interfaces to other organizational units/projects are identified and monitored.
- Project plans are created and followed.
- Project progress against plan is monitored and reported.
- Project deviations are identified and actions taken as needed to achieve goals and targets.

The project management process defines 15 Base Practice indicators [BP] to achieve the above outcomes. These are covered in the assessment explanation.

General Interpretation

When performing an assessment, the assessor needs to determine that what activities are performed and how they meet the purpose of the base practice indicators. An activity may be called something different or occur in a different process, for example 'Define the scope of work' may already have occurred in a project tendering activity. In this situation, the evidence that the activity has occurred is the important fact, not when or in which process it has occurred. An organization may have an activity that meets more than one base practice, and the assessor should judge whether it meets the purpose of each of these base practices.

Important reminder: The processes, base practice indicators, generic practices and work products in ISO/IEC 15504-5 are defined for process assessment purposes and not as process implementation rules!

When looking at evidence of process performance, the assessor needs to determine whether the evidence supports the purpose of the base practice. The evidence may range from verbal statements of events to formally documented work products.

Assessors need to be reasonably familiar with the purpose and contents of the listed work products. In many situations, organizations will use work product titles similar to those listed in the work products list, which obviously makes the assessment evidence easier to collect. However, an organization may use entirely different names for work products or combine work products that are shown separately in the above work product table. Therefore, the assessor needs to ensure that the content of the evidence meets the purpose of the base practice, and not look for specific work products/documents with titles as above. Assessors need to be ready and willing to explain what evidence they are looking for and why it is important (what base practices it helps to achieve), and help the assessed organization that provides evidence in their own format and conventions to interpret and judge it meets the required assessment evidence.

If assessments are well planned, the processes and work products should already have been interpreted during the process mapping activities before the assessment interviews start. However, it is likely that some interpretation and judgment will still be called upon during the assessment interviews.

In the following interpretation, we assume the use of the standard work product titles for convenience.

Interpretation for large and complex projects

The main document to describe the project management process is likely to be the PROJECT PLAN.

Main inputs include: AGREEMENT or COMMITMENT, and/or a CONTRACT and/or a REQUIREMENTS SPECIFICATION. These are likely to be used as inputs to most Base Practices and therefore are only shown for BP1 in this description.

BP1: The scope of work covers the project goals and the tasks/activities to be performed in the project. Inputs are likely to be an AGREEMENT or COMMITMENT, a CONTRACT or a REQUIREMENTS SPECIFICATION. The main output document is initially likely to be a statement of the major project goals, major work activities and major outputs for these activities and the overall nature and quantity of resources estimated/guessed. In many cases, the initial scope may already have been submitted as a supplier offer or an internal draft. As the project is further specified, the PROJECT PLAN will list the subsidiary goals and how they will be achieved, and match this to the WORK BREAKDOWN STRUCTURE (see BP5). The outputs should reflect the general estimation of quantity and type of resources needed, the project structure, and resource availability. Constraints may include schedule, (customer) specified outputs or products, and methods. Sub-plans may include a supplier PROJECT PLAN(s), QUALITY, CM, System Engineering, and Software Plans when they explicitly contain project and subproject management aspects.

BP2: The project lifecycle and strategy inputs are the REQUIREMENTS SPECIFICATION, RISK STRATEGY and QUALITY POLICY. The strategy covers aspects such as in-house development or subcontracting for various activities. For larger projects, a SOFTWARE DEVELOPMENT PLAN may be specified.

BP3: When evaluating the feasibility of the project, inputs include a SOFTWARE DEVELOPMENT METHODOLOGY if one already exists or is customer specified. The PROJECT PLAN should describe/refer to the LIFECYCLE MODEL to be used (perhaps in an existing PROCEDURE or SOFTWARE DEVELOPMENT PLAN.

BP4: Inputs to project estimates can include any proposal/tender documents, the WORK BREAKDOWN STRUCTURE, PROJECT MEASURES and PROCESS MEASURES, and RISK ANALYSIS if they exist. This practice refines the initial scope from BP1. The output is ESTIMATES that may be part of the PROJECT PLAN. These would list each major task, duration and resources (persons, infrastructure).

BP5: Main outputs of defining project activities and teaks are the WORK BREAKDOWN STRUCTURE and a DELIVERABLES and MILESTONE LIST. Normally work breakdown structures do not show scheduling and sequencing but the PROJECT PLAN may show relationships between main activities. Some projects will have separate resource plans.

BP6: The human resources are likely to be described in the PROJECT PLAN. Very large projects may use a separate RESOURCE and TRAINING PLAN.

BP7: Main output is a SCHEDULE; in large projects, there may be master and subordinate schedules. Complex projects should use a project scheduling tool, but less complex projects may have hand drawn schedule. Projects using rolling scheduling may only show the schedule for the next planning period. The planning period will depend upon the total project length, the major milestones and major activity durations. In rolling planning, the planning period could be anything from one month to six months in which detailed planning occurs and all future activities/milestones are only listed without details.

BP8: Project Interfaces are both internal (between teams in a project) and external (to customer, other projects, other organization units, and other suppliers/partners). The interfaces define to whom the project delivers products, communicates with and receives products from, both internally and externally (customer, other project/units). This is described in the PROJECT PLAN or in INTERFACE documents.

BP9: Inputs may include PERSONNEL RECORDS and JOB PROCEDURES. The generalized resources identified in BP6 are now specifically allocated to groups, teams and individuals. The key personnel are listed in the PROJECT PLAN.

BP10: The main activity is collecting all the information from BP1 to BP9 into the PROJECT PLAN. The plan may need to be further developed/maintained over time as the project evolves and activities change.

BP11: Main activity is implementing the prepared PROJECT PLAN. Implementation is also likely to be recorded through PROJECT STATUS REPORTS, COMMUNICATION MECHANISMS and REVIEWS (Strategy/Plan).

BP12. Main input is a TRACKING SYSTEM, PROJECT PLAN and SCHEDULE. Progress is likely to be recorded through PROJECT STATUS REPORTS, COMMUNICATION MECHANISMS and REVIEWS (Strategy/Plan). PROJECT MEASURES such as completion of activities against the requirements, performance against cost, resource usage, quality, schedule and risks all provide a basis for higher Capability Level performance. Where no metrics are used, it may be sufficient to regularly report 'all is ok' for Capability Level 1 tracking (depends upon project complexity).

BP13: Main input to reviewing progress is a TRACKING SYSTEM and applicable STANDARDS. Outputs can be PROJECT or PROGRESS STATUS REPORTS or COMMUNICATION MECHANISMS.

BP14: The main inputs to acting on deviations are the same as BP13 and any outputs it created. Outputs can be CORRECTIVE ACTIONS or

COMMUNICATION MECHANISMS. Not all problems may require immediate or even eventual corrections, so assessors should determine whether unsolved problems have caused major schedule, scope, activity or output problems and is this is a consistent pattern indicating lack of sufficient tracking and/or correction.

BP15: The project close-out or completion review uses the status reporting from BP13, actions from BP14 and measures from BP 12. Outputs can be PROJECT STATUS REPORTS or COMMUNICATION MECHANISMS highlighting any major schedule, scope, activity or output issues and also positive aspects. Lessons learnt as well as comparisons between hard data (measures) that help improve future project estimations and activities are important to record and communicate.

Note: As can be seen, work products from one activity are used in another activity – this is normal as the many of the activities occur in parallel, incrementally, or iteratively in sequence as project process planning and performance occurs.

Interpretation for medium projects

The will be a gradual decrease in the number of separate work products – they will be amalgamated into fewer documents, as the project size decreases. Assessors should expect to see most of the evidence required by the base practices, but less data and in less detail as project size decreases.

Interpretation for small projects

The initial project planning may be as simple as a statement of project purpose and outcomes, either verbally agreed by the project team or contained on a single form or document.

A formally documented project process will probably be described in one document, most likely called the Project Plan, containing brief details of activities meeting all of the above base practices, but it may be as small as 2 to 5 pages for very small projects (< 1 man year effort).

Interpretation for mission and safety critical projects

Even small projects may require as much evidence as large, complex projects. Note however, that the majority of additional mission and safety critical requirements will be placed upon product related aspects (engineering processes) than on the project management process.

Capability Level 0 - General Interpretation

A Capability Level 0 assessment for a process means that the process has not largely or fully achieved Capability Level 1. This means that for any particular project, there is either insufficient evidence that the process achieved its purpose and outcomes, or several required base practices were not performed.

For an assessment across several projects, it means that there is no consistent application of the practices that shows that the process is effective (meets its purpose). This consistent application of the practices (activities, tasks) is termed systematic achievement of the process purpose and outcomes.

When a process is at Capability Level 0, then the probability of success is strongly reduced. This has been clearly shown is several studies of process improvement (refer to the business case for software improvement section). However, there are still a few projects that succeed, even when their processes are at Capability Level 0 [47].

Many commentators suggest that the only way a project achieves its goals is by the heroics of an individual or team. While this may not be an ideal situation, it should be recognised and used as a basis for improvement.

Unlike some commentators, I don't denigrate the efforts of 'heroes'. In this context, I describe heroes as individuals or teams that display extraordinary skills and motivation to succeed under great pressure. Every organisation eventually needs a hero to 'save the day' (save a particular project). By nature, many of these people spend a lot of time thinking (no they are not being lazy when the pressure is 'off'). They become motivated to ACT when there is a great need. Of course, you don't want to rely on heroes to complete every project. However, in some projects, these highly talented people are the only means to succeed. As an improvement facilitator, I recommend you should work with people (and especially the heroes) to improve the organisation (after all the heroes have shown how to succeed). There is nothing more powerful than having a hero as your improvement champion!

---

[47] For a reminder of how few software projects succeed– reread the section on the software crisis.

Capability Level 1: Performed Process

Process Attribute PA1.1 Process Performance Attribute

The project management process attribute measure the extent that a process achieves its intended outcomes and the activities achieve the intent of the base practice indicators. To evaluate the activities, assessors use the indicators of process performance defined in clause 5 (Base Practices) and Annex B (Work products associated to processes).

General Interpretation

A good indication of a Fully achieved project management process is that the project plan reflects the current status of the project. This means that either the project is still 'on track' (very little deviation from plan and demonstrating reasonable initial planning) or the plan is being maintained. If the plan is being maintained, check how much it has changed from the original plan to see whether original planning was reasonable given the known scope of work at the start of the project (this will also provide some indication of process management at Capability Level 2 and 4 as we will discuss later).

Many projects use rolling planning – this means that only a limited forward time period has been planned in detail, and further future activities are merely listed at a more abstract level of detail. It is common for rolling planning to be anything from one week (for agile development projects) to 3-6 months for long-lived projects (that run for years) often using spiral, incremental or waterfall development strategies. So long as the rolling planning activities occurs before the next time period being planned, rolling planning can be a powerful and accurate method of project planning. In general, rolling planning will affect the level of evidence for all the base practices, including the scope (the scope may only be known for the rolling planning period). In an assessment, the assessor should take care to determine if this is the case.

In some organizations, where projects are performed in the same way, it is possible that a project handbook/procedure/method/standard or even a published book[48] could describe many of activities meeting the purpose of the base practices. If the project is explicitly following this, it may be assessed to be sufficient evidence of process performance. This applies in particular for activities meeting the following base practices:

---

[48] Such documents could include using the Project Management Handbook of Knowledge®, or PRINCE® Project Management handbook.

- BP2: Define project lifecycle.
- BP5: Define project activities and tasks.
- BP8: Define project interfaces.
- BP9: Allocate responsibilities.
  - Which could all be standardized for the project.

When assessing for process performance (PA1.1), there may be a wide variation in how well the activities are performed, for example the current project status may not match the planned schedule, the work breakdown and allocation of resources may have changed. The progress tracking against plan and the actions taken to correct deviations may not be timely and very effective. However, if all of these activities are performed and the impacts of the deviations/variations are not catastrophic or highly disadvantageous for the project, then the assessor should not consider them when assessing achievement of PA1.1. These deviations/variation will be considered in assessing achievement of PA2.1 and PA4.2.

Interpretation for large and complex projects

Large projects with extensive initial planning will use many of the work products listed in the base practices interpretation section. There will be records of distribution of the planning work products and evidence of performance of updates/maintenance.

When the organization's project management process specifies work products, and not all of these are produced when required, the assessor should take this onto account in the rating of the process performance. Depending upon the impact or potential impact of the missing work products, this may affect the achievement of a particular base practice.

Interpretation for medium size projects

As projects become less complex and smaller, expect to find fewer or smaller work products (less content). Work Breakdown Structures may become a simple list of activities/tasks rather than using a structure showing the relationships between activities/tasks (most Work Breakdown Structures use a tree paradigm to show relationships).

In addition, the engineering, customer-supplier, quality management and support processes may also be partially or fully included/integrated within the project management work products.

Interpretation for small projects

Small project may have written planning documents or even verbal planning. In the case of formally documented projects look for a project plan together with a maintained action item list as the main evidence of the project management process.

When verbal project planning occurs (for example in some agile methodologies) or no permanent evidence is retained (for example use of a white board for plans, story cards), the assessor will need to ensure that all interview participants agree on how the project is planned and performed. Any temporary evidence available at the time of assessment should also be assessed and the assessor should judge how consistent are the participants' perception of performance of the project. In the case where there is little formally documented evidence, the assessor needs to ask project participants the following:

- Describe the project scope. [BP1: Define the scope of work.]
- Describe the project activities. [BP5: Develop work breakdown structure. BP10/BP11: Establish and implement project plans]
- What is the timing of project activities? [BP7: Establish project schedule], who does what [BP4: Size and estimate tasks and resources, BP9: Allocate responsibilities, BP8: Identify interfaces]
- How is the work performed? [BP2: Determine development strategy, and life cycle model]
- Are changes and problems that affect project progress dealt with in a timely manner? [BP13: Track progress against plans, BP14: Act to correct deviations].

For partial or substantial achievement of the process attribute (in this case PA 1.1) we need to judge the degree of achievement of the base practice indicators using the NPLF rating scale. As described earlier, N means 'Not achieved'; there is little or no evidence of achievement. P means 'Partially achieved'; there is some evidence of a systematic approach and achievement of the defined attribute. L means 'Largely achieved'; there is evidence of a systematic approach to and significant achievement of the defined attribute but performance of the assessed process may vary. F means 'Fully achieved'; there is evidence of a complete and systematic approach to and full achievement of the defined attribute. There are no significant weaknesses in the performance of the assessed process. The NPLF Rating scale uses the following percentages of achievement:

N   Not achieved   0 to 15% achievement
P   Partially achieved >15% to 50% achievement
L   Largely achieved >50% to 85% achievement

F   Fully achieved   >85% to 100% achievement

Note that a rating is not just a matter of counting the number of practices achieved and dividing by the total number defined in the standard. It is also necessary to judge the relative importance of the various practices. It may be that one or two practices are the most important to perform for a particular process or capability level. This can only be judged in context, no universal rule is applicable.

Sample Scenarios – Capability Level 1

Scenario 1

The assessor finds that the current status of the project reflects the project plan(s). All base practices are fulfilled and there is evidence (including input and output work products) that meets the scope of the process and produces the desired process outcomes within the project constraints and meeting the organizations' business goals. The project participants are aware of who is responsible for each activity. The assessor can judge that PA1.1 is fully achieved. The process can be rated as **Fully achieving Capability Level 1**.

Scenario 2

The assessor finds that a few of the specified work products are missing or not adequately maintained. Alternatively, the assessor finds that Progress Tracking [BP13] is inadequately performed, however the current project status still substantially reflects the planning and the project is (more or less) in control. Some actions to correct deviations have been taken (although they may not have been timely or totally adequate). The assessor judges that there is less than 100% achievement of PA1.1 but no significant weaknesses in achieving the purpose of the project management process (better than 85% achievement). The process can be rated as **Fully achieving Capability Level 1**.

When the project management process does not fully achieve its purpose and outcomes, there are two possible groups of causes. The first group of causes is inadequate planning. The second group of causes is inadequate implementation.

In general the assessor is likely to find that planning related activities meeting the purpose of following base practices are more often likely to have been adequately performed. The planning activities address the following base practices:

- BP1: Define the scope of work.
- BP2: Determine strategy.
- BP4: Size and estimate project attributes such as tasks and resources.
- BP5: Define project activities and tasks.
- BP7: Establish project schedule.
- BP8: Identify interfaces.
- BP10: Establish project plans.

The assessor is more likely to find that the ongoing maintenance and progress tracking/deviation activities meeting the purpose of the following base practices are not adequately performed. The implementation activities address the following base practices:

- BP11: Implement project plans.
- BP9: Allocate responsibilities.
- BP12 and BP13: Track progress against plans.
- BP14: Act to correct deviations.

Note: ongoing maintenance and implementation performance activities are a common cause of failure to achieve Capability Level 1 in many processes, not just project management.

Scenario 3

Project participants agree that the project was planned and is being managed, but disagree on how the project management is being performed. This is likely to mean that project performance is varying across the project, and could either be inadequate allocation of responsibilities, or lack of communication (especially of changes), or that the planned project performance has varied since the project planning took place. The assessor should look particularly at:

- BP9: Allocate responsibilities. Do participants know who does what?
- BP8: Identify interfaces. Are parts of the project work being performed outside of the project team? Is this known to participants?
- BP10: Establish project plans. Are plans established, agreed and **communicated**?
- BP12 and BP 13: Track progress against plans. Is some form or progress tracking done and communicated to affected project participants?
- BP14: Act to correct deviations. Are some actions taken and some problems fixed?

The assessor may find that the most common activities that are inadequately performed are related to the above base practices. If actions are taken to correct deviations [BP14] without application of project tracking mechanisms [BP12], the project may under or over correct (this will affect PA 2.1 as we will describe later). If these 3 activities are not performed or fail to achieve the purpose of the base practices, then the assessor should judge that the highest rating will be **Largely achieved for Capability Level 1.**

Scenario 4

Project participants indicate that the way the project is being performed seems to vary over time without their understanding of the reasons for change. The assessor should look particularly at:

- BP4: Has any re-sizing or re-estimation occurred? Were the results used to change the tasks and resources? Was this communicated to those who interface with the changed areas?
- BP10 & BP11: Establish and implement project plans. Is the plan up to date and communicated?
- BP12: Track progress against plans. Is progress being tracked? If not, how do participants know what is causing problems in process performance?
- BP14: Act to correct deviations. Is there an action list? Are actions being performed?

The assessor may find that the most common activities that are inadequately performed related to BP10, BP11, BP12 and BP14. The assessor should judge that the highest rating will be **Largely achieved for Capability Level 1.**

Scenario 5

Project participants indicate that they do not know exactly how the project process is being performed. This is likely to mean that the planning activities are inadequate or not communicated to project participants. The assessor should look particularly at:

- BP5: Define project activities and tasks. Is the work known and defined in a way that will allow each participant to be made responsible for part of the work? Is the relationship between the work activities understandable?
- BP9: Allocate responsibilities. Do participants know who does what?

- BP8: Identify interfaces. Are parts of the project work being performed outside of the project team?
- BP7: Establish project schedule. Do participants know when activities are meant to occur and what outputs are associated with each?
- BP10: Establish project plans. Are plans established, agreed and **communicated**?
- BP11: Implement project plans.

If 3 to 4 of the planning activities are inadequately performed (for example, BP5, BP8, BP9, BP10) and activities related to BP11 are inadequately performed, then the assessor should judge that the highest rating will be **Partially achieved for Capability Level 1**.

Scenario 6

The assessor may find that the planning activity was not performed or poorly performed, thereby failing to achieve the purpose of several of the above base practices [BP1 to BP9]. This could occur if there is an inexperienced person performing the project planning and/or no project management standard/guidance available (for example, no defined project management procedure or handbook).

If the planning activities are not performed or very inadequately performed, then it is unlikely that implementation activities will be adequately performed [BP8, BP10 to BP14]. The assessor in this situation would rate the process performance as **Not achieved for Capability level 1**.

Scenario 7

The implementation activities of BP11: Implement project plans are not performed (and yet a project plan exists). The assessor should judge that the overall process purpose will not be achieved and must rate the process as **Not achieved for Capability level 1**.

Although the rating scale allows for 50 to 85% achievement of base practices for Largely achieved, the standard also states that the overall process purpose must be achieved, and this applies in this situation.

Note.
We will only consider the scenarios that are likely to Largely or Fully achieve Capability Level 1 when assessing Capability Level 2 in the next section. Normally the assessor would not further assess the scenarios that only Largely achieve Capability Level 1 if performing a Capability Determination. In the improvement business case, the assessor would consider the

scenarios at higher Capability Levels in order to suggest suitable improvement opportunities.

Capability Level 2 – Managed Process

Process Attribute 2.1 Performance Management Attribute

The performance management attribute measures on the extent to which the performance of the process is managed to produce work products that meet the defined objectives. It has six Generic Practices.

GP 2.1.1 identifies the objectives for performing the process, the scope of the process performance and any assumptions and constraints on performance.

GP 2.1.2 plans and monitors process performance. Planning covers the process cycle, milestones, schedule, estimation, activities and tasks, and reviews. Performance is monitored against the plan. Note here that the practice does not specify a formal project plan document, but normally a Generic Work Product (plan) is produced.

GP 2.1.3 adjusts the performance of the process by identifying performance issues and taking action when objectives are not met. Normally performance is adjusted to meet the plan, but this may include rescheduling and adjusting plans.

GP 2.1.4 defines, assigns and communicates the responsibilities, commitment and authorities of people/organizational units performing the process. This includes both implementing and verifying the work products produced. The personal skills, experience and knowledge required are also defined.

GP 2.1.5 identifies human, information and infrastructure resources needed to perform the process and ensures they are made available. It uses outputs from the previous Generic Practice.

GP 2.1.6 identifies and manages the interfaces between persons and groups using the process. It relies upon GP 2.1.4 to assign responsibilities.

In addition to the Generic Practices, there are 7 Generic Resources identified. These include human resources, facilities and infrastructure, project management tools, workflow tools, communication mechanisms, information storage mechanisms, and problem and issue management mechanisms. These resources should be used as supplemental evidence to the practices. The use of a resource is often good evidence that the related practice is being performed and one of the stated outcomes is achieved. In part 5, it identifies the outcomes related to each Generic Resource.

Finally there are 4 Generic Work Products identified; plan, record, register and report. As noted in the chapter on Process Assessment Models, these generic work products are simplified variants of specific work products that are universally applicable.

General Interpretation

Assessment of the set of Generic Practices GP 2.1.1 to 2.1.6 is related to how well the process is performed. At Capability Level 2 the assessor expects to see the actual project performance is better planned and managed than is required at Capability Level 1. In summary, the assessor should ask "*Is the project management process being actively managed against objectives and plans with review/feedback used to take actions including adjusting planning as needed?*"

If we take the statement of purpose for each indicator, it becomes clear that they are related and follow a sequence from objectives through to ongoing performance of project management.

- Identify the objectives for the performance of the process (for example, time-scale, and cycle time and resource usage).
- Plan the performance of the process according to the identified objectives by identifying the activities of the process, the expected time schedule and allocation of resources for each activity.
- Adjust performance to plan or adjust plans.
- Plan and assign the responsibility and authority for developing the work products of the process.
- Ensure people can manage performance of the process.
- Ensure the people and groups are well organized (interfaces)

In this example, the project management process is performed to achieve the six practices (in fact it is shown as a Generic Resource for the practices). This simplifies the ability to obtain evidence from the base practices meeting the above purposes and their associated characteristics. For other processes, especially in the primary lifecycle process area (customer-supplier and engineering), the assessor may look to the project management process to help supply some of this evidence.

The assessor should consider the practices initially as a group. Is there a clear and apparent connection between all the actual activities performed that achieve these practice indicators? If the project management participants are able to describe:

- the project management[49] objectives;
- identify activities to achieve each objective;
- the project management activity times and resources needed/used;
- who specifically does each activity;
- examples of ongoing progress tracking (for example project status reports, meetings with customer and supplier project representatives); and
- re-planning (for example new dates for project management actions).

If these are described, then the assessor will have a good general indication that the purpose of the generic practices is being met. The assessor may need to judge what level of evidence is needed in addition to the statements of the interviewed persons (generally there will be a need for more evidence as project size and complexity increases). The assessor then uses the Generic Practice characteristics and the Generic Resource and Work Product characteristics to ask for further evidence. The evidence may consist of what is expected and/or estimated. In this context, expected means it is based upon the judgment of a person with some experience in this type of project (qualitative evidence), and estimated means it is based upon previous project data[50] (quantitative evidence).

Normally, quantitative evidence is considered better than only relying upon an individual's experience (qualitative evidence) but both should be used. If a project management group gathers their experience using techniques such as Delphi[51] to set objectives/estimates without quantitative measurement data, the results can also often be better than relying upon an individual's experience alone. Since project management uses some data based estimation and tracking (for example, cost, time, and effort) it is likely that some measurement data will be collected and used. This may be historical and could consist of productivity and effort data, project and technical work sizing, and process related data (for example, time to produce a project plan).

The assessor should judge whether the evidence (qualitative and/or quantitative) meets the needs of managing the performance of the project (GP

---

[49] To generalize this example, the assessor should substitute 'project management' with the process being assessed.

[50] There are three common ways to set objectives. Estimation is based upon previously collected quantitative measurement data; guess is based upon a person's experience or intuition without any measurement data, and 'guesstimate' is an experienced person making a judgment based upon incomplete data (somewhere in between a guess and an estimate).

[51] Delphi is a group technique where individual make (independent) estimates, they are then compared and group estimation created using agreed statistical techniques with mean, deviations and outlying values.

2.1.2, GP 2.1.3). Such evidence should exist within the work products produced in the project management process (for example in the project plan or project reports). The evidence should include:

- Performance objectives which may include several of the following (the first two are commonly required):
  - The project time scale – how long the project will run, how many project iterations (cycles) and how long each cycle will run (cycle time) and major dates (milestones) with associated deliverables.
  - The required project resources, number and type of people and skills, plus any specific technology, tools or environment.
  - The project price, cost, profit, and management margin (project management margin is a budget that a project manager may have to use when problems occur).
  - Project customer satisfaction (people) and quality goals, product related objectives, and process related objectives for both the project management process itself and for all project processes (for example, design and implement a new software development process of lifecycle, train project participants in required processes).
- Performance planning which is commonly documented in a project plan, containing:
  - Work activities and their relationships are identified (for example in a work breakdown structure).
  - Standard and special project needs are identified.
  - Identified schedule constraints, cost constraints, resource availability and utilization, and the technical work.
  - Risks related to the constraints, resources and technical work are identified.
  - Plan and schedule covering the objectives and the actual planning performed.
- The activity of allocation of work (plan and assign responsibility and authority):
  - The activities and production of require work products are allocated to resources and there is evidence that the responsibility for the activities and work products is assigned together with the authority to perform the work.
  - The availability of work products is scheduled (e.g. by milestones).
  - The need for verification and who is responsible is identified.
- The activities to manage, track and replan the performance of the process are performed and records show that:
  - Plans are communicated to project participants.

- Corrective action mechanisms are communicated to project participants.
- Ongoing project management activity evidence is created and used. Commonly the evidence may be described in a variety of media. It covers:
  - Planned and actual performance in relation to schedule, milestones, cost and resources.
  - Task completion, work product and quality criteria planned and met, and risk tracking.
  - Project communication methods including project meetings, stand-up information meetings, project progress reports (status reports), email and threaded electronic communications are used.
  - Action tracking (for example, corrective actions) information.
  - Reviews, verification activities, audits and assessments of project management are planned and performed.
  - Estimates and measurements from planning are used.
  - Lesson learnt and other qualitative forms of feedback and control.

The associated Generic Resources can provide both evidence and a way to perform processes that contribute to achieving the purpose of the project management process. Therefore, if the assessor does not find the evidence of process planning and performance within the project management process, the assessor may need to consider the generic resources. The following examples may help interpret how associated processes may provide generic resources.

- MAN.2 Organization Management– provides objectives that apply to all projects.
- ENG.1 Requirements elicitation process – provide means to capture customers project management requirements, e.g. project reporting.
- MAN.4 Risk management process – risk assessment, analysis, mitigation, and reporting.
- SUP.4 Joint review process – verification of process performance.
- MAN.4 Quality management – quality related activities – corrective actions.
- RIN.1 Human resource management – resources allocation.
- RIN.4 Infrastructure – provision of infrastructure and planning tools.
- SUP.1 Quality assurance – internal verification and review actions.
- SUP.5 Audit – internal audit and assessment.
- SUP.9 Problem resolution – project action tracking and problem activities.
- SUP.10 Change request management.

Interpretation for large and complex projects

The assessor should determine whether the project management in large projects is centralized within one group, or delegated/allocated to several groups. It is quite common in large projects to have multiple project managers, for example an overall project manager, a software project manager, a hardware project manager, an integration manager, a project test manager and project quality manager. The managers working on a part of the project are often called sub-project managers.

When there are multiple project managers, the assessor needs to determine whether they each have their own project/subproject plans and in the case of multiple plans, the relationships between them. In the situation where multiple project plans exist, the work breakdown structure at the first or second level will normally show each separate area for which a project plan exists.

Large projects often have the most to gain from using quantitative data in managing projects. Assessors are more likely to find reasonable quantitative data gathered and used in running projects, than in estimating projects. Cost/Schedule Control Systems coupled to PERT/CPM scheduling techniques can provide a means to specify, collect and use detailed cost and schedule data as an aid to project management, including the use of trends for prediction and corrective actions.

Interpretation for medium projects

The assessor should expect to find that centralized project management is more common than in large projects, but not exclusively used. The assessor should expect to see all the types of evidence in a variety of documented formats. As noted earlier, several forms of evidence may be amalgamated into one or few documents.
For a medium size project to be successfully managed it will be insufficient to only use verbal means of management and control of process performance, as the number of people involved will lead to interpretation and project memory problems. The assessor should expect to see schedules using PERT/CPM techniques. The work breakdown should be associated to the resources and costs in a clearly documented manner.

Interpretation for small projects

The assessor may need to rely more heavily on interviews with the project management personnel to determine how project management is planned and performed. The amount of documented evidence is likely to be much less than for medium size projects, and will be for a shorter duration. The small team also means that only one person is likely to perform the project management activities. The project manager is likely to vary the project management process performance more widely than in larger projects, for example, project progress reporting may be suspended during a period where other activities take precedence.

For an organization that regularly performs many small projects, the experience of the project manager's may be heavily relied upon. Project communication mechanisms, especially verbal and email are likely to be more common than more formal project progress reports. This may make some progress tracking activities evidence such as corrective actions more difficult to verify.

The assessor should therefore assess the actual performance against the planned performance of the project management process taking into account the small team size and its schedule flexibility.

Interpretation for mission and safety critical projects

Standards associated with mission and safety critical projects will often require highly formal planning, risk activities, corrective actions, and performance progress monitoring and reporting.

Process Attribute 2.2 - Work product management attribute

The work product management attribute measures the extent that work products that are appropriately managed. It has four Generic Practices that form a coherent group managing the lifecycle of work products.

GP 2.2.1 defines the requirements for work products such as content, quality, structure, review and approval criteria.

GP 2.2.2 defines the requirements for control of work products, such as identification, distribution, traceability, dependencies and approval.

GP 2.2.3 specifies how to identify and control work products, including changes to them. In addition it specifies versioning, product configurations and access mechanisms.

GP 2.2.4 specifies reviewing work products against requirements and the need to resolve issues arising from review.

In addition to the Generic Practices, there are 8 Generic Resources identified. These include a requirements management method, configuration management, document identification and control, review methods, communication mechanisms, problem and issue management mechanisms. Finally there are 7 Generic Work Products, the four already specified in PA2.1 plus a Standard, a Template and the highly generic 'Work product'.

General Interpretation

Assessment of the work product management attribute is relatively straight-forward. The set of indicators specify, control, manage relationships and the quality of the work products in support of process performance (hence PA2.2 supports PA2.1). In summary, the Generic Practices:

- Identify the requirements for the work products, including both functional and non-functional aspects.
- Manage the documentation, configuration management and change control of the work products.
- Identify and define any work product dependencies.
- Manage the quality of work products to ensure that they meet their functional and non-functional requirements.

Assessor should find that most organizations with an ISO 9000 based quality system would perform the activities meeting all these indicators. For many organizations that regularly work in projects, there will be a guide/handbook/standard that specifies the requirements for the project management process. This should specify how the project will be performed, and the quality aspects of the work products being produced (for example, the project plan). It should also specify acceptance criteria and/or methods.

The requirement traceability from customer requirements to the project management process is likely to be satisfied by explicit statement from a contract or project review, rather than an alphanumerical traceability matrix approach.

The main aspect that the assessor may find is poorly handled is the ongoing management or maintenance/adjustment of the work products (GP 2.2.4) and the distribution or access by personnel (GP 2.2.3). The assessor should not assume that the work product is up to date, or that when it is not up to date, that it does not meet the criteria in GP 2.2.4. The assessor must determine how the criteria of the process work products trigger review and adjustment – this may use interval (for example, yearly) or event triggers (for example, a major change in project goals or a major schedule slip, or change of the project personnel). In addition, the assessor should judge whether the interval is appropriate based on the amount of deviation from desired performance. If deviation is causing major project problems, then GP 2.2.4 may not be achieved, but if the deviation is not having a major impact on performance of the project management process, then GP 2.2.4 may be fully or largely achieved. The assessor should also consider whether the configuration management and control requires an on-line system (this is preferable but not mandatory).

The assessor should find that work product dependencies from the project plan to other work products are generally well handled; many project plans explicitly refer to other project process work products (for example, the schedule and the work breakdown structure if separately maintained, sub-project plans, reports). The assessor should determine how well the project participants (especially the project manager) are following any existing standards for the project (either internal or external, and including such standards as a project management handbook).

The assessor should determine that the quality of the work products is maintained through standards for their production (see characteristics in GP 2.2.1) and for their verification/review. Any changes required for the work product should be tracked and evidence of closure available. Work product change management of the managed work product may also include changes caused by other work product changes. This is best handled by ensuring that there is minimal duplication of information between work products so that it is clear which work product is maintained when changes in the project performance occur.

The assessor should judge the acceptable time interval between project performance changes occurring and the update of work products. This should be based upon the project duration and importance of the changes. The acceptable time interval will be different for a major change occurring in a project of several years duration to one of several months duration. The assessor should also judge whether less formal methods (for example, email, intranet and extranet, or verbal communication to affected persons) are capable for short periods of being sufficiently acceptable in place of formal work product changes, again based in part of the scope of change and the project duration, and also upon the organization's defined approach to handling such changes.

The assessor may need to consider the Generic Practices for guidance or evidence such as the quality, configuration management, documentation, and verification and validation requirements for work products.

Interpretation for large and complex projects

The assessor may find that large projects have a large number of work products that they manage and control. For these large projects, it is advantageous for the organization to have a formally defined configuration management system to manage work product configuration (version, status), change control and dependencies. The system should have archive and retrieval capabilities, accessible via several mechanisms (for example, index and search), and controlling who has read and who has write access.

The assessor may need to restrict their survey of evidence to a few work products rather than all the possible work products for a large project, and should be guided by the persons interviewed to determine the most important products to look at.

Interpretation for medium projects

As medium size projects increase in size, the advantages of a formally defined configuration management system increase.

Interpretation for small projects

The assessor may find for small projects, especially those of short duration, that there is no evidence of maintenance of work products. This is acceptable when the duration is short and when the change(s) in process performance are either minor or replanning within the remaining project duration does not provide sufficient benefit, compared to the effort required. In this situation, the assessor should determine that the changes required are communicated to the project participants and are used as the basis for completion of project management activities. Traceability may be neither explicit nor required, especially when all activities are described within one document.

Interpretation for mission and safety critical projects

The assessor should find that configuration management and control of the project management work products follows the same rigorous configuration management requirements for all work products in a mission and safety critical project. Of particular importance is assuring that versions of work products are properly assigned to product configurations (GP 2.2.3) and proper quality criteria have been established (GP 2.2.1) and used (GP 2.2.4).

Sample Scenarios– Capability Level 2

Scenario 1

The assessor finds that the current status of the project reflects the project plan(s). All base practices are fulfilled and there is evidence (including input and output work products) that meets the scope of the process and produces the desired process outcomes within the project constraints and meeting the organizations' business goals. The project participants are aware of who is responsible for each activity.

The assessor should first assess that the project management objectives are able to achieve the purpose of project management (that is to run the project against cost, schedule and resource constraints to achieve the project goals). The assessor can then assess that the process was planned (project plan fulfils GP 2.1.1 and GP 2.1.2)

If all base practices are being fulfilled, then someone is doing them, however the assessor may need to check that responsibility and authority are explicitly assigned. If responsibility and authority are assigned and being performed, then the assessor can judge that GP 2.1.4 and GP 2.1.5 are fulfilled.

For projects that have been running over a longer duration, the general indication that current status reflects project plans is a positive indicator of a well-managed process. The assessor should look at how the project management progress tracking is performed (GP 2.1.3) and interfaces between parties (GP 2.1.6). For projects running over a shorter duration, the assessor may need to look at the planned way to track and re-plan, as there will be less evidence indicating tracking and re-planning. If project management process execution is being tracked and re-planned when needed then GP 2.1.3 is fulfilled (current status reflects project plans, GP 2.1.3).

If the objectives are fulfilled, then the assessor should judge that PA 2.1 is fully achieved.

If the assessor finds evidence (input and output work products) that meet the scope of the process and achieve the desired process outcomes, then GP 2.2.1, GP 2.2.2 and GP 2.2.4 are likely to be fulfilled. The assessor should check that configuration and change control are fulfilled (GP 2.1.3) to judge if PA 2.2 is fully achieved.

The process should be rated as **Fully achieving Capability Level 2.**

Scenario 2

The assessor finds that a few of the specified work products are missing or not adequately maintained. Alternatively, the assessor finds that Progress Tracking [BP13] is inadequately performed, however the current project status still substantially reflects the planning and the project is (more or less) in control. Some actions to correct deviations have been taken (although they may not have been timely or totally adequate).

The assessor needs to determine what work products are required to be created (GP 2.2.1). Depending upon project size and complexity, a few or many of the work product examples in ISO/IEC 15504 may not be needed. Therefore the assessor should first ask the project participants whether they are following a specified project management method, and to what extent (for example, is it tailored according to guidelines or implemented totally?). The assessor can ask participants what this method requires and may need to see the method to determine the work products to be used and produced. Do the produced work products achieve the requirements of the method and the project management base practices? (GP 2.2.4). If the project management method being followed is inadequate then the requirements on work products may be inadequate (GP 2.2.1).

If the maintenance of the work products is inadequate, then the assessor should assess the configuration management and control (GP 2.2.3) and also whether the lack of maintenance is caused by inadequate project tracking (GP 2.1.2) and adjustment (GP 2.1.3). In this scenario, there is evidence of project tracking and actions taken, but concern that they may not be adequate. The assessor needs to make an experienced judgment on what is a reasonable level of project tracking, re-planning and work product maintenance. The assessor should pose the following questions:

- Is the project performance generally well managed and still under control?
  - What are the project management objectives - are there any major or minor deviations from these? How many minor deviations are there?
  - What are the major project constraints (cost, schedule, resources) - are there any major or minor deviations from these?
- What is the impact of work products being out of date? Is it affecting project performance in a major or minor way? (For example, staff performing the wrong tasks or lack of coordination).
- Are there alternative mechanisms mitigating the effect of out of date work products?
- Is project tracking detecting the deviations?
- Is project tracking triggering actions?

It is quite common for projects to not have all the resources they desire and need. This commonly affects activities such as maintenance of project documentation. Project staff may create alternative (and simpler) mechanisms to manage the project performance, some of which may not even be specified in the project management method. The assessor therefore should look at whether maintenance of work products first affects project performance (PA 2.1) and then whether the project tracking (GP 2.1.2) is ensuring a lack of major deviations from planned performance. If there are no major deviations, then the assessor should assess that PA 2.1 is still fully achieved. If there are major deviations in project management performance, then GP 2.1.3 is not achieved.

The assessor should then specifically check the requirements on maintenance of work products.

- Is there a specified way to manage the configuration and change of work products?
- If the specified way to manage is not being fulfilled, then GP 2.2.3 is not achieved.

In summary, we have three potential results.

Scenario 2A

If there are no major deviations in project management performance then PA2.1 is fully achieved. If configuration management and change of work products is not achieved (GP 2.2.3), then PA 2.2 is still largely achieved.

The process should be rated as Fully achieving Capability Level 2.

Scenario 2B

If project tracking is inadequate (GP 2.1.2) and there are several minor deviations in project performance, then PA 2.1 can only be considered as largely achieved. If configuration management and change of work products is not achieved (GP 2.2.3), the PA 2.2 is largely achieved.

The process should be rated as Largely achieving Capability Level 2.

Scenario 2C

If project tracking is inadequate (GP 2.1.2) and there are many minor or (one or more) major deviations in project performance, then PA 2.1 can only be considered as partially achieved. If configuration management and change of work products is not achieved (GP 2.2.3), the PA 2.2 is largely achieved.

The process should be rated as Partially achieving Capability Level 2.

Scenario 3

Project participants agree that the project was planned and is being managed, but disagree on how the project management is being performed. This is likely to mean that project performance is varying across the project, and could either be inadequate allocation of responsibilities, or lack of communication (especially of changes), or that the planned project performance has varied since the project planning took place.

The assessor should look at activities associated with GP 2.1.4 & GP 2.1.5 (plan and assign the responsibility and authority, and resource allocation) and at GP 2.1.3 (project tracking and re-planning).

The second area that the assessor should look at is the management of work products in activities associated with GP 2.2.3 (configuration management and change) and GP 2.2.2 (work product dependencies). When work product dependencies are not well documented, then it is possible to change one work product and forget or miss making the associated changes in another work product. The result may be that persons that principally rely upon different work products as the basis for their understanding and actions have different perceptions of what they need to do.

Scenario 3A

In this scenario, GP 2.1.2 and GP 2.2.2 are associated with planning activities. If these are inadequately performed, the assessor should find evidence relatively early in the performance of project management when problems occur. If the assessor finds that this planning is inadequate, it is also will impact upon the project tracking and adjustment activities later in the project management performance (GP 2.1.3 and GP 2.2.4).

The assessor should judge that the highest rating will be **Partially achieved for Capability Level 2**.

Scenario 3B

GP 2.1.3 and GP 2.2.4 are associated with implementation of tracking and adjustment activities. If only these activities are inadequately performed, the assessor should find evidence only later in the performance of project management of problems occurring. If the impact is minor deviations in project performance, the assessor should judge the rating will be **Largely achieved for Capability Level 2**.

If the impact is major deviations in project performance, the assessor should judge the rating will be **Partially achieved for Capability Level 2**.

Scenario 4

Project participants indicate that the way the project is being performed seems to vary over time without their understanding of the reasons for change. The assessor should look at activities associated with GP 2.1.2 and GP 2.1.3 (project tracking and adjustment). Is performance of project management and the project tracked? Are deviations causing actions to be taken? Are these actions being communicated?

The assessor should also look at activities associated with GP 2.1.4 to see if adequate resources were planned (responsibility and authority are assigned) and activities associated with GP 2.1.5 to check if adequate resources are provided. Finally, the assessor should check activities associated with GP 2.2.4 (work products are updated) and made available to project participants.

Scenario 4A

If the primary cause of problems begins in the planning (GP 2.1.2), then this is likely to affect the implementation activities (GP 2.1.3 and GP 2.2.4).

In this scenario, the assessor should judge the rating will be **Partially achieved for Capability Level 2**.

Scenario 4B

If the primary cause of problems is inadequate project tracking and actions to correct deviations (GP 2.1.3), together with communication of these changes to project participants, the assessor must judge whether there are major deviations in project performance or minor deviations. If the impact is minor deviations in project performance, the assessor should judge the rating will be **Largely achieved for Capability Level 2**.

If the impact is major deviations in project performance, the assessor should judge the rating will be **Partially achieved for Capability Level 2**.

Capability Level 3: Established process

Capability Level 3 specifies standard and defined processes. The purpose of Capability Level 3 remains similar to what was defined in the technical report version of the standard. This is to specify organizational standard processes that are tailored and deployed as defined processes with associated human and infrastructure resources. However, the definition of Capability Level 3 practices has altered from the technical report version. In the technical report, PA3.1 covered process aspects, and PA3.2 covered resources.

Now PA3.1 covers standard process definition and refinement, and PA3.2 covers defined process deployment. PA3.1 is an overall organizational responsibility, while PA3.2 is a specific to the project/organizational unit deploying the process. The main interacting Generic Practices from each Process Attribute interact as shown in the following diagram.

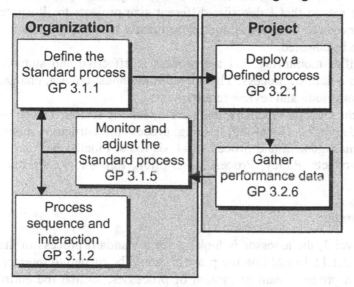

Fig. 49. Standard and Defined Process interactions.

Process attribute 3.1 – Process definition attribute

The process definition attribute measures the extent to which a standard process is maintained to support deployment of a defined process. This covers both definition and monitoring of a standard process elements and interaction with other processes, as well as people aspects and infrastructure support. It has five Generic Practices that aim to specify a process that can be used throughout the organization.

GP 3.1.1 defines a standard process which has the main required process elements and guidance on how to tailor, deploy and implement it.

GP 3.1.2 determines inter-process sequences and interactions so that they create an integrated process chain (system of processes). This intent of this practice to highlight inter-process dependences was previously poorly covered in the technical report. Assessors sometimes made the mistake of expecting all base practices to occur within one process or ignoring the effect of associated or related processes.

GP 3.1.3 identifies the roles of people and the competencies needed to perform the process.

GP 3.1.4 identifies process support infrastructure and the environment in which the process is valid. The environment can greatly affect process execution; hence the reason that I describe different size projects to illustrate how the process needs to be adapted and consequently how the process assessment needs to be adjusted.

GP 3.1.5 specifies monitoring that the process is effective and suitable when deployed as a defined process. This includes methods, criteria, change mechanisms and any audit and review requirements.

In addition to the Generic Practices, there are 6 Generic Resources identified. These include process modelling, training, process infrastructure, monitoring, resource management and process analysis tools. Finally there are 5 Generic Work Products, Policy, Process description, Repository, Standard and Strategy.

General Interpretation

At Capability Level 3, the assessor is looking for a standard process in the organization (GP 3.1.1). In addition the process should be related to interacting processes in a process chain or system of processes, so that the entire process chain is effective and supportive (GP 3.1.2). The standard process should define information/data/methods to monitor the performance of the defined process (GP 3.1.5). In addition, the process should be changed as needed based upon this monitoring. Note: this is a form of continual process improvement, even if it is not called that in the standard. [52]

---

[52] The process change (improvement) covered by the fifth practice in GP 3.1.5 does not rely upon quantitative measurement (part of Capability Level 4). It may be based upon qualitative information, for example lessons learnt using the defined process. In comparison to part 5, the FAA iCMM explicitly defines these types of improvement as a Capability Level 3 process attribute.

The persons defining the standard process also need to define the human resource requirements (roles and competences) needed for performing the process (GP 3.1.3) and the process infrastructure and working environment for the process (GP 3.1.4).

The assessor should first look at the overall cycle shown earlier. Is there evidence that the standard process is refined based upon its implementation in the defined process within projects? If this is occurring then it is likely that all the generic practices are being performed to some extent.

The assessor, when looking at activities associated with GP 3.1.1. (Define the standard process) has a set of generic resources with which the organization's process documentation can be assessed (process modelling, process infrastructure). The standard process must both guide and reflect the way the organization defines and implements the process currently – it is not valid to have a standard process that does not act as the basis for the actual process in use. The assessor should particularly look at how the standard process specifies objective criteria for task completion, and process entry and exit points, which sometimes are poorly specified. Another characteristic that is often poorly defined is the process performance data/information that has to be collected. For the project management process, information/data may include:

- Cost and schedule data, including absolute data (budget, time elapsed, effort spent) and variation data (estimated versus actual values).
- Resource data including the number and type of people required and used, the skills required and available, and training data.
- The use of specified infrastructure and tools.
- Qualitative information such as problems encountered, actions taken, lessons learnt, ease/difficulty of defining, tailoring and implementing the project management process.

The assessor may find that the standard process is either an internal or an external 'document'. It is valid to use a project management handbook such as the PMBOK® [47] or PRINCE © [48] project methodology, or alternately an internal procedure or handbook. The assessor when looking at activities associated with GP 3.1.1 expects to find guidance on process implementation and tailoring. Tailoring may consist of:

- Adopting the standard process without change.
- Adding, deleting or modifying parts of the standard process.
- Adopting a substantially different process when appropriate, allowed by the standard process and agreed by the persons responsible for the process.

The tailoring guidelines should provide criteria on what can be tailored and to what extent. Factors to consider include:

- Project environment and size.
- Product domain and complexity.
- Personnel available and involved in both the tailoring and implementation.
- Interfaces/dependencies to other organizations.
- Selecting processes, activities, and tasks.
- Associated training required.

The assessor should expect to see project performance data (GP 3.1.5) that aids understanding and refinement of the standard process. Process performance data for all processes must include at least some qualitative data and for the project management process should also include some quantitative data. Examples of data include:

- Qualitative data: project progress/status reports, project completion reports, lessons learnt, review reports, problem reports, corrective actions raised/performed and their results, resource capability, skills requirements, and training feedback.
- Quantitative data: actual cost, schedule, effort, process duration/cycle time, and resource utilisation.

When the assessor finds quantitative performance data for a process, it is also applicable to PA4.1, and a likely positive sign that the process owner has deliberately considered performance data in the definition and refinement of the standard process.

For GP 3.1.3 the assessor should expect to find the needs for people are identified and documented. This covers the roles (e.g. project manager, sub-project manager, team leader) and the responsibilities (e.g. plan, manage, review, report) and competencies (e.g. report writing, people and team management and leadership, communication skills, planning and forecasting ability) required for each role. There should be guidance on whether one person or a team covering the project needs is acceptable and preferably for what types of projects. The performance standards must also be defined (e.g. ability to prepare a project plan within a specified duration and level of effort). The details may be contained in the standard process for project management, or it may refer to an organization's Human Resource Management process (RIN.1).

For GP 3.1.4, the assessor should look at what process infrastructure is in place (via generic resources including process modelling and process/methods library, standard process description or procedures). In addition, the work environment requirements are identified, such as what the combination of project support tools are needed for various projects. For example, in very small projects the work environment may consist of on room with all personnel collocated, using an electronic printing whiteboard and an information wall to show all project management information. For a large project, the work environment will require more sophisticated project scheduling and tracing tools.

Interpretation for large and complex projects

The assessor should expect to find a requirement for more extensive project performance data in large projects. The assessor should also check whether the organizational processes (PIM.1 – Process Establishment, PIM.2 – Process Assessment and PIM.3 Process Improvement) are defined and used, as a source of additional evidence of a process focused organizational culture.

The assessor may also need to consider how the standard process handles projects that span organizational boundaries (across different organizations). How are the interfaces and dependencies across different organizations managed? This should be defined in the standard process to adequately cover the requirements of GP 3.1.2.

Interpretation for medium projects

As projects become shorter in duration and/or smaller in scope and effort, the requirement for performance data may also decrease.

The assessor should determine from the interviews whether there are distinct rules guiding the implementation and tailoring of the Standard Process depending upon the project duration/scope. This is particularly important if the assessor is assessing several project instances that vary widely in duration and scope, to avoid assuming that all projects have to be run the same way.

The organization should consider carefully how to optimise the tailoring to benefit from the performance data collected versus the effort expended.

Interpretation for small projects

For small projects, especially those of short duration, the assessor should expect that feedback of performance data to the standard process will occur upon project completion, and may also be by exception (only significant data is fed back). The creation and analysis of comparative data, both combinations of quantitative data and comparison to historical data is less likely within the project, however the assessor should judge this as a very positive indicator is performed.

The assessor should also determine the level of training and understanding of the persons implementing and tailoring the process (e.g. the project manager), as it is more likely that persons of less project management experience are allocated to small projects (this is a standard experiential learning technique).

Interpretation for mission and safety critical projects

Mission and safety critical projects will probably have well defined standard processes, strict tailoring and implementation rules.

Process attribute 3.2 – Process deployment attribute

The process deployment attribute measures the extent to which a standard process is deployed effectively as a defined process. This covers the process tailoring and deployment and associated resources; human, informational and infrastructural. There are six Generic Practices.

GP 3.2.1 specifies the need to deploy a defined process to suit the environment or context in which it is used. This may be via selecting or tailoring a standard process (for example there may be several standard processes for project management depending upon project parameters such as size, duration, communication level and co-location of people). The process as deployed must also be verified to conform to the standard process requirements.

GP 3.2.2 specifies the roles, responsibilities and authorities of individuals and groups performing the process. These are communicated so that all parties know 'who does what' and 'who is responsible for what'.

GP 3.2.3 identifies the competences of individuals and groups and relevant training.

GP 3.2.4 requires that competent human resources are available and perform the defined process. The required information resources are also made available and used as needed. This practice uses the outputs of GP 3.2.2 and GP 3.2.3.

GP 3.2.5 requires process infrastructure that supports the defined process. The infrastructure must be managed and maintained. The work environment needed for the defined process is made available, managed, used and maintained.

GP 3.2.6 requires the people performing the process to identify, collect and analyse process performance data. The data should enable the people to understand process behaviour and judge the effectiveness and suitability of the process as deployed. In addition the data and analysis should identify where the deployed and standard processes can be improved.

There are 9 Generic Resources for this process attribute, including resource management, process, information and knowledge management systems, process assessment, audit and review. There are 8 Generic Work products, all of which were previously defined.

General Interpretation

The management practices are grouped into three related areas. GP 3.2.1 and GP 3.2.6 cover the process deployment and monitoring. GP 3.2.2, GP 3.2.3 and GP 3.2.4 cover human resources. GP 3.2.4 and MP 3.2.5 cover information and infrastructure resources.

As noted earlier, GP 3.2.1 and GP 3.2.6 have clear interaction with the standard process Generic Practices GP 3.1.1, GP 3.1.2 and GP 3.1.5. The assessor when looking at activities associated with GP 3.2.1 expects to find that the standard process is implemented and/or tailored to prepare a defined process for a particular project. Tailoring may consist of:
- Adopting the standard process without change from a process library.
- Adding, deleting or modifying parts of the standard process.
- Adopting a substantially different process when appropriate, allowed by the standard process and agreed by the persons responsible for the process (both at organization and project levels).

The tailoring guidelines should provide criteria on what can be tailored and to what extent. Factors to consider include:
- Project environment and size.
- Product domain and complexity.
- Personnel available and involved in both the tailoring and implementation.
- Interfaces/dependencies to other organizations.
- Selecting processes, activities, and tasks.
- The degree of co-location of personnel and communication mechanisms.
- Associated training required.

It is important to ensure that the persons doing the tailoring are trained in the standard process and how to tailor it. This is to ensure that they understand how each part of the standard process is meant to be implemented and also to provide useful feedback. They need to document tailoring decisions and rationale for these decisions. For each project, this is likely to be a one-time event, unless major project reorganization has to occur and the project management process subsequently revised.

The assessor may find that in companies having projects of similar nature, that the project manager (or other person tailoring and implementing the process), will use an existing document (e.g. project plan) as the basis for creating the new process description. This is a common practice and the standard process and tailoring guidelines should allow this, while specifying a suitable review (against the standard process requirements) to check applicability/effectiveness.

The assessor should determine in the assessment interview, how well the project participants understand the use of performance data to manage the process (GP 3.2.6). In the project, the primary focus will be on the defined process within the project. Is the data used by participants to improve their performance of the defined process, and to take corrective actions? Is data collected and analysed with respect to process interactions (in process chains or systems of processes)? Is the performance data also collected over time (historical data established) and current data and performance analysed against this historical project management data? Is data combined to improve the analysis? Such combinations may indicate a more active use of data and resultant feedback. Combinations of quantitative data could comprise:

- cost/schedule,
- process duration/effort,
- process duration/resource utilisation,
- actual cost, schedule, and effort data versus plan/estimates, and
- trends in performance.

Is data made available to the owner of the Standard Process? This data may be all the data analysed in a project, or may be a subset of the data analysed within a project highlighting exceptions/best practice/problems that are only relevant to the standard process.

The project performance data analysis may be more frequent than the analysis of data relevant to the Standard Process. For example, the analysis and feedback to refine the standard process and its performance data needs (GP 3.1.5) may only be performed upon project closure or at the end of a major project phase. The analysis frequency and trigger events should be defined in the standard and defined processes. The assessor should determine from the interviews reasonable intervals for the project related analysis of the defined process, and for the standard process related analysis. This should be based in part upon the project duration (for example, if a project runs more than five years, waiting for project closure is probably unacceptable, but if it runs 6-18 months it is more acceptable) and the expected/actual scope of the changes found when analysis is performed.

The assessor should determine how changes to the standard process are implemented/tailored in the defined process. The organization should define when changes impact upon existing projects, and when they are implemented only in new projects (GP 3.1.1).

For GP 3.2.2, GP 3.2.3 and GP 3.2.4, the assessor should first interview the project participants to determine how the project needs for people are identified and documented. This covers the roles (e.g. project manager, sub-project manager, team leader) and the responsibilities (e.g. plan, manage, review, report) and competences (e.g. report writing, people and team management and leadership, communication skills, planning and forecasting ability) required for each role. There should be guidance on whether one person or a team covering the project needs is acceptable and preferably for what types of projects. The guidance should be contained in the standard process (GP 3.1.3). The performance standards must also be defined (e.g. ability to prepare a project plan within a specified duration and level of effort). The details may be contained in the Standard Process for project management, or it may refer to an organization's Human Resource Management process (RIN.1).

One particular aspect that the assessor should interpret carefully is the statement in GP 3.2.4: *"Required human resources are made available, allocated and used"*. Many project managers and participants will often state the opposite – that there are insufficient resources allocated. This has become a fact of modern cost control affecting project management (or any process in fact). When this statement is encountered, the assessor needs to determine from the project participants (and maybe also from organizational management) the impact of the lack of sufficient resources. If the impact is major upon the performance of the project management process, it should already have been evident in assessing PA2.1 – Performance Management Attribute. Alternatively, it should be evident in the overtime records of project personnel. People who have to work large amounts of overtime to perform the process are doing so in an unsustainable manner. This is likely to fail and cause major impacts on the project (or another project) in the future. Another aspect that the assessor needs to judge is whether the lack of resources is systematic (e.g. across all projects) or only for a particular project. Only if it is a systematic problem, should the assessor judge that GP 3.2.4 is only partially achieved or not achieved. If the impact is not major or systematic then the assessor may judge that GP 3.2.4 is largely or fully achieved.

GP 3.2.4 and GP 3.2.5 cover the activities to satisfy the information and infrastructure resource needs of the project. They should also reflect what was defined in the standard process (GP 3.1.4). Process infrastructure for the project management process may consist of facilities, hardware, software, methods, techniques, standards and equipment. These may comprise some or all of the following:

• Paper and/or electronic process documentation and guides.
• Physical workspaces.

- Project management tools including as scheduling tools, cost/schedule control systems, project coordination and team management systems, and electronic workspaces.
- Training systems and equipment.
- Communications tools including email, threaded communications tools, conferencing and meeting tools.
- Problem and action tracking tools.
- Product domain specific environments where they impact upon performance of project management (otherwise they these environments support the engineering processes).

The support must also allow funding to implement and use the infrastructure. The assessor will find it easiest to assess from the interviews what process infrastructure is in use (GP 3.2.5) and refer from there to if it has been provided in an acceptable way (GP 3.2.4).

Interpretation for large and complex projects

The assessor should focus initially on the top level of project management, in interviews with the project manager and the project management team, to determine whether and how the human resources and infrastructure are identified and implemented. Based upon interviews with the top-level project management, the assessor may then select further second level (sub-project) management personnel/teams to interview.

The top-level project management should be able to indicate if they define the resource and infrastructure requirements consistently across large projects, or allow sub-projects to use their own infrastructure.

The assessor may also need to consider projects that span organizational boundaries (across different organizations). The author's experience is that infrastructure that is consistent and compatible across organizations will reduce the effort of personnel implementing the project. This is very important for engineering processes, but also an advantage for project management (for example, using the same scheduling tool allows organizations to exchange data and analysis electronically).

The assessor should expect to find more extensive project performance data in large projects. There should be historical data available, especially for projects running longer than one year. Organizations that perform large projects will normally have created a Standard Process internally, or if using an externally acquired project management process document/standard/book, will probably have defined an application guide. Large projects are also often required to gather quantitative project performance data, by both their organizational management and the customer.

The assessor should also check whether the associated organizational processes (PIM.1 – Process Establishment, PIM.2 – Process Assessment, and PIM.3 Process Improvement) are defined and used, as a source of additional evidence of a process focused organizational culture.

The assessor may also need to consider projects that span organizational boundaries (across different organizations). How are the interfaces and dependencies across different organizations managed?

Interpretation for small projects

Small projects are often under even greater pressure to minimise the use of resources for project management and often lack infrastructure that reduces effort in performing the process. The assessor may find that the project manager is a part time role, combined with other technical/quality/ management roles. The assessor may also find that small projects are used as experiential learning/training for the project manager. In these situations, the assessor needs to judge whether the resource requirements are well identified and necessary training provided.

Small projects have an advantage in requiring less or simpler process infrastructure due to the ability to use communication within small teams to handle many project management activities that would require more extensive infrastructure in large projects. The assessor will need to judge the effectiveness and appropriateness of these simpler communications based methods/mechanisms versus more formal project management, progress tracking and reporting methods/mechanisms.

The assessor may also find that human resource management is a part time role within the organization, in many small organizations, it may even be an undocumented process, relying upon the experience of a senior manager/Managing Director.

The assessor's fundamental judgment will need to focus on whether major problems are impacting project management performance or whether excessive overtime is needed to perform the activities.

Interpretation for mission and safety critical projects

The assessor should find that human resource and infrastructure are also stringently specified for mission and safety critical projects.

Sample Scenarios – Capability Level 3

Scenario 1

The assessor finds that the current status of the project reflects the project plan(s). All base practices are fulfilled and there is evidence (including input and output work products) that meets the scope of the process and produces the desired process outcomes within the project constraints and meeting the organizations' business goals. The project participants are aware of who is responsible for each activity.

The assessor should first question project participants whether they are following a project management method, procedure or handbook when planning and implementing the project. Questions include:

- Is the method described?
- Did it guide users in applying it to a project (tailoring)?
- Is the method applicable to multiple projects (standard process)?
- Did it specify mechanisms and data to help the project participants understand and refine the process (and inter-process) behaviour in the project?
- Did it specify monitoring and feedback mechanisms to refine the process?
- Did it specify roles, responsibilities and competences of personnel?
- Did it specify infrastructure and work environment?

If the project participants are able to positively answer these questions and refer to information that addresses these questions (covering GP 3.1.1 to GP 3.1.5, GP 3.2.1 and GP 3.2.6), then the assessor should judge that PA 3.1 is fully achieved.

If the project participants can describe how roles and activities are assigned and delegated, and that persons are adequately trained to be competent in their defined roles, then the activities associated with GP 3.2.2 and GP 3.2.3 are fulfilled. Similarly, if the project participants are able to describe the way infrastructure is identified and provided to support the implementation of the project management process, then the activities associated with GP 3.2.4 and MP 3.2.5 are fulfilled.

The process should be rated as **Fully achieving Capability Level 3**.

Scenario 2

The assessor finds that a few of the specified work products are missing or not adequately maintained. Alternatively, the assessor finds that Progress Tracking [BP13] is inadequately performed, however the current project status still substantially reflects the planning and the project is (more or less) in control. Some actions to correct deviations have been taken (although they may not have been timely or totally adequate).

In this scenario the work products were specified but some were missing/not maintained, and project tracking may be inadequately performed. Therefore, the main issue for the assessor to judge is whether activities associated with process resources are adequately specified and implemented and/or process infrastructure is adequate. The assessor should interpret the process resource attribute as a systemic issue. To determine if the problem is systemic, the assessor should ask:

- Are roles, responsibilities and competencies identified in the standard process and implemented in the defined project management process? (GP 3.1.3, GP 3.2.2, GP 3.2.3)
- Is the process infrastructure identified and implemented? (GP 3.1.4, GP 3.2.4)
- Is this project implementation typical (systemic) or unique?
  - Check with the project manager/leader.
  - Check with participants (who may have a different view to the manager/leader).
  - Check with the responsible upper management or process owner.
  - If possible, check other projects.

The assessor needs to judge the extent of the systemic problem. Does the systemic problem affect the activities associated with one, two, three or all five resource related practices (GP 3.1.3, GP 3.1.4 to GP 3.2.2 GP 3.2.3, GP 3.2.4)? We provide guidance below for scenario 2A.

The assessor should also question project participants whether they are following a project management method, procedure or handbook when planning and implementing the project (as in Scenario 1) and hence if both a standard and defined process exist. In general, if a standard process exists and is properly implemented in a defined project process, the assessor should expect that deviations in project performance should mostly be minor, and when major deviations in project performance are detected, then action is taken to correct the performance in a timely manner (but not necessarily immediately). If the assessor sees examples of corrective actions that refine the standard process (GP 3.1.5), then there is a reasonable probability that all the associated practices are also performed (GP 3.1.1 to MP 3.1.4) and PA 3.1 is fully achieved.

Scenario 2A

In scenario 2A, there are no major deviations in project management performance. If the assessor finds that PA 3.1 is fully achieved, then the ratings for PA 3.2 will determine the overall rating of the Capability Level.

Scenario 2A-1

If no systemic problems affect the activities associated with the practices, but only one project instance is affected then the assessor should judge that PA 3.2 is fully achieved. The process should be rated as **Fully achieving Capability Level 3**.

Scenario 2A-2

If the systemic problem affects the activities associated with one of the deployed process practices, then the assessor should judge that PA 3.2 is largely achieved. The process should be rated as **Largely achieving Capability Level 3**.

If the systemic problem affects the activities associated with the two practices, then the assessor should judge that PA 3.2 is partially achieved. The process should be rated as **Largely achieving Capability Level 3**.

Scenario 2A-3

If the systemic problem affects the activities associated with three of the practices, then the assessor should judge that PA 3.2 is only partially achieved. The process should be rated as **Partially achieving Capability Level 3**.

Scenario 2A-4

If the systemic problem affects the activities associated with all four practices, then the assessor should judge that PA 3.2 is not achieved. The process should be rated as **Partially achieving Capability Level 3**.

Capability Level 4: Predictable process

Process attribute 4.1 - Measurement attribute

The process measurement attribute measures the extent to which the process is measured to ensure it meets the performance and business objectives and goals. This covers the establishment of process information to support business goals, measurement (quantitative) objectives, measures, frequency of measurement and results. There are six Generic Practices.

GP 4.1.1 identifies process information needs relevant to business goals of stakeholders. It is important that business goals drive the information and measurement requirements, and not vice versa.

GP 4.1.2 identifies process measurement objectives that meet the information needs.

GP 4.1.3 requires establishment of quantitative process performance objectives meeting the stakeholders' business goals.

GP 4.1.4 identifies process and product measurement that allows monitoring and analysis of process and product goals. This includes the types of data collected, frequency of measurement and data collection, methods, processing algorithms and verification mechanisms. This practice requires a competent measurement system.

GP 4.1.5 specifies the collection and analysis of the process and product measurements as part of the defined process. In other words, the measurement and analysis is an integral part of process performance. The results are reported to parties responsible for setting and monitoring quantitative objectives.

GP 4.1.6 specifies the use of measurement results to monitor and verify that the process is meeting its objectives. This focuses on quantitative process control techniques such as statistical process control. It includes process trend behaviour as well as process capability. The use of process trends implies an active, predictive control of the process, not just a reactive control of the process.

There are 5 Generic Resources defined for this process attribute, including management information, measurement techniques frameworks and tools, and analysis tools. There are 5 Generic Work products defined, the most important being Measures and Data.

General Interpretation

The measurement process attribute is focused on specifying, collecting and analysing quantitative measurement of processes with the aim to better achieve the business goals. These business goals should be used to derive both quantitative process and product goals for the process. This not only includes measurement of the defined process as deployed but also trend analysis of the process in order to predict future process behaviour. For the project management process, the following example is illustrative:

- The business goal is to profitably run projects that satisfy customer needs. This goal requires the following process and product goals in a project:
  - Provide the customer with a clear plan for the project, addressing the customer's goals, desired cost and schedule constraints (product). [Measurements include quantifiable customer goal metrics, cost and schedule for activities.]
  - Provide the customer with their desired/required products and services (product). [Measurements include quantifiable product and service met-

rics such as number of requirements specified/met, service times, satisfaction index.]

- Provide the customer with progress tracking and reporting meeting their needs (product) [Measurements include budgeted cost versus expenditure, planned versus actual schedule performance.]
- Perform the project management process within the organizational cost, schedule and resource constraints (process). [Measurements include Budgeted Cost of Work Performed, Actual Cost of Work Performed, Budgeted resources versus actual resources, Earned Value, Schedule Variance, Cost Variance, Price Variance, and Usage Variance.]
- Perform the project management process to minimise risks and problems (process). [Measurements include risk estimation, risk actions taken, number of problems encountered, number of corrective actions, and success rate for actions.]
- Additional goals include:
  - Perform the project management process so that performance data is used to refine the process performance and provide feedback to the organization's standard process (process). [Measurements include number of changes to project plans and performance of the process, number of feedback items, and quantifiable impact of changes (e.g. cost savings).]
  - Perform the project management process at Capability Level 5, assess using ISO/IEC 15504 process assessment and make corrections as needed (process). [Measurements include Capability Level, opportunities for improvement.]
  - Use trend analysis to predict possible process and product risks and problems and use to mitigate or prevent risk or problems (process). [Measurements include use in various combinations over time to track trends, the effect of improvements upon trends.]

As described, the project management process is by its nature, a good candidate process to achieve the process measurement attribute (PA 4.1) of Capability Level 4. In the technical report version of the standard, it was noted as an associated process that helps other processes achieve the management practices of PA 4.1. Alignment with business goals is one of the outcomes of another associated process: MAN.1 Organizational Alignment.

The assessor should determine that the measurements taken are used to support the achievement of the business goal(s) and are applied consistently across the organization (and not just in one project). The assessor should determine if the use of measurement is aiding the project participants to refine their understanding and implementation of the project management process.

For an organization just beginning to adopt process measurement, the assessor should determine the organization's plan to deploy measurement across its projects. In practice, it is often easiest to deploy measurement at the start of a new project, rather than later in the project lifecycle and in some cases it may be better to deploy measurement in specific sub-projects first.

The organization must take care when deploying measurement to focus on products and processes in a way that motivates people to the desired mode of behaviour. If measures are not carefully selected, they can promote negative behaviour, for example people may not report problems if the number of problems reported is used as a negative personal performance indicator by management.

In general, when measurement is carefully deployed within the project management process, the activities will be better managed and more often meet their process and product goals.

Interpretation for large and complex projects

Large projects may require deployment of measurement in specific sub-projects. The organization should recognize which sub-projects and which processes benefit most from measurement. In addition, the measurements used should vary from sub-project to sub-project, especially the product measurements, which are related to the products that each sub-project produces. Measurement should consider the level of detail required when activities 'roll up' from sub-projects to project level.

Trend analysis is more important for larger projects, as their duration will be longer, costs correspondingly higher and risks of greater severity.

Interpretation for small projects

Small projects will normally only support quantitative measurement at project level, and not for lower level sub-projects (if any exist). The most useful measures to consider are schedule variance, cost variance and resource usage.

Interpretation for mission and safety critical projects

Mission and safety critical projects often have specific product measures, for example the number of software problems, their severity and to which criticality class of software they apply. There will be fewer specific process measurements – the generic ones already described will apply.

Process attribute 4.2 – Process control attribute

The process control attribute measures the extent that a process is quantitatively managed to create a capable and predictable process performance[53]. There are five Generic Practices.

GP 4.2.1 defines process control analysis methods and techniques that meet control objectives. The objectives were defined in practices as part of PA 4.1.

GP 4.2.2 defines process control parameters and limits that allow quantitative process control.

GP 4.2.3 specifies analysis of process and product measurements that identify variations in process performance. This includes identifying when the process exceeds control limits, and the potential assignable cause(s) – both common causes and special causes. It also includes ensuring that the analysis results are provided to people who can take action to correct the out of control variations.

GP 4.2.4 specifies identification, implementation, monitoring and evaluation of corrective actions for the identified assignable causes.

GP 4.2.5 specifies the re-establishment of control limits. These limits may need to change if the process is changed, but should not change if corrective action did not change the process but rather its implementation. There may be situations where the control limits are tightened because they were incorrectly specified.

There are 3 Generic Resources covering process analysis, control and statistical control techniques. There are 7 Generic Work Products, all of which were previously specified.

General Interpretation

If the measurement process attribute (PA 4.1) is implemented, then it is possible to use these process measures as a quantitative basis for control of the performance of the defined project management process in a project (PA4.2). If process assessment (for example using ISO/IEC 15504) of the project management process is performed, then the results of the assessment can be used to implement or better perform the activities associated with the base practices and the management practices. The assessor should determine

---

[53] Note that the standard also uses the term 'stable' and 'within defined limits'. In this definition, stability is concerned with ensuring the standard and deployed process(es) are not changed so often that it is impossible to quantitatively control them. The term 'within defined limits' is redundant because quantitative control (particularly statistical control) requires defined control limits.

what additional measurement analysis and control techniques are used, for example for cost/schedule/resource usage. The organization should specify for process control practices:

- How often the process is measured or sampled. Is the measurement interval able to detect useful process variations without requiring excessive analysis?
- What the control limits or parameters are so that measures that deviate from these are detected. For example, a control parameter may allow up to 15% short-term schedule delay or 10% cost overrun, and any greater deviation requires analysis.
- The way that the selected technique allows trends or non-normal process behaviour patterns to be detected. For example, plotting cost and schedule variance over time allows patterns and trends to be visualised.
- The way that the validity and accuracy of the source data, the analysis and the results is assured. For example, are a number of projects compared?
- The applicability and usability of the analysis and results. Do the results lead to understanding of problems and subsequent actions that help refine performance of the process?
- Do corrective actions change project management process performance to keep performance more often within the control parameters/limits?
- Are corrective actions also monitored using the process measurement data, especially trend data?
- Are new control parameters set over time that when met ensure that better control of the process is occurring?

The assessor should determine how the organization defines, implements and uses the process control practices to better control the project management process. The simplest evidence is graphical charting such as Pareto charts or process control charts.

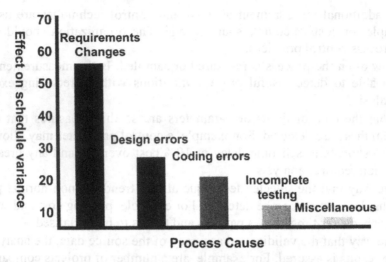

Fig. 50. Pareto chart example – process causes for schedule variance.

Organizations using formal Cost/Schedule Control Systems will meet most of the data capture and analysis practice requirements. The assessor should determine how this information is used to manage the project management process.

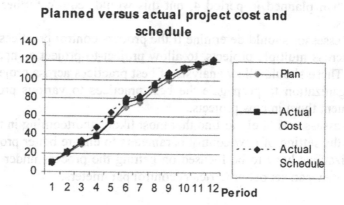

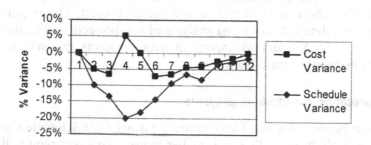

Fig. 51. Example of Cost/Schedule Control charts.

In the above example, the control parameter for cost and schedule variation (Control Limit: CL) is set to 15 percent variance. In time period 4, the schedule variance is 20% and would be a trigger to take project management actions to analyse and correct this deviation. In addition, the chart illustrates that there was a distinct negative schedule trend from period 1 to 4 (the trend indicates schedule slip), which should also be a cause for trend analysis (preferably at the latest in period 3). The example assumes a corrective action was taken resulting in improvement in schedule variance.

The cost variances do not exceed the control parameter or show any strong trends for this example. There is a positive trend between periods 6 to 12, in which the cost meets the planned budget by period 12. One may infer that the schedule slip may be related to the expenditure (cost), which was lower than planned in period 4, but this would require further quantitative analysis.

The assessor should determine if the process control practices are also applied across multiple projects, to allow project-to-project comparisons to be made. These should allow analysis of best practices across projects, to allow the organization to propagate the best practices to various projects and/or implement them in new projects.

The assessor is likely to find that most likely shortcoming in the organization is the setting of new control parameters to ensure better process control. Organizations have to be focused on getting the process under control first, before they can set better (stricter) control parameters.

Interpretation for large and complex projects

Large projects are likely to use formal Cost/Schedule Control Systems that provide the necessary data for process control. Well-run projects will use the system for sub-projects as well as the overall project. The responsibility to perform the data collection and analysis of sub-projects will be the responsibility of Cost Account Managers, in many projects this will be the sub-project manager or team leader.

Interpretation for medium projects

Medium projects are less likely to use a formal Cost/Schedule Control System, particularly when they are smaller in size. This will require the project to collect the required data separately. In these situations, it is of benefit to the project to work with the section of the organization that collects the effort (hours worked per person) against specified sub-projects and work packages. For the labour component of a project, the project manager should have a labour rate so that the effort can be related to the cost. This can then be collated with the project schedule data, to produce cost/schedule/resource usage data.

The data collection and analysis interval should be specified against both the overall project duration and the likelihood of deviation from plan (for example, if it is likely that a significant variation against plan can occur within a three month period, then data collection and analysis should be monthly so that negative trends can be detected).

Interpretation for small projects

Small projects will generally have very informal methods of process control. If the project duration is short (for example, less than 3 months), then process control within a project may not be needed or even viable. If this is the case, the assessor may need to look at how process control is managed across several projects and whether the historical data is collected, analysed and used when planning and implementing new projects.

The assessor should determine whether the process control applied at project commencement has aided the control of the project in this situation.

For small projects of longer duration, simple techniques such as Pareto analysis may be sufficient.

Interpretation for mission and safety critical projects

Many mission and safety critical projects have specified measurement requirements that can be used for process control purposes. Normally however, the measurements will relate more to the engineering and customer-supplier primary lifecycle processes.

Sample Scenarios – Capability Level 4

Scenario 1

The assessor finds that the current status of the project reflects the project plan(s). All base practices are fulfilled and there is evidence (including input and output work products) that meets the scope of the process and produces the desired process outcomes within the project constraints and meeting the organizations' business goals. The project participants are aware of who is responsible for each activity.

The assessor should determine what process measurements are being performed and how they are used to control process performance. Since the current project status reflects the project plans, the assessor should first determine whether the project was recently re-planned. If the project was not re-planned, has been running for a significant period and process measurements are being used for process control purposes, the process should be rated as **Fully achieving Capability Level 4.**

If the project has been re-planned, the assessor should determine whether process measurement was used to detect whether it was within the process parameters/control limits; detect the problems; and plan corrective actions including the re-planning. The assessor should also determine for how long the process was outside the control parameters to determine if timely action was taken. If the answer to all these issues is positive, the process should be rated as **Fully achieving Capability Level 4.**

However, if the project management process was outside the control parameters for a significant time with adverse affect upon project performance and/or process measurement and control did not trigger re-planning, then the assessor needs to determine the extent, applicability and usability of process measurement and process control. If the process measurement and analysis activities are occurring, then the process should be rated as **Largely achieving Capability Level 4**.

Scenario 2

The assessor finds that a few of the specified work products are missing or not adequately maintained. Alternatively, the assessor finds that Progress Tracking [BP13] is inadequately performed, however the current project status still substantially reflects the planning and the project is (more or less) in control. Some actions to correct deviations have been taken (although they may not have been timely or totally adequate).

In scenario 2A-1, there are no major deviations in project management performance (Capability Level 2) and there were no systemic problems affecting the standard and defined process activities (Capability Level 3).

However, the assessor is likely to find that inadequate progress tracking is a result of inadequate process measurement and also indicates a lack of process control. The inadequate or untimely corrective actions also indicate that not all the activities associated with process control are fulfilled.

In this scenario, the assessor should therefore judge the extent of process measurement, its applicability and usability to track progress and its use in process control. If limited process measurement is occurring, the process should be rated as **Partially achieving Capability Level 4**.

Capability Level 5: Optimising process

Process attribute 5.1 – Process innovation attribute

The process innovation attribute measures the extent to which changes to the definition and deployment of the process are identified by common cause performance variation analysis and innovative approaches. There are five Generic Practices.

GP 5.1.1 defines objectives for process innovation to meet new business goals[54]. This includes setting the overall direction for process innovation and relevant quantitative and qualitative improvement objectives.

GP 5.1.2 specifies analysis of process performance measurement data to identify common and special cause variations, and to understand the impact of common cause variation. Common cause variation is an inherent property of a defined process as deployed in its environment.[55]

GP 5.1.3 identifies improvement opportunities due to emergence of new industry best practices, and user feedback on process improvement and innovation opportunities.

GP 5.1.4 derives and evaluates improvement opportunities due to new process concepts, technologies and emergent risks.

GP 5.1.5 defines an implementation strategy. This includes longer term organization planning, evaluation, trials, classification and prioritization, review and validation measures and methods and implementation is a project or program. Examples of this include the 9-Step improvement approach and Team Based Business Design Improvement described in the Practical Guide.

There are 3 Generic Resources, a process improvement framework such as supported by the PIM processes, process information capture and analysis and a trial/pilot system. There are 10 Generic Work Products, Strategy being the main addition.

---

[54] Business goals may be explicitly stated, or may be derived from Vision and Mission statements, business opportunities and competitive business analysis. Note that business here does not imply a profit motive, rather the defined purpose and activities of any organization.

[55] Special cause variation is literally variation caused by special or one-off events that should be handled separately. Special causes do not cause normal process variation. The normal approach is to find and remove the special cause.

General Interpretation

An organization that implements activities associated with the process innovation attribute is focused on creation and implementation of changes to the standard project management process based upon new business goals and directions. While this purpose appears to be similar to the purpose of GP 3.1.1 and GP 3.1.5, in PA 5.1 the process change is also based upon quantitative based understanding, analysis and evaluation of the variation in process performance.

The Generic Practices are a mix of innovation centric change (GP 5.1.1, GP 5.1.3 GP 5.1.4) and process performance variation based change (GP 5.1.2). Therefore, the assessor should identify the person(s) responsible for process change and ask for the following evidence:

- In there an approach/activity to relate business goals to process implementations (GP 5.1.1)?
- Is there a strategy for regular scanning of industry process innovations and best practices to identify new opportunities (GP 5.1.3, GP 5.1.4)?
- Is a systematic review of implementation of historical changes to the defined project management process in projects? Is there quantitative analysis of historical changes (including causal analysis focused on identifying how best to eliminate process defects)? (GP 5.1.2)
- Are the process changes planned, documented and subject to trial/pilots to assess their effectiveness before the standard process is updated throughout the organization (GP 5.1.5)?
- Does the process change implementation has defined goals (for example the achievement of a target process capability, Return on Investment), based upon quantitative analysis of cost/benefit, risks, resource usage constraints and analysis of process performance trends (GP 5.1.5)?
- Do the goals and implementation strategy take into account organizational impact factors including economic, human, management and technology factors, which impact or may be impacted by the proposed process changes (GP 5.1.5)?
- Are information/data collected and analysed according to a standard/defined process to determine the effectiveness of the process change and make adjustments as needed (GP 5.1.5)?

The data collected when the change is implemented, then becomes part of the historical data for the process, which can be used when planning further changes. The organization should be collecting and using both quantitative and qualitative data. Qualitative data consists especially of information related to human factors including job satisfaction, motivation, morale, and consensus/conflict, which are at least partially subjective.

The organization must balance the amount of change it can sustain beneficially against the disruptive and negative effects of change (for example, personnel being confused over how to do an activity, training time, learning curve effects). Properly planned change should lessen the negative effects, but there is still a limit to the ability of people to absorb change.

The assessor should expect to see evidence that there is a *sequence* of related activities associated with the management practices in PA 5.1 (in other words, the activities relate to each other in a logical order). This sequence of activities does not stipulate a regular cycle of activity or specific trigger events to commence the identification of change.

The assessor should expect to find that organizations that have performed the process change activities would have institutionalised these activities. These activities will meet the requirements of the associated organizational processes: PIM.1 – Process Establishment and PIM.2 Process Improvement. Depending upon the way the organization defines its quality system, it may also use MAN.4 Quality Management, and a separate innovation process.

The assessor should expect to find that process change is not specifically addressed in the organization's project management process description, but is in fact in a separate organizational document/procedure/handbook.

Interpretation for large and complex projects

Process change may have benefits for large projects running over a significant duration. In a large project, the organization may use one sub-project as a pilot before implementing the process change in all sub-projects and the main project.

It is often simpler to make the change when starting a new sub-project preferably with an experienced and willing manager. This is likely to minimize any negative impacts including resistance to change and change of performance monitoring that may affect personal evaluation of the manager. It takes advantage of sub-project start-up activities, which could include training, and the use of a willing champion for the change.

Reviews/evaluation of changes in larger projects of significant duration (greater than two years) should be performed more frequently than only once at the end of the project, otherwise the ability to use the process change throughout the organization may be limited. The organization should consider phase end reviews or regular (periodical) reviews, even those these are based upon intermediate results, rather than the final project results. Collecting information on this basis will also help determine whether the results obtained are consistent over the duration of the project or one-time or start-up effects.

Interpretation for small projects

Process change in small projects is best performed when a new project starts, rather than during its execution. An organization that runs many small projects has an opportunity to use each new project start to trial or pilot changes to different processes, however the organization has to take care that not too many changes occur simultaneously as it may make the ability to quantitatively analyse what changes are beneficial more difficult to do. For example, if project management and an engineering process are changed in one project, with a positive effect, it may not be possible to determine whether one or both changes caused the positive effect.

Another benefit of small projects is that project review based upon the actual *final* results is possible within a short time, unlike projects of longer duration.

Interpretation for mission and safety critical projects

Process change for mission and safety critical projects may be driven by externally imposed standards, in addition to internal sponsored change.

Process attribute 5.2 – Process optimisation attribute

The process optimisation attribute measures the extent to which changes to the process ensure an effective process result meeting improvement objectives. There are two Generic Practices.

GP 5.2.1 assesses the impact of each proposed change to both the standard and defined processes. This is based upon prioritised process and improvement objectives, including product quality, process performance and impact on interacting processes. Some of these objectives come from GP 5.1.1, GP 5.1.3 and GP 5.1.4.

GP 5.2.2 defines an implementation strategy and approach. This includes identifying and managing various business factors such as economic, human, technology and management factors that affect deployment. GP 5.1.5 can provides an input to this practice.

GP 5.2.3 evaluates the effectiveness of the change. This includes measurement of process performance and capability, analysis to determine common and special causes and feedback on any further opportunities for improvement.

There are 2 Generic Resources, a change management system and a process evaluation system. There are 5 Generic Work Products, all of which were previously identified.

General Interpretation

An organization that implements activities associated with the process optimisation attribute is focused on implementation of an institutional improvement process (rather than on adhoc, irregular or one-off improvement activities). The organization's institutional process should take input from all
levels of the organization (from top management to junior staff) for improvement opportunities.

The successful implementation of process optimisation requires an appropriate organizational culture (see the Practical Guide chapter on Improvement and Culture). Otherwise, it will not be sustained when business cost
cutting and downsizing pressures occur.

The process innovation attribute (PA 5.1) can also act as an input to the
activities associated with process optimisation (PA5.2). The assessor should
expect to find evidence of a *sequence* of activities associated with process
optimisation to:

- A mechanism for evaluation and review of process and product to identify
  potential improvement opportunities (GP 5.2.1).
- A mechanism to establish an improvement programme and improvement
  teams, and help them identify and communicate improvement opportunities (GP 5.2.2).
- A mechanism for discussion and feedback on improvement opportunities
  between staff and also with users/customers (GP 5.2.3).
- Analyse the source of real problems and risks in the current process, identifying improvement opportunities in a systematic and proactive manner
  including (GP 5.2.1):
  - A documented, systematic mechanism or process exists to identify, re-
    cord and analyze improvement opportunities arising from: senior man-
    agement, customer surveys, employee surveys and feed-
    back/suggestions, competitor and market surveys, business benchmarks
    and best practices, research and development, new technologies, infor-
    mation databases, process measurements and process assessments.
  - Causal analysis to identify the best way to eliminate process defects.
  - A culture that stimulates all parties to contribute to continual improve-
    ment and provide feedback (management, staff, users and customers).
  - A mechanism to use and analyse product and process measures both for
    detecting improvement opportunities and for selecting the most suitable
    opportunities.
- Implement changes to selected areas of the defined process according to
  the implementation strategy (GP 5.2.2), including:

- Planning for potential improvements including expected organizational and project impacts (for example, the impact on project schedules and costs), evaluation against process measurement and control criteria (what measured, frequency of measurement, control parameters, data sources, calculated measurements), use of pilots or trials of the improvement(s), objectives of the improvement, target date for completion, benchmarks against which the improvement can be measured, and monitoring the effectiveness of the improvement activities and result.
- Implementation of improvements is managed in a controlled manner.
- Measures of the improved process are collected for validation against the expected impacts and the organization's goals, and become part of the historical improvement records.

• Validate the effectiveness of process change and provide feedback to the standard process definition (GP 5.2.3), including:
- The collected measures are analysed according to a standard/defined process to determine the effectiveness of the process improvement and make adjustments as needed.
- A mechanism is used for documenting and reporting results to improvement sponsors.
- The standard organizational process is used to update the standard process definition and propagate the improvements as planned.

In general, organizations striving to reach this level of process capability will have deliberately designed their business processes (i.e. quality management system) to fully achieve both the process innovation and process optimisation attributes. The assessor should expect to find that organizations have institutionalised these activities. These activities will meet the requirements of the associated organizational processes: MAN.1 – Organisational alignment, PIM.3 Process Improvement and MAN.4 Quality Management.

Therefore, the assessor should expect to find that process optimisation is not specifically addressed in the organization's project management process description, but is in fact in a separate organizational document/procedure/handbook.

Organizations that strongly embrace process assessment and an improvement culture are likely to have some or all of the activities associated with continuous process improvement in place. This also applies to organizations that strongly embrace Total Quality Management.

For organizations beginning to perform process optimisation activities, the assessor may find that there is little historical evidence available. In this situation, the assessor should look primarily at the definition of the activities in a standard process and how well any improvements follow this process.

Interpretation for large and complex projects

Large projects can benefit from process optimisation and provide a good basis for benchmarking and measuring the effect of improvement actions when they are operating in a 'stable' state or phase. A 'stable' state means they are not in project start-up, a major growth/shrinkage phase, or a wind-down/completion phase, where changes in the project itself may make assessing the change created from process improvements difficult to determine.

Large projects may be good candidates for improvements as they can benefit from improvement over a significant duration. In a large project, the organization may use one sub-project as a pilot before implementing the process change in all sub-projects and the main project.

It is often simpler to make the change when starting a new sub-project preferably with an experienced and willing manager. This is likely to minimize any negative impacts including resistance to change and change of performance monitoring that may affect personal evaluation of the manager. It takes advantage of sub-project start-up activities, which could include training, and the use of a willing champion for the change.

Interpretation for small projects

Process improvement in small projects is best performed when a new project starts, rather than during its execution. An organization that runs many small projects has many opportunities to use new projects to trial or pilot improvements to different processes, however the organization should also consider the possibility to trial improvement in one project while running a similar project without improvements to better evaluate the effectiveness of the improvements.

Another benefit of small projects is that project review based upon the actual *final* results is possible within a short time, unlike projects of longer duration.

Sample Scenarios – Capability Level 5

Scenario 1

The assessor finds that the current status of the project reflects the project plan(s). All base practices are fulfilled and there is evidence (including input and output work products) that meets the scope of the process and produces the desired process outcomes within the project constraints and meeting the organizations' business goals. The project participants are aware of who is responsible for each activity.

The scenario itself does not provide any hint that it is achieving Capability Level 5. The assessor needs to assess the organizational activities associated with process change (PA 5.1) and continuous improvement (PA 5.2), as noted above it is most likely these activities are institutional (organization processes) and not in the project management process itself.

The assessor should determine what process innovations and changes have been performed of the standard project management process.

Have these improvements and changes been based upon the criteria, mechanisms and activities associated with PA 5.1 and PA 5.2, as described in the general interpretation section above? Does the project management process historical evidence show that improvements and changes have improved the organization's ability to manage projects and achieve business goals? If the answer to all these issues is positive, the process should be rated as **Fully achieving Capability Level 5**.

SW CMM and CMMI

SW CMM® and CMMI®

In this chapter, I describe some of the most important features of the Software Engineering Institute Capability Maturity Models because they are popular Process Assessment Models. I also compare them to ISO/IEC 15504. This chapter will be of interest to anyone wishing to decide which assessment model and method to choose, particularly quality professionals.

The Software Engineering Institute has developed maturity models for software development since 1989, based upon the needs of the United States Department of Defence. The first major published model was the Capability Maturity Model for Software (SW CMM®).

The Software Engineering Institute has researched the relationship between capability, process performance and maturity and provides the following definitions in the SW CMM® V1.1 [49].

Software process capability describes the range of **expected** results that can be achieved by following a software process. The software process capability of an organization provides one means of predicting the most likely outcomes to be expected from the next software project the organization undertakes.

Software process performance represents the **actual** results achieved by following a software process. Thus, software process performance focuses on the results achieved, while software process capability focuses on results expected. Based on the attributes of a specific project and the context within which it is conducted, the actual performance of the project may not reflect the full process capability of the organization; i.e., the capability of the project is constrained by its environment.

Software process maturity is the extent to which a specific process is explicitly defined, managed, measured, controlled, and effective.

Note: In the CMMI® this has been replaced by a definition for organisational maturity.

In the same introduction, the Software Engineering Institute states that it defined the staged structure of the SW CMM® based on principles of product quality that have been formulated over the last sixty years, and based in part upon the work of Walter Shewart (principles of statistical quality control), W. Edwards Deming and Joseph Juran. The Software Engineering Institute adopted the principles into a maturity framework that establishes a project management and engineering foundation for quantitative control of the software process, which is the basis for continuous process improvement.

This staged representation for implementation of processes has specific processes needed to achieve a particular maturity level.

Table 15. SW CMM® Maturity Levels and Processes.

Maturity		Processes – additional processes per maturity level
Maturity Level 1	Initial	no processes, chaos
Maturity Level 2	Managed	Requirements Management, Software Project Planning, Software Project Tracking and Oversight, Software Subcontract Management, Software Quality Assurance, Software Configuration Management.
Maturity Level 3	Defined	Organizational Process Focus, Organizational Process Definition, Training Program, Integrated Software Management, Software Product Engineering, Intercrop Coordination. Peer Reviews
Maturity Level 4	Quantitatively Managed	Process Measurement and Analysis, Quality Management
Maturity Level 5	Optimising	Defect Prevention, Technology Innovation, Process Change Management

The staged representation was a model that software organizations found easy to understand due to the explicit processes to be deployed at each maturity level. Many organizations in North America and India (and to a much lesser extent in Europe and Asia) have adopted SW CMM® V1.1[56] as their preferred assessment framework and their preferred process deployment approach.

---

[56] The Software Engineering Institute released a draft version 2 of the SW CMM® in 1997. It proposed new processes/practices and revisions to existing processes/practices with greater coverage of ISO/IEC 15504 processes. However due to the nature of changes in the model, the USAF sponsor's desire to integrate various CMMs and achieve conformance to ISO/IEC 15504 it was decided not to adopt it. Hence SW CMM® V1.1 is still in use. There is planning in the SEI to retire the SW CMM® with a target date by the end of 2005, so users will need to consider migrating to CMMI® or ISO/IEC 15504.

The model reflects its original client and industrial organizations; covering large and/or complex software projects in organizations delivering mission critical systems (initially for military purposes). It is by nature prescriptive in terms of assessing the staging of process implementation.

An advantage of a SW CMM® assessment is that it gives a single Maturity Level (ML) for the assessed organization. The result can be expressed as a single number and this is attractive to clients and organizations, who do not wish to investigate in detail the meaning of the result (for example, to which domains it applies).

Due to the staged nature of process deployment, it is restrictive in terms of adaptability/flexibility; an organization cannot decide to adopt processes in a different order to that described in the model without ramifications on the assessed maturity level. While it does suit many organizations to use this staged approach, they need to be aware that it is not conformant to the international standard ISO/IEC 15504, which has ramifications on comparability of assessment results with other assessment methods.

The Software Engineering Institute had in parallel to the later development of the SW CMM®, also developed a System Engineering CMM®, an Integrated Product Development CMM® and a Software Acquisition CMM®. It became apparent that there were inconsistencies, overlaps and duplications between the models. They made a decision that the most important aspects of these models should be integrated. This decision resulted in creation of the Capability Maturity Model Integration (CMMI®) [50] which has been developed in several variants (the Systems Engineering, Software Engineering, and Integrated Product and Process Development variant is referred to here as it is the most comprehensive variant).

Capability Maturity Model Integrated

The CMMI®[57] was conceived to both comply with the emerging ISO/IEC 15504 standard and also as a staged representation, thereby maintaining representational consistency with SW CMM®. The staged representation of CMMI® can be shown in a simplified form as maturity levels that indicate Process Areas (the set of processes in the table below).

---

[57] CMMI and CMMI® are used interchangeably in this book. Both forms acknowledge that CMMI® is a registered trade mark of the SEI[SM].

Table 16. CMMI® Maturity Levels and processes.

Maturity		CMMI Processes – additional processes per maturity level
Maturity Level 1	Initial	No processes
Maturity Level 2	Managed	Requirements Management, Measurement and Analysis Project Monitoring and Control Project Planning Process and Product Quality Assurance Supplier Agreement Management, Configuration Management
Maturity Level 3	Defined	Decision Analysis and Resolution, Product Integration Requirements Development Technical Solution Verification Validation, Organizational Process Focus, Organizational Process definition, Integrated Project Management, Risk management, Organizational training
Maturity Level 4	Quantitatively Managed	Organizational Process Performance Quantitative Project management
Maturity Level 5	Optimising	Organizational Innovation and Deployment Causal Analysis and resolution

Source: Software Quality Institute. CMMI Evaluation. Capability Maturity Model Integration Mapping to ISO/IEC TR 15504-2:1998

It is apparent that the processes in the CMMI are different to those in the SW CMM®. The system engineering aspects are the major source of additional processes, but there are also additional advanced support and organizational processes. The United States Air Force Software Technology Support Center has prepared a mapping between the SW CMM® V1.1 and the CMMI® [V0.2]. I will not focus on the mapping here but provide the reference [51] for those interested in further research.

While developing the CMMI, the Software Engineering Institute has been involved in the development of ISO/IEC 15504 and therefore has also created a continuous representation of CMMI. This representation is still structurally different to the Process Assessment Model in ISO/IEC 15504-5 but is intended to be mapped to a conformant Process Reference Model. In version 1.2 the CMMI model is further aligned to the ISO/IEC 15504 process reference model requirements and terminology.

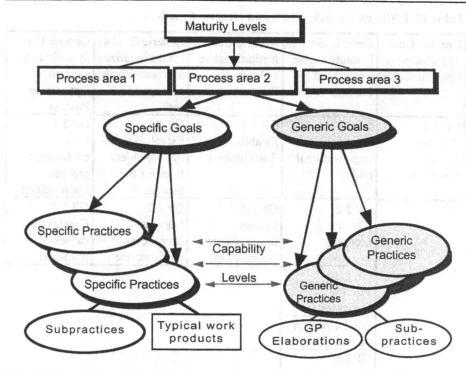

Fig. 52. Continuous representation of CMMI.

Each Process Area has Specific Goals achieved by Specific Practices, and Generic Goals that are achieved by Generic Practices. The Generic Goals can be summarized as:

- Achieve Specific Goals
- Institutionalize a Managed Process
- Institutionalize a Defined Process
- Institutionalize a Quantitatively Managed Process
- Institutionalize an Optimizing Process.

For the five generic goals, there are seventeen generic practices. Generic Goal 2 has ten of the fifteen practices.

Table 17. CMMI® Generic Goals and Generic Practices

Generic Goal 1: Achieve Specific Goals	Generic Goal 2: Institutionalize a Managed Process	Generic Goal 3: Institutionalize a Defined Process	Generic Goal 4: Institutionalize a Quantitatively Managed Process	Generic Goal 5: Institutionalize an Optimizing Process
GP 1.1 Perform specific practices	GP 2.1 Establish an organizational policy	GP 3.1 Establish a defined process	GP 4.1 Establish quantitative objectives for the process	GP 5.1 Ensure continuous process improvement
	GP 2.2 Plan the process	GP 3.2 Collect improvement information	GP 4.2 Stabilize subprocess performance	GP 5.2 Correct root causes of problems
	GP 2.3 Provide resources			
	GP 2.4 Assign responsibility			
	GP 2.5 Train people			
	GP 2.6 Manage configurations			
	GP 2.7 Identify and involve relevant stakeholders			
	GP 2.8 Monitor and control the process			
	GP 2.9 Objectively evaluate adherence			
	GP 2.10 Review status with higher level management			

The SEI compares the advantages of the continuous and staged representations. The following tables summarises these (including my notes).

Table 18. CMMI Continuous and Staged Models.

Continuous Representation	Staged Representation
Freedom to select the order of improvement that best meets the organizations business objectives and mitigates the organizations areas of risk. (Note there are no explicit risk analyses and relationships in the model.)	Provides a pre-defined and proven improvement path. (Note the model assumes a 'heavy' process orientation which is generally unsuited to agile methods or knowledge centric approaches.)
Enables increased visibility of the capability achieved in each individual process area. (Note it does not exclude the ability to focus on sets of processes.)	Focuses on a set of processes that provide an organization with a specific capability characterized by each maturity level. (Note that the process set may not suit each organization.)
Allows improvements of different processes to be performed at different rates. (Note this allows critical business processes that have a management multiplier quality effect to be improved faster.)	Summarizes process improvement results in a simple form – a single maturity level number. (Note that Mark Paulk advises not to focus on the maturity level, rather on the value of the improvements).
Reflects a newer approach that does not yet have the data to demonstrate its ties to return on investment. (Note that the SEI does not believe there is no return on investment, only that the data does not yet exist in the SEI. Also note that limited data exists from the SPICE trials.)	Builds on a relatively long history of use that includes case studies and data that demonstrate return on investment. (Note the SEI publishes this data on their web site regularly.)

For organizations that wish to pursue a risk oriented approach to improvement, they should look at the author's work as described in the Process Assessment and Improvement book [5]. A risk oriented approach means that process improvement is based upon a risk analysis of the enterprise. This approach means that not only are problems reduced (as in typical process improvement using CMMI) but also risks are explicitly reduced.

Version 1.2 of the CMMI, has integrated the designated System Engineering and Software Engineering representations. It is now called CMMI for Development. The Integrated Product and Process Development (IPPD) practices were also consolidated and simplified. There are no longer any separate IPPD process areas. The SEI uses the term constellation to define two variants of the CMMI, one with IPPD and one without. Hence you may choose to use the IPPD practices (or not by ignoring all practices marked as IPPD). Other changes include:

- Supplier Agreement Management (SAM) and Integrated Supplier Management (ISM) were consolidated and Supplier Sourcing was removed (Staged representation).
- The advanced practice and common feature concepts have been removed.
- Hardware amplifications were added.
- Generic practice (GP) elaborations were added to the level 3 GPs.
- An explanation of how process areas support the implementation of GPs was added.
- Material was added to ensure that standard processes are deployed to projects at their start-up.

One personally interesting addition to the CMMI is on page 4 of the introduction where the new Figure 1.1 titled 'The Three Critical Dimensions' reflects my People-Process-Product model and the inclusion of Cultural factors in improvement. See the Process Assessment and Improvement book for more on both the model and the cultural factors in improvement [5].

Scope of CMMI compared to ISO/IEC 15504

The first important aspect when comparing the scope of CMMI® and ISO/IEC 15504 is that the technical solution processes in the CMMI® cover both Systems Engineering and Software Engineering. This broader scope of the CMMI® is an important reason for large system integrators and acquirers to consider using it. If ISO/IEC 15504 uses ISO/IEC 15288 and ISO/IEC 12207 to create a composite process dimension, then a similar (but not the same) scope covering systems and software engineering is possible.

CMMI® Continuous Representation Model Process Dimension

The CMMI® Continuous Representation Model is the simpler representation to compare to ISO/IEC 15504. In this representation, there are four major process categories as shown in the following table.

Table 19. CMMI® continuous representation model process areas.

Category	Process Area
Process Management	Organizational Process Focus Organizational Process Definition Organizational Training Organizational Process Performance Organizational Innovation and Deployment
Project Management	Project Planning Project Monitoring and Control Supplier Agreement Monitoring Integrated Project management Integrated Teaming Risk Management Quantitative Project management
Engineering	Requirements Management Requirements Development Technical Solution Product Integration Verification Validation
Support	Configuration Management Process and Product Quality Assurance Measurement and Analysis Causal Analysis and Resolution Decision Analysis and Resolution Organizational Environment for Integration

CMMI as defined in the Continuous Representation Model has some differences to the process dimension of ISO/IEC 15504-5. The CMMI technical solution processes can be mapped in part against ISO/IEC 15288 as a Systems Engineering Process Reference Model. CMMI addresses all of the processes of ISO/IEC 15504 Process Reference Model, with the exception of the processes specifically identified below.

- OPE.1 - Operation Process
- MAN.2 - Management Process
- MAN.1 - Organizational Alignment Process

The following processes are not completely addressed in the CMMI:

- SPL.2 - Supply Process
- ENG.12 - Software Maintenance Process
- RIN.1 - Human Resource Management Process
- REU.2 - Reuse Programme Management

In addition, CMMI® does not have a Customer-Supplier process category but contains the Customer - Supplier processes and sub-processes in the Engineering and Project Management Process Areas. Establish Supplier Agreements and Satisfy Supplier Agreements in the Project Management Area partially cover the Acquisition Process and the Supply Process in

ISO/IEC 15504. Manage Requirements in the Engineering Process Area provides equivalent coverage to Requirements Elicitation in ISO/IEC 15504. The CMMI® uses a cyclic model for the Engineering processes, while ISO/IEC 15504 does not specify (either may be valid).

CMMI ^{Continuous} Representation Model Capability Dimension

In CMMI® the capability dimension is represented by the Generic Practices, plus some process areas.

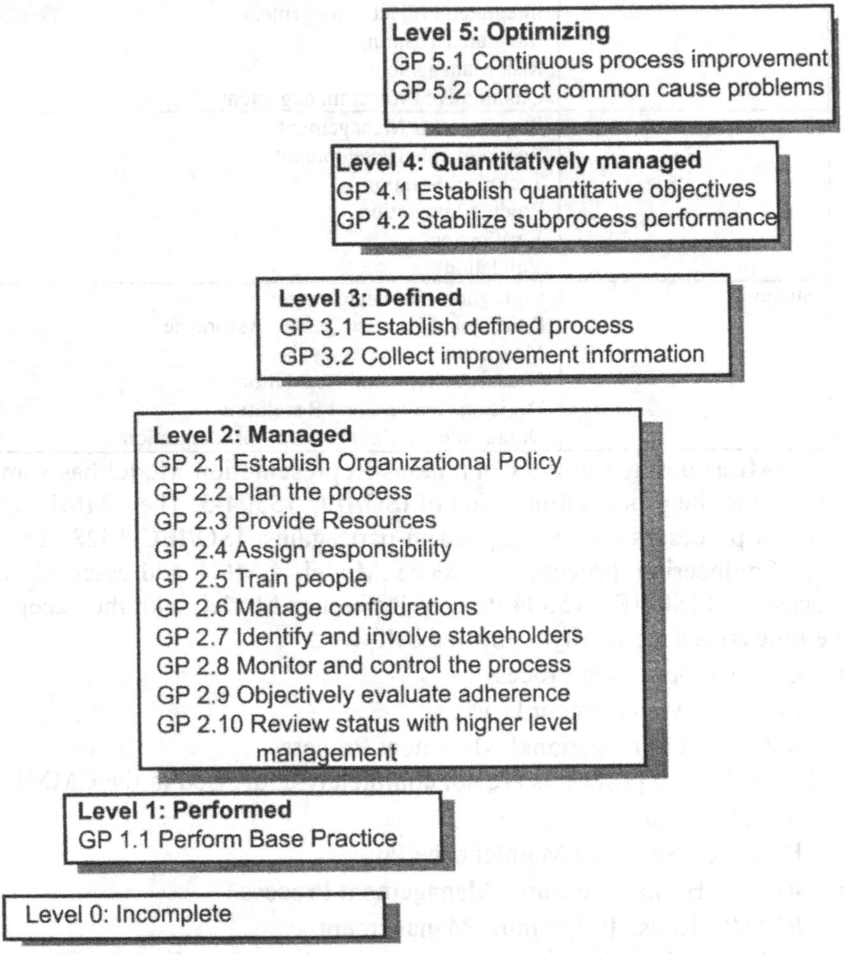

Level 5: Optimizing
GP 5.1 Continuous process improvement
GP 5.2 Correct common cause problems

Level 4: Quantitatively managed
GP 4.1 Establish quantitative objectives
GP 4.2 Stabilize subprocess performance

Level 3: Defined
GP 3.1 Establish defined process
GP 3.2 Collect improvement information

Level 2: Managed
GP 2.1 Establish Organizational Policy
GP 2.2 Plan the process
GP 2.3 Provide Resources
GP 2.4 Assign responsibility
GP 2.5 Train people
GP 2.6 Manage configurations
GP 2.7 Identify and involve stakeholders
GP 2.8 Monitor and control the process
GP 2.9 Objectively evaluate adherence
GP 2.10 Review status with higher level
         management

Level 1: Performed
GP 1.1 Perform Base Practice

Level 0: Incomplete

Fig. 53. CMMI® Capability Dimension.

The Generic Practices in CMMI do not fully cover all of the Process Attributes in ISO/IEC 15504. As stated in the SQI report: Two of the process attributes of the Capability Dimension of ISO 15504-2 are not addressed in any of the Generic Practices of the CMMI Continuous Model. These are PA3.2 - Process Resource Attribute, and PA5.1 - Process Change Attribute. However the SQI mapping shows that these two process attributes are addressed in process areas of the CMMI so that coverage of all attributes is achieved.

Process attribute PA 3.2 is addressed in Organizational Process Focus, Organizational Process Deployment, and Organizational Training and Integrated Project Management process areas. This means that any assessment to cover ISO/IEC 15504 Capability Level 3 would require these process areas to be in the assessment scope in order to be able to translate the results.

Process attribute PA 5.1 is addressed in Organizational Innovation and Deployment and Causal Analysis and Resolution. This means that any assessment to cover ISO/IEC 15504 Capability Level 5 would require these process areas to be in the assessment scope in order to be able to translate the results. On the other hand, most of the Work Product Management aspects in Process Attribute PA 2.2 are not explicitly addressed in the CMMI.

The need to assess process areas in order to obtain Capability Level ratings is a possible disincentive to use the continuous representation. The increase in assessment scope also works against making narrower scope assessments of other process areas if wishing to determine higher Capability Levels for those processes.

While I am unaware of organizations using CMMI and translating the results into ISO/IEC 15504 Capability Levels (rather than using the staged model maturity levels), this may not remain an academic concern as ISO/IEC 15504 gains wider acceptance.

CMMI areas outside the scope of ISO/IEC TR 15504-2

Some elements in the CMMI Continuous Representation - the whole of the Decision Analysis and Resolution process area and parts of the Technical Solution process area (particularly systems engineering aspects) are outside the scope of the earlier technical report version of ISO/IEC 15504-2. The technical solution processes can be mapped in part against ISO/IEC 15288 as a Systems Engineering Process Reference Model and is now covered in the proposed Part 6 of ISO/IEC 15504.

There is no precise or simple one-to-one mapping between CMMI and ISO/IEC 15504, the assessor needs to take care when translating the results of a CMMI conformant assessment to the standard. Some processes, for example SUP.1 - Documentation Process and ORG.4 - Infrastructure Process, are addressed rather generally in CMMI® over a wide range of process areas. It is probable in an assessment that insufficient data would be collected to permit rating of these processes using any feasible translation mechanism. There is work being performed to address this in a proposed new Part 8 of the ISO/IEC 15504 standard covering maturity level assessments.

In some process areas, especially for Requirements Management and Integrated Project Management, the mapping (even at the sub-practice level) is to a wide range of process outcomes. This will lead to significant problems in attempting to use observations recorded in these process areas in any translation. It also implies that the definition of these process areas is inadequately detailed; for example, Requirements Management has only one Specific Goal and four Specific Practices.

In version 1.1 of the CMMI there were concerns relating to the use of advanced practices in the CMMI Continuous Model. However the SEI has now removed these advanced practices from the CMMI.

CMMI Staged Representation Model

The primary difficulty in mapping the CMMI® Staged Representation Model is in relation to the Capability Dimension as only Level 2 and Level 3 Generic Practices are explicitly identified, and these are established within each Process Area, rather than being seen as common capabilities across all areas. In undertaking this mapping, therefore, the mapping to the Generic Practices previously established was taken, and in each process area the relevant Process Attributes were seen as applying to the cited Processes. In describing this coverage, the following guidelines were adopted:

- If all outcomes of a Process are addressed in the Basic Practices of the Process Area, the attributes derived from the relevant Generic Practices are seen as applying *completely* to that Process.
- If more than one outcome of a Process is addressed, the attributes derived from the relevant Generic Practices are seen as applying *partially* to that Process.
- If only a single outcome of a Process is addressed, the attributes derived from the relevant Generic Practices are regarded as applying *slightly* to that Process.

Within a single Process Area, therefore, the Performance Management, Work Product Management and Process Definition process attributes (for Process Areas at Level 3 and higher) can be seen as applying to different extents to different Processes in the Reference Model.

Table 20. CMMI® Staged Representation and ISO/IEC 15504.

Maturity		CMMI Processes – additional processes per maturity level	ISO/IEC 15504 mapped processes
Maturity Level 1	Initial	No processes	No direct equivalent
Maturity Level 2	Managed	Requirements Management, Measurement and Analysis, Project Monitoring and Control, Project Planning, Process and Product Quality Assurance, Supplier Agreement Management, Configuration Management	Supplier Selection Process, Supplier Monitoring Process, Customer Acceptance Process, Documentation Process, Configuration Management Process, Quality Assurance Process, Joint Review Process, Audit Process, Problem Resolution Process, Project Management Process, Measurement Process
Maturity Level 3	Defined	Decision Analysis and Resolution, Product Integration, Requirements Development, Technical Solution, Verification, Validation, Organizational Process Focus, Organizational Process definition, Integrated Project Management, Risk management, Organizational training, Integrated Teaming, Organizational Environment for Integration	Requirements Elicitation Process, System requirements analysis and design process, Software requirements analysis process, Software design process, Software construction process, Software integration process, Software testing process, System integration and testing process, Verification Process, Validation Process, Risk Management, Process establishment process, Process assessment process,
Maturity Level 4	Quantitatively Managed	Organizational Process Performance, Quantitative Project management	Quality Management, Infrastructure Process.
Maturity Level 5	Optimising	Organizational Innovation and Deployment, Causal Analysis and resolution	Process Improvement process

In terms of the scope of the model, it is clear that the process dimension of the CMMI Continuous Representation Model covers the same scope as does the Staged Representation.

The SEI provides information comparing continuous representation capability levels and maturity levels. This is based on the work of the SQI. The following table shows equivalent staging as a sequence of target profiles, each of which is equivalent to a maturity level rating of the staged representation. The result is a target staging that is equivalent to the maturity levels of the staged representation. The table shows a summary of the target profiles that must be achieved when using the continuous representation to be equivalent to maturity levels 2 through 5. Each shaded area in the capability level columns represents a target profile that is equivalent to a maturity level.

Table 21. Comparison of Capability and Maturity Levels.

Name	ML	CL1	CL2	CL3	CL4	CL5
Requirements Management	2					
Project Planning	2	Target Profile 2				
Project Monitoring and Control	2					
Supplier Agreement Management	2					
Measurement and Analysis	2					
Process and Product Quality Assurance	2					
Configuration Management	2					
Requirements Development	3					
Technical Solution	3					
Product Integration	3					
Verification	3					
Validation	3		Target Profile 3			
Organizational Process Focus	3					
Organizational Process Definition +IPPD	3					
Organizational Training	3					
Integrated Project Management +IPPD	3					
Risk Management	3					
Decision Analysis and Resolution	3					
Organizational Process Performance	4					
Quantitative Project Management	4		Target Profile 4			
Organizational Innovation and Deployment	5					
Causal Analysis and Resolution	5		Target Profile 5			

The following rules summarize equivalent staging:
- **To achieve maturity level 2, all process areas assigned to maturity level 2 must achieve capability level 2 or higher.**

- To achieve maturity level 3, all process areas assigned to maturity levels 2 and 3 must achieve capability level 3 or higher.
- To achieve maturity level 4, all process areas assigned to maturity levels 2, 3, and 4 must achieve capability level 3 or higher.
- To achieve maturity level 5, all process areas must achieve capability level 3 or higher.

These rules and the table for equivalent staging are complete. Note that target profiles 4 and 5 do not extend into the CL 4 and CL 5 columns. The reason is that the maturity level 4 process areas describe a selection of the subprocesses to be stabilized based, in part, on the quality and process-performance objectives of the organization and projects. Not every process area will be addressed in the selection and CMMI does not presume in advance which process areas might be addressed in the selection.

So, the achievement of capability level 4 for process areas cannot be predetermined because the choices depend on the selections made by the organization in its implementation of the maturity level 4 process areas. Thus the table does not show target profile 4 extending into the CL 4 column, although some process areas will have achieved capability level 4. The situation for maturity level 5 and target profile 5 is similar.

CMMI Assessments

There are three defined classes of CMMI assessments. The SEI document Appraisal Requirements for CMMI [52] provides the details, that are summarised here.

Class A assessments are required in order to derive Maturity levels for an organization, while Class B and Class C are less rigorous and can provide a less time consuming alternative when Maturity levels are not required. SCAMPI (Standard CMMI Appraisal Method for Process Improvement) meets the class A requirements.

The need to be able to achieve translation to ISO/IEC 15504 Process Profiles is only required for Class A methods, and the SEI document specifies some additional requirements to meet this need.

The following table provides a high level summary of the appraisal classes.

Table 22. Classes of Appraisal Methods.

Characteristics	Class A	Class B	Class C
Usage mode	1. Rigorous and in-depth investigation of process(es) 2. Basis for improvement plan	1. Initial (first-time) 2. Incremental (partial) 3. Self-assessment	1. Quick-look 2. Incremental
Principal Outcomes	1. Findings adequate as a basis for process improvement activities 2. Buy-in and ownership of results 3. CMMI measurement framework rating(s) to characterize assessment scope	1. Findings adequate as a basis for process improvement program 2. Buy-in and ownership of results.	1. Findings adequate to expose gaps in implementation of processes
Advantages	Thorough coverage; strengths and weaknesses for each PA investigated; robustness of method with consistent, repeatable results; provides objective view; option of 15504 conformance.	Organization gains insight into own capability; provides a starting point or focuses on areas that need most attention; promotes buy-in.	Inexpensive; short duration; rapid feedback.
Disadvantages	Demands significant resources.	Does not emphasize depth of coverage and rigor and cannot be used for level rating.	1. Provides less buy-in and ownership of results. 2. Not enough depth to fine-tune process improvement plans.
Sponsor	Senior manager of organizational unit.	Any manager sponsoring an SPI program.	Any internal manager.
Team composition	External and internal.	External or internal	External or internal.
Team size	4-10 persons + assessment team leader.	1-6 + assessment team leader.	1-2 + assessment team leader.
Team qualifications	Experienced.	Moderately experienced.	Moderately experienced.
Assessment team leader requirements	Lead assessor.	Lead assessor or person experienced in method.	Person trained in method.

Source: The Software Quality Institute CMMI Evaluation report. See Table 1 and Appendix A of the SEI document: Appraisal Requirements for CMMI for the details used to create this table.

Advantages and Disadvantages

CMMI is about 560 pages and the Standard CMMI Appraisal Method for Process Improvement (SCAMPI^{SM}) is 245 pages long. CMMI provides a much greater level of detail for the processes (except for the primary engineering software development processes). It describes sub-practices, which are actually implementation hints under the specific practices. CMMI defines typical work products on the level of specific practices and these are not always consistent with the same or similar work products in other practices. It also shows the typical relationship between process areas.

CMMI Staged Representation Model suits larger process-centric organizations, but often does not suit smaller organizations. It is also requires more effort with organizations that allow high project independence in terms of process implementation (this is because when assessing the maturity level, the organization as a whole needs to be assessed and if it has wide variations in project implementations, then it requires more project assessments).

CMMI assessments use a procedure described in SCAMPI based upon findings, observations and evidence to determine a maturity level. This is more complicated (requires more judgment) than the Capability Level rating mechanism in ISO/IEC 15504. A Class A (e.g. SCAMPI) assessment requires extensive and time consuming participation of a wide section of an organization. Generally certified Lead Assessors do not provide a maturity level report unless a Class A assessment is performed. Type B and Type C assessments require less time and effort but do not provide a maturity level rating. The CMMI Lead Assessor is totally responsible for the assessment result, even though the assessment team makes a collective judgment on each item in the assessment.

A formal CMMI certification of an organization's maturity level does not exist.

When an assessor submits an assessment result to the CMMI Steward, the steward only registers the assessment and does not certify that the Lead Assessor has correctly assessed the maturity level of the organization.

The SW CMM introduced the Software Engineering Process Group (SEPG) and this has further been developed into Software Process Improvement Networks (SPINs) spanning multiple organizations using both SW CMM and CMMI. While Software Engineering Process Groups are not the only improvement team approach (and not always the best, especially when organizational improvement are needed), they have proven to be useful when supported by senior management in process oriented organizations. Readers are advised to read the chapters on process improvement in the Process Assessment and Improvement book [5].

CMMI maintains a benchmarking database: Process Appraisal Information System, which has collected data on 1900 assessments since 1989. The analysis provided is at organizational level not process level, which is interesting for managers, but not useful for selecting process improvement projects.

ISO/IEC 15504 is about 300 pages long. With the latest revision, the standard itself (part 2) is much shorter and applicable to all process oriented standards, but readers may have to refer to Process Reference Models from these other standards such as ISO/IEC 12207 or ISO/IEC 15288. The new part 5 is about 200 pages long and the new Part 6 will be of somewhat shorter length.

ISO/IEC 15504-5 specifies work products in a generic manner so that they are consistently defined, but sometimes are too generic to be used without further knowledge or assistance. A similar issue exists with part 6.

ISO/IEC 15504 assessments are generally less time consuming than a Class A CMMI assessment and assessors are better able to maintain the expected schedule. An ISO/IEC 15504-2 assessment is possible for the entire organization, for a single project or organizational unit or even a single process while still being able to provide a Capability Level result. Class A CMMI assessments are always across the organization (cannot be tailored down).

The rating mechanism for determining Capability Levels uses a defined method partly based on simple mathematics, and partly based on the judgment of the assessors (each practice indicator may require assessor judgment but the summation of practice indicators is mathematical). This rating method is easier to use than that in SCAMPI.

ISO/IEC 15504-2 specifies a Competent Assessor for a conformant assessment, but in the case that a team makes collective judgment on the assessment result; the Competent Assessor can state this in the report. The assessment team or Competent Assessor can decide upon the how the assessment rating is made (individual, team, voting, consensus) involving the sponsor if desired.

ISO/IEC 15504-2 provides for multiple process reference and assessment models, while CMMI specifies their own specific assessment model. ISO/IEC 15504-2 is therefore more flexible and can be tailored to suit particular industry and business needs.

SW CMM and CMMI have built up a solid following in some countries, particularly USA and India. When the business needs match these models, they are viable assessment models to adopt.

On the other hand, the flexibility of ISO/IEC 15504 both in terms of process coverage and assessment scope, plus its adaptability to specific industries is a strong advantage of the standard. The ability to perform assessments ranging in scope from one process in one project (or organizational unit) to a complete organization-wide assessment means it is possible to perform very quick to very comprehensive assessments. In addition, as is described in the practical guide, the ability to use the capability scale independently of the process dimension to design higher capability business processes provides a powerful business advantage. The adoption of ISO/IEC 15504 is growing steadily as more industries realize these benefits.

For organizations looking for a general process assessment and improvement approach, either model is acceptable, but my preference would be to use ISO/IEC 15504 because of its assessment flexibility and the power of having various process reference models.

A Short History and Harmonization

Annex 1: ISO/IEC 15504 A Short History and Harmonization

The development of process assessment illustrates the improvement in understanding and application of process assessment for business purposes. Some key milestones in this development include:

- Research into process assessment techniques in IBM in the late 1970s early 1980s, including Ron Radice's Programming Process Study.
- The first publicly available process assessment method in 1987 [53].
- The start of the SPICE project in 1993 (which developed the early drafts of ISO/IEC 15504)
- The handover to an international standards working group of ISO/IEC DTR 15504 (Draft Technical Report) in 1997.
- The change from a software process assessment standard to a process assessment standard applicable to any process, in 2002.
- Ratification of the new international standard ISO/IEC 15504-2 in 2003.

The United States Department of Defence sponsored the Software Engineering Institute at Carnegie Mellon University to produce a process assessment standard for use in assessing Defence contractors. A preliminary version of the technical report was produced in 1987 [54]. This led to the production of the Software Capability Maturity Model. The Software Engineering Institute released the SW CMM V1.0 in 1991 [55].

From 1982, Bell were involved in process assessment methods (Bellcore Process maturity audit), and Bell Canada with Northern Telecom were investigating creation of process assessment standards to assess their major suppliers, eventually to release in 1991 the first version of Trillium [56]. In Europe there was a research group sponsored by the European Union that created the Bootstrap assessment methodology [57] in 1993-4.

In 1992, the United Kingdom Ministry of Defence through the Defence Research Agency sponsored a study called Improve-IT [58]. Based on study work, the British Standards Institution (BSI) proposed to that software process assessment be considered as an area for standardization and that the international community pool its resources to develop a standard for software process assessment, including the best features of existing software assessment methods [59]. The BSI suggested that a three part approach be used:

- A study period would be undertaken.
- Development of a draft international standard (Technical Report Type 2).
- Registration as a full international standard.

The ISO/IEC JTC1/SC7 WG10[58] study group met throughout 1992 and 1993 to specify the requirements for a common, international standard [60]. The new standard should be a software process assessment standard that provided both capability determination and a basis for process improvement, harmonize existing efforts, be flexible, consistent and reliable, yet be simple to use and understand. These requirements became the basis for starting the SPICE[59] project, which should then rapidly produce the software process assessment standard.

The SPICE project was administered by Alec Dorling with the project editor being Terry Rout of the Software Quality Institute, Brisbane, Australia. It began in 1993 and up until 1995 produced a series of draft documents to address the following requirements:

- Process assessments should be a basis for both process improvement and capability determination.
- It should be flexible with regard to applications, sectors, size, projects and organizations.
- Its coverage should encompass process, people and technology (products).
- Its outputs should be shown as profiles (process and capability).
- It should support existing standards such as ISO 9000 and ISO/IEC 12207.
- It should provide reliable and consistent assessment results.
- It should be simple to use and understand.
- It should be objective and provide quantitative results wherever possible.
- It should not be presumptive of specific organization structures, management philosophies, lifecycle models, technologies or development methods.

---

[58] ISO/IEC – International Standards Organization / International Electrotechnical Committee

[59] SPICE originally stood for Software Process Improvement and Capability Evaluation but due to French translation issues was changed to become Software Process Improvement and Capability dEtermination.

These requirements formed a basis for the conformance requirements of the standard (chapter 3) specifically in relation to the Process Reference Models, Process Assessment Models and the Capability dimension.

In addition to preparing documentation, the project also sponsored trials of the developing SPICE Process Assessment Model. The first phase trial occurred in 1995.

In 1995, the study group decided that an evolutionary approach would be taken to harmonize the software process assessment standard and ISO/IEC 12207 [61]. In addition, a reference model would replace the definitive process model, process descriptions would be restricted to more general statements of purpose, the capability dimension would become 'Process Capability Attributes' and there would be a section on conformance of process models. This was documented in the Kwa Maritime Agreement [62].

After the documentation was revised, the second phase trials occurred in 1996-1997, in which the author participated. At the conclusion of the second phase trials and inclusion of changes from the trials participants, the preliminary draft technical report was balloted. This consisted of nine parts [63] and was for a Software Process Assessment standard.

From 1997 to 2003, primary responsibility for the work was passed back to the joint ISO/IEC JTC1/SC7 WG10 working group. This group is responsible for the standardization process. This included a focus on the relationship to other standards and also transforming the draft and preliminary technical reports into what is now known as ISO/IEC 15504.

The five part document set of the standard was completed in 2005 (part 5 being the last part to be completed). Part 6 is due to approved by 2007.

General Process Assessment standard
Because of harmonization with other standards (specifically ISO/IEC 12207, ISO/IEC 15288 and ISO 9000), ISO/IEC 15504 has become a general Process Assessment standard, and not just a Software Process Assessment standard.

It no longer specifies a single Process Reference Model, but specifies requirements for Process Reference Models. This allows the organization to select the most suitable existing model or create a model to suit their particular needs.

ISO/IEC 15504's development has been a worldwide collaborative effort, with input from twenty countries and many organizations from each country that are involved in the software and Information Technology industries, standards setting bodies, consultants and firms using and trying it within their own business.

Standards Development in ISO

The International Organization for Standardization (ISO) is a worldwide federation of national standards bodies from some 100 countries, one from each participating country. ISO's work results in international agreements, which are published as International Standards. ISO consists of many study and working groups.

Initially it was decided to create a Software Process Assessment standard, and it would be carried out under the auspices of a joint technical committee of the International Standardization Organization and the International Electrotechnical Commission. ISO/IEC JTC1 is the joint ISO and IEC technical committee, which deals with information technology. In 1993, this joint technical committee approved a new work item proposal, thus establishing working group WG10.

An early decision was made to pursue full standardization by first producing an International Organization for Standardization/International Electrotechnical Commission (ISO/IEC) Type 2 Technical Report (TR), and then converting it to a full international standard. As the subject of process assessment was still under technical development and there was the possibility of major changes subject to further agreement, the publication of a Type 2 Technical Report was deemed (by JTC1) to be more appropriate (than an International Standard).

The successive stages of the technical work for a Type 2 Technical Report were:

- Stage 1 (proposal stage): A New Work Item Proposal was under consideration (1993).
- Stage 2 (preparatory stage): A Working Draft was under consideration (1993-1995).
- Stage 3 (committee stage): A Proposed Draft Technical Report (PDTR) was under consideration (1995-1996).
- Stage 4 (approval stage): A Draft Technical Report (DTR) was under consideration (1996-1997).
- Stage 5 (publication stage): A Technical Report (TR) was prepared for publication (1998).

Note: the reader will see reference to ISO/IEC TR 15504 throughout this book as some parts of the standard are from a Technical Report that are still current. The decision to publish a Technical Report was taken by JTC1 1 ballot on the Draft Technical Report in 1998.

Once the ISO/IEC TR 15504 document set was published, SC7 made a recommendation to JTC1 1, stating whether the Technical Report should be revised and published as an International Standard. This revision has in fact been a major change from a 9 part standard in 1998 Technical Report focused on Software Process Assessment to a 5 part International Standard focused on Process Assessment in 2005 and a 6 part standard in 2007.

This major change was due to the harmonization work occurring between the ISO/IEC JTC1 working groups responsible for ISO/IEC 15504, ISO/IEC 12207, ISO/IEC 15288 and ISO 9000.

The result is that the ISO/IEC 15504 was balloted in 2003 as an International Standard for Process Assessment and part 5 in 2005. Due to the changes made in the past two years, it is now possible to use the standard with a wider variety of Process Assessment Models, covering the entire organizational process spectrum.

Note: a normative part of a standard is the formal part of the standard that must be complied with (i.e. it is mandatory), while an informative part of a standard is for information purposes or guidance and compliance is optional or voluntary.

ISO/IEC 15504-2 is a normative part of the standard, while ISO/IEC 15504-5 is an informative part. When the reader looks at the standard, they should determine which version they have (for example, the Technical Report version).

Some of the ISO/IEC TR 15504 (Technical Report) informative parts are highly useful and form part of many implementations of the standard. Reference is made to these parts as they provide very useful guidance. The main Technical Report parts of general interest are:

ISO/IEC TR 15504-7 – the process improvement part.

ISO/IEC TR 15504-8 – the capability determination part.

Glossary

Annex 3: Glossary of Acronyms and Terms

assessed capability
the output of one or more recent, relevant process assessments conducted in accordance with the provisions of ISO/IEC TR 15504

assessment constraints
restrictions placed on the freedom of choice of the assessment team regarding the conduct of the assessment and the use of the assessment outputs

assessment indicator
an objective attribute or characteristic of a practice or work product that supports the judgment of the performance of, or capability of, an implemented process

assessment input
the collection of information required before a process assessment can commence

assessment instrument
a tool or set of tools that is used throughout an assessment to assist the assessor in evaluating the performance or capability of processes and in handling assessment data and recording the assessment results

assessment participant
Person of the organizational unit, who is interviewed by members of the assessment team for the acquisition of data on one or more processes to be assessed.

assessment purpose
a statement, provided as part of the assessment input, which defines the reason for performing the assessment

assessment record
an orderly, documented collection of that information which is pertinent to the assessment and adds to the understanding and verification of the *process profiles* generated by the assessment

assessment scope
a definition of the boundaries of the assessment, provided as part of the assessment input, encompassing the organizational limits of the assessment, the processes to be included, and the context within which the processes operate (see *process context*)

assessment sponsor
the individual, internal or external to the organization being assessed, who requires the assessment to be performed, and provides financial or other resources to carry it out

capability dimension
the set of process attributes comprising the capability aspects of the reference model of processes and process capability

conformant process assessment model
an operational model, used for performing assessments, which meets the defined requirements (for model purpose, scope,

	elements and indicators, mapping to the reference model, and translation of results) for conformance to the reference model
competent assessor	a person who has demonstrated the necessary skills, competencies and experience for performing process assessments
constructed capability	a capability constructed from elements of organizational units or of different organizations that are assembled for the purposes of achieving a particular specified requirement
defined process	the operational definition of a set of activities for achieving a specific purpose
enhanced capability	a capability greater than current assessed capability, justified by a credible process improvement programme
objective evidence	qualitative or quantitative information, records, or statements of fact pertaining to the characteristics of an item or service or to the existence and implementation of a process element, which is based on observation, measurement, or test and which can be verified
organizational unit	That part of an organization that is the subject of an assessment. An organizational unit (OU) deploys one or more processes that have a coherent process context and operates within a coherent set of business goals. NOTE: An organizational unit is typically part of a larger organization, although in a small organization, the organizational unit may be the whole organization. An organizational unit may be, for example: A specific project or set of (related) projects; a unit within an organization focused on a specific lifecycle phase (or phases) such as acquisition, development, maintenance or support; a part of an organization responsible for all aspects of a particular product or product set
practice	a software engineering or management activity that contributes to the creation of the output (work products) of a process or enhances the capability of a process
process	A set of interrelated activities that transform inputs into outputs. NOTE: The term 'activities' covers use of resources (see ISO 8402:1994, 1.2). [ISO/IEC 12207]
process assessment	a disciplined evaluation of an organization's software processes against a model compatible with the reference model
process attribute	a measurable characteristic of process capability applicable to any process
Process Attribute rating	a judgment of the level of achievement of the defined capability of the Process Attribute for the assessed process
process capability determination sponsor	the organization, part of an organization or person initiating a process capability determination
process capability determination	a systematic assessment and analysis of selected software processes within an organization against a target capability, carried out with the aim of identifying the strengths, weaknesses and risks associated with deploying the processes to meet a particular specified requirement
process Capability Level rating	a representation of the achieved process Capability Level derived from the Process Attribute ratings for an assessed process

process Capability Level	a point on the six-point ordinal scale (of process capability) that represents the increasing capability of the performed process; each level builds on the capability of the level below
process capability	the ability of a process to achieve a required goal
process category	a set of processes addressing the same general area of activity
process context	the set of factors, documented in the assessment input, that influence the judgment, comprehension and comparability of Process Attribute ratings
process dimension	the set of processes comprising the functional aspects of the reference model of processes and process capability
process improvement	action taken to change an organization's processes so that they meet the organization's business needs and achieve its business goals more effectively
process improvement programme	All the strategies, policies, goals, responsibilities and activities concerned with the achievement of specified improvement goals. A process improvement programme can span more than one complete cycle of process improvement
process improvement project	any subset of the process improvement programme that forms a coherent set of actions to achieve a specific improvement
process outcome	an observable result of the successful implementation of a process
process performance	the extent to which the execution of a process achieves its purpose
process profile	the set of Process Attribute ratings for an assessed process
process purpose	the high level measurable objectives of performing the process and the likely outcomes of effective implementation of the process
proposed capability	the process capability that the organization proposes to bring to bear in meeting the specified requirement
provisional assessor	a person who has the skills and competencies to carry out assessments under the guidance and supervision of a competent assessor
software process assessment	A disciplined evaluation of an organization's software processes against a reference model.
software process	the process or set of processes used by an organization or project to plan, manage, execute, monitor, control and improve its software related activities
standard process	the operational definition of the basic process that guides the establishment of a common process in an organization
supplier	organization that provides a product or service to the customer
target capability	the process capability which the process capability determination sponsor judges will represent an acceptable process risk to the successful implementation of the specified requirement
work product	an artefact associated with the execution of a process
Architectural design	Describes the division of the software into software components, their interfaces, the control structures and the implied mechanisms necessary to satisfy requirements. The architectural design can be documented in different views.
ECU	Electronic Control Unit - A computing device consisting of hardware, software, communication interfaces and locally con-

	nected sensors and actuators
Resource consumption of the software	specifies among others, the consumption of memory space and CPU time in sufficient detail
Release strategy	defines the sequence for realizing the software requirements according to the internal and external needs
Software	Common name used for different types of software components such as application software or system software usually executed in an ECU. Software consists of software components. Software components consist of software units
Software component	An identifiable Part within the software that realizes a function on a particular ECU. The software component realizes vehicle functions (e.g. close sliding roof with transmitter key) as well as functions required ECU-internally (e.g. fail-safe-software)
Software design	super ordinate concept of architectural design, dynamic behaviour of the software and detailed design
Software requirements specification	Specifies the requirements for an instantiation of a function on a particular ECU
Software requirement	a single entity within the software requirements specification
Software units	The building blocks of software components. A Software unit is a small entity that can perform a coherent set of operations
Software integration test case	a test case used within the software integration to verify that the previously performed integration step has produced completely or partially integrated software that complies with the corresponding requirements
System	A system consists of several ECU's interconnected by a communication network for the purpose of realizing the coherent functions of a functional area
System design	the system design specifies the required sensors, actors, computing devices, internal and external interfaces, communication media and communication paths and the possible structuring into subsystems
System integration test case	a test case used within the system integration to verify that the previously performed integration step has produced a completely or partially integrated system that complies with the corresponding requirements
System requirements	The system requirements are specified by the customer and are among other relevant specifications: functional area requirements specifications, customer ECU requirements specifications, network specification
Test case	a description of the ordered steps necessary to decide upon the fulfilment of a requirement, together with the required preconditions and test setup (test object and test equipment). In case a corresponding verification criteria is defined, the test case contains a reference to it
Verification criteria	specifies the conditions under which the fulfilment and the non-fulfilment of a requirement can be objectively decided upon

Index

Index

Bibliography

Bibliography

[1] Han van Loon, Reach for the STARS. Leadership and management in the new millennium. LC Publishing. ISBN 0-9758325-0-6

[2] ISO/IEC 15504 standard consists of five ratified parts and 2 in draft:

ISO/IEC 15504-1 Information Technology — Process Assessment - Part 1 - Concepts and vocabulary

ISO/IEC 15504-2 Information Technology — Process Assessment - Part 2 - Performing an assessment

ISO/IEC 15504-3 Information Technology — Process Assessment - Part 3 - Guidance on performing an assessment

ISO/IEC 15504-4 Information Technology — Process Assessment - Part 4 - Guidance on use for process improvement and process capability determination

ISO/IEC 15504-5 Information Technology — Process Assessment - Part 5 - An exemplar process assessment model

ISO/IEC TR 15504-6 Information Technology – Process Assessment – Part 6: An exemplar system process assessment model.

ISO/IEC 15504-7 (WD) Information Technology – Process Assessment – Part 7: Assessment of Organizational Maturity.

[3] International Standard ISO/IEC 12207, Information Technology - *Software Life Cycle Processes*, International Organization for Standardization, International Electrotechnical Commission, 1995.

[4] International Standard ISO/IEC 15288, Systems Engineering - *System Life Cycle Processes*, International Organization for Standardization, International Electrotechnical Commission, 2002.

[5] Han van Loon. Process Assessment and Improvement. A Practical Guide. Springer. ISBN 0-387-23182-X

[6] International Standard ISO 9000:2000: Quality Management Systems: Fundamentals and Vocabulary.

ISO 9001:2000: Quality Management Systems - Requirements.

ISO 9004:2000: Quality Management Systems - Guidelines for performance improvements.

[7] ISO 9001:1994: Quality systems - Model for quality assurance in design, development, production, installation and servicing

[8] Annex A: ISO 9004:2000: Quality Management Systems - Guidelines for performance improvements.

[9] ISO/IEC 14598:1998 Software Engineering – Product Evaluation. International Organization for Standardization, International Electrotechnical Commission.

[10] ISO/IEC 15939 Software Engineering – Software Process Measurement. International Organization for Standardization, International Electrotechnical Commission.

[11] ISO/IEC 12207:2002/Amd 2:2004, Information Technology - Software Life Cycle Processes, Amendment 2 International Organization for Standardization, International Electrotechnical Commission.

[12] IEEE Std. 1517 – 1999 Standard for Information Technology – Software Life Cycle Processes – Reuse Processes.

[13] Carma McClure. Software Reuse – A Standards-Based Guide. IEEE Software Engineering Standards Series. ISBN 0-7695-0847-X

[14] ISO/IEC 15288 FDIS 15288 (E) Systems Engineering – Systems Life Cycle Processes.

[15] Han van Loon, Reach for the STARS. Leadership and management in the new millennium. LC Publishing. 2006 ISBN 0-9758325-0-6

[16] V-Model Development Standard for IT-Systems of the Federal Republic of Germany, Federal Ministry of the Interior for the civilian Federal Administration. www.v-modell.iabg.de

[17] See www.itil.org, The Office of Government Commerce, British Government.

[18] The British Standards Institute: BS 15000:2000, Specification for IT Service Management

[19] John Torgersson, University of Boras. OOSPICE – The Road to Qualitative CBD. SPICE2002 Conference. www.oospice.com

[20] B. Henderson-Sellers, F. Stallinger, R. Lefever: Bridging the Gap from Process Modelling to process Assessment: the OOSPICE Process Specification for Component Based Software Engineering. Proceedings of the 28th EUROMICRO conference. Sept 2002, Dortmund, Germany. IEEE Computer Society. Loa Alamos, CA 2002.

[21] John Henderson-Sellers, COTAR UTS. The OOSPICE Project: Capability Assessment for CBD Methodology. SPICE 2001 Conference.

[22] Franck Barbier LIUPPA Université de Pau, France. Business Component-Based Software Engineering. Kluwer International Series in Engineering and Computer Science: Volume 705. ISBN 1-4020-7207-4

[23] Specifically the following standards were considered:
ISO 9000:2000 Quality Management Systems – Fundamentals and Vocabulary.
ISO 9001:2000 Quality Management Systems – Requirements.
ISO 9004:2000 Quality Management Systems – Guidelines to performance improvements.

[24] Application of Process Capability Determination to Quality Management. ESTEC Study Contract No. 14617/00/NL/CK. SYNSPACE AG, InterSPICE and Alenia Spazio, ESA.

[25] Automotive SIG, Automotive SPICE Process Reference Model. The Procurement Forum. The SPICE User Group. V4.2 August 2005

[26] ISO/IEC 15504-5:2005 Information Technology — Process Assessment — Part 5: An exemplar Process Assessment Model

[27] ESA/ESTEC Study Contract No. 10662/93/NL/NB WO6-CCN5: ISO/IEC TR 15504 Conformant Method for the Assessment of Space Software Processes 14.7.1995

[28] ECSS standards included, among others: ECSS–E–40B Draft: Space Engineering – Software. ESA-ESTEC Requirements & Standards Division, Noordwijk, 28.6.2000.

ECSS-M-00A: Space Product Management - Policies and Principles. ESA-ESTEC Requirements & Standards Division, Noordwijk, 19.4.1996.

ECSS-M-00-03A: Space Product Management – Risk Management. ESA-ESTEC Requirements & Standards Division, Noordwijk, 25.04.2001.

ECSS-Q-80B Draft: Space Product Assurance - Software product Assurance. ESA-ESTEC Requirements & Standards Division, Noordwijk, 3.4.2000.

[29] F. Stallinger, B. Henderson-Sellers, J. Torgersson: The OOSPICE Assessment Component: Customizing Software process Assessments to CBD. F Bartier (ed): Business Component-Based Software Engineering. Kluwer Academic Publishers. 2002.

[30] Gerhard Wagner, AUDI AG. SPICE im AUTOMOBIL. ASQF-02.11.2003 SPICE Days 2003 Nürnberg.

[31] Automotive SIG, Automotive SPICE Process Assessment Model. The Procurement Forum. The SPICE User Group. V2.2 August 2005.

[32] Carnegie Mellon, Software Engineering Institute. Mary Beth Chrissis, Mike Konrad, Sandy Shrum. CMMI®: Guidelines for Process Integration and Product Improvement. Addison Wesley.

[33] http://www.sei.cmu.edu/cmmi/

[34] CMMI® for Development (CMMI-DEV, V1.2)

[35] Taken directly from section 7 of CMMI® for Systems Engineering, Software Engineering, and Integrated Product and Process Development (CMMI-SE/SW/IPPD, V1.1)

[36] EIA/IS 731 Electronic Industries Alliance. *Systems Engineering Capability Model (EIA/IS-731)*. Washington, D.C.: 1998.

[37] The Federal Aviation Administration Integrated Capability Maturity Model ® FAA-iCMM ® Version 2.0 An Integrated Capability Maturity Model for Enterprise-wide Improvement. Linda Ibrahim et al. September 2001. http://www1.faa.gov/aio/common/documents/iCMM/FAA-iCMMv2.htm

[38] The Federal Aviation Administration Integrated Capability Maturity Models (FAA-iCMM®) Appraisal Method (FAM). www.faaa.gov/aio

[39] Development Standard for IT-Systems of the Federal Republic of Germany. General Directive No. 250 "Lifecycle Process Model" (description of activities and products as an answer to the question of *"what"* will be done), General Directive No. 251 "Allocation of Methods" (description of the minimum requirements with regard to methods as an answer to the question of *"how"* it will be done), General Directive No. 252 "Functional Tool Requirements" (standardized criteria for the selection of tools which explain *"with what"* it will be done).

[40] The complete V-Model is available from IABG (Industrieanlagen-Betriebsgesellschaft.GmbH) in German at www.v-modell.iabg.de and in English at www.v-modell.iabg.de/vm97.htm#Engl

There is also an electronic process guide format at Fraunhofer IESE at www.iese.fhg.de/Vmodell/

[41] See section: The V-Model in the ISO and AQAP environment of General Directive No. 250 "Lifecycle Process Model".

[42] Davor Gornik, Rational® Software White Paper 2001. IBM ® Rational Unified Process: Best Practices for Software Development Teams

[43] Rational Software White Paper 2000: Assessing the Rational Unified Process against ISO/IEC 15504-5: Information Technology – Software Process Assessment Part 5: An Assessment Model and Indicator Guidance.

[44] A comparison of the IBM Rational Unified Process and eXtreme Programming. John Smith. 2003 Rational Software. IBM.

[45] Software Quality Institute, Professor G. Dromey. Griffith University, Brisbane. Australia. www.sqi.gu.edu.au

[46] Director of Certification, International Assessors Certification Scheme (INT-ACS). Manchester, United Kingdom www.int-acs.org. See also the ASQF website for documents including www.asqf.de/asqf/documents/INT-ACS-100.pdf and www.asqf.de/asqf/documents/INT-ACS-4.pdf

[47] A Guide to the Project Management Handbook of Knowledge. 2000 Edition. Project Management Institute. www.pmi.org

[48] Managing successful projects with PRINCE 2 ®. Office of Government Commerce. United Kingdom.

Also Tailoring PRINCE 2 ®. www.ogc.gov.uk/prince/

[49] M. Paulk, B. Curtis, M.B. Chrissis et al. Capability Maturity Model for Software. Software Engineering Institute. CMU/SEI-91-TR-24, August 1991

[50] Software Engineering Institute, Capability Maturity Model® Integration, Version 1.2 for Systems Engineering, Software Engineering, and Integrated Product and Process Development (CMMI-DEV, V1.2) CMU/SEI-2006-TR-008 August 2006.

[51] Charles Weber, Description of CMMI Staged Model Representation. USAF Software Technology Support Center. 9 June 1999.

[52] Software Engineering Institute technical report, Appraisal requirements for CMMI version 1.1. CMU/SEI-2001-TR-034 December 2001.

[53] W.S. Humphrey and W.L. Sweet, A method for Assessing the Software Engineering Capability of Contractors. Technical Report CMU/SEI-87-TR23 September 1987.

[54] W.S. Humphrey and W.L. Sweet, A method for Assessing the Software Engineering Capability of Contractors. Technical Report CMU/SEI-87-TR23 September 1987.

[55] M. Paulk, B. Curtis, M.B. Chrissis et al. Capability Maturity Model for Software. Software engineering Institute. CMU/SEI-91-TR-24, August 1991.

[56] Coallier, F. (and others) (1991) The Trillium Model. Bell Canada.

[57] Koch, G. E. et al. 1993. Maturity Assessments: The BOOTSTRAP Approach.

[58] *ImproveIT*, 1991, ISO/IEC JTC1/SC7 N865.

[59] Proposal for a Study Period on Process Management, 1991, ISO/IEC JTC1/SC7 N872.

[60] Study Report: The Need and Requirements for a Software Process Assessment Standard, 1992, ISO/IEC JTC1/SC7 N944R.

[61] International Standard ISO/IEC 12207, Information Technology - *Software Life Cycle Processes*, International Organization for Standardization, International Electrotechnical Commission, 1995.

[62] WG10 Meeting Kwa Maritane: *Proposal for Changes to the Architecture*, 1995, ISO/IEC JTC1/SC7/WG10 N080

[63] ISO/IEC TR 15504 Technical Report consists of nine parts.
ISO/IEC TR 15504-1: Information Technology - Software Process Assessment Part 1: Concepts and Introductory Guide, 1996, ISO/IEC JTC1/SC7 N1592
ISO/IEC TR 15504-2: Information Technology - Software Process Assessment Part 2: A Reference Model For Processes And Process Capability, 1996, ISO/IEC JTC1/SC7 N1594
ISO/IEC TR 15504-3: Information Technology - Software Process Assessment Part 3: Performing An Assessment, 1996, ISO/IEC JTC1/SC7 N1596
ISO/IEC TR 15504-4: Information Technology - Software Process Assessment Part 4: Guide To Performing Assessments, 1996, ISO/IEC JTC1/SC7 N1598.
ISO/IEC TR 15504-5: Information Technology - Software Process Assessment Part 5: An Assessment Model And Indicator Guidance, 1996, ISO/IEC JTC1/SC7 N1601.
ISO/IEC TR 15504-6: Information Technology - Software Process Assessment Part 6: Guide To Qualification Of Assessors, 1996, ISO/IEC JTC1/SC7 N1603.
ISO/IEC TR 15504-7: Information Technology - Software Process Assessment Part 7: Guide For Use In Process Improvement, 1996, ISO/IEC JTC1/SC7 N1605.
ISO/IEC TR 15504-8: Information Technology - Software Process Assessment Part 8: Guide For Use In Determining Supplier Process Capability, 1996, ISO/IEC JTC1/SC7 N1607.
ISO/IEC TR 15504-9: Information Technology - Software Process Assessment Part 9: Vocabulary, 1996, ISO/IEC JTC1/SC7 N1609.

About the Author

Han van Loon

Han van Loon is a practicing consultant in the management field as well as Visiting Professor at Nottingham Trent University in the UK and the University of Business and International Studies in Switzerland. He is the copyright owner of this work. Han has published articles on quality management topics over a period of two decades, and worked with the ISO/IEC 15504 standard since 1994. He has successfully led organizations to the highest levels of process capability. Han is an accomplished international speaker and teacher. He has presented at conferences, led seminars and workshops and conducted training in Australia, Asia, Europe and North America.

Han consults to companies and organisations wishing to improve their enterprise results through holistic improvement facilitation, including the use of process assessments and human centred improvement. He specialises in helping clients wishing to achieve business enterprise excellence and world class performance.

Han may be contacted via email: welcome@lc-stars.com or via his web site: http://www.lc-stars.com. His web site provides more details of his holistic management and improvement methodologies and publications.

About the cover

The cover is a combination of the symbol for Yin and Yang, the symbol for Infinity ∞ and the Team Based Business Design Improvement cycle. It symbolizes the balance and tension between process performance and process change, the continuity required for quality and change implied in improvement, and a holistic balance between people and process. The symbol is copyright of Han van Loon and is used as his corporate trademark.